Robert Needham Cust

Essay on the Common Features which Appear in all Forms of Religious Belief

Robert Needham Cust

Essay on the Common Features which Appear in all Forms of Religious Belief

ISBN/EAN: 9783337262365

Printed in Europe, USA, Canada, Australia, Japan

Cover: Foto ©Lupo / pixelio.de

More available books at **www.hansebooks.com**

COMMON FEATURES, WHICH APPEAR

IN ALL

FORMS OF RELIGIOUS BELIEF.

PUBLICATIONS BY THE SAME AUTHOR.

ETON ADDRESSES TO KING WILLIAM IV. 1840.
HAILEYBURY-OBSERVER CONTRIBUTIONS. 1840-1842.
CALCUTTA-REVIEW CONTRIBUTIONS. 1845-1893.
HISTORY OF COCKAYNE-HATLEY CHURCH. 1851.
MANUALS FOR GUIDANCE OF NATIVE OFFICIALS IN THE URDU-LANGUAGE. 1855 to 1859.
PANJÁB REVENUE-MANUAL. 1865.
REVENUE-LAW OF NORTH-WEST PROVINCES OF INDIA. 1867.
LAND-REVENUE-PROCEDURE FOR NORTHERN INDIA. 1870.
MODERN LANGUAGES OF THE EAST INDIES. 1878.
LES RELIGIONS ET LES LANGUES DE L'INDE (FRENCH). 1880.
LA RELIGIONE ET LE LINGUE DELL' INDIA (ITALIAN). 1882.
LAS RELIGIONES Y LOS IDIOMAS DE LA INDIA (SPANISH). 1884.
Θρησκείαι καὶ Γλῶσσαι τῆς 'Ινδίας (GREEK). 1884.
MODERN LANGUAGES OF AFRICA. 2 Vols. 1883.
LES LANGUES DE L'AFRIQUE (FRENCH). 1885. (GERMAN. 1881.)
LE LINGUE DELL' AFRICA (ITALIAN). 1885.
MODERN LANGUAGES OF OCEANIA. 1887. (GERMAN. 1887.)
LES RACES ET LES LANGUES DE L'OCEANIE (FRENCH). 1888.
MODERN LANGUAGES OF THE CAUCASIAN-GROUP. 1887.
LANGUAGES OF THE TÚRKI BRANCH OF THE URAL-ALTAIC FAMILY. 1889. (GERMAN AND ENGLISH.)
LINGUISTIC AND ORIENTAL ESSAYS. Series I. 1880.
LINGUISTIC AND ORIENTAL ESSAYS. Series II. 1887.
LINGUISTIC AND ORIENTAL ESSAYS. Series III. 1891.
PICTURES OF INDIAN LIFE. 1881.
THE ROMAN CATHOLIC SHRINES OF LOURDES, ZARAGOSSA, LORETTO, Etc. 1885 and 1892.
POEMS OF MANY YEARS AND PLACES. 1887.
SUMMER-HOLIDAYS OF AN ETON BOY. 1887.
THE SORROWS OF AN ANGLO-INDIAN LIFE. 1889.
NOTES ON MISSIONARY SUBJECTS. 1889.
BIBLE-LANGUAGES. 1890.
CLOUDS ON THE HORIZON, OR THE VARIOUS FORMS OF RELIGIOUS ERROR. 1890.
BIBLE-TRANSLATIONS. 1890.
AFRICA REDIVIVA, OR MISSIONARY OCCUPATION OF AFRICA. 1891. (FRENCH AND ENGLISH.)
ADDRESSES ON BIBLE-DIFFUSION. 1892.
ESSAY ON THE METHODS OF EVANGELIZATION OF THE WORLD. 1894.
COMMON FEATURES, WHICH APPEAR IN ALL THE RELIGIONS OF THE WORLD BEFORE ANNO DOMINI. 1895.
THE GOSPEL-MESSAGE. (*In the Press.*)

BY

ROBERT NEEDHAM CUST, LL.D.,

BARRISTER-AT-LAW,
HONORARY SECRETARY OF THE ROYAL ASIATIC SOCIETY,
LATE MEMBER OF HER MAJESTY'S INDIAN CIVIL SERVICE.

I. Who in times past suffered all nations to walk in their own ways. *Acts*, xiv, 16.
II. Other sheep I have, which are not of this fold. *John*, x, 16.
III. They are less to be blamed, for they peradventure seek God and desire to find Him. *Wisdom of Solomon*, xiii, 6.
IV. He hath made of one blood all nations of men for to dwell on all the face of the earth . . . that they should seek the Lord, and find Him, though He be not far from every one of us. *Acts*, xvii, 26, 27.
V. And the times of this ignorance God winked at, but now commandeth all men everywhere to repent. *Acts*, xvii, 30.
VI. One God and Father of all. *Ephesians*, iv, 6.
VII. The world by wisdom knew not God. 1 Cor. i, 21.
VIII. God, who at sundry times. *Hebrews*, i, 1.
IX. No respecter of persons. *Acts*, x, 34.

LONDON:
LUZAC & CO., 46, GREAT RUSSELL STREET,
1895.

HERTFORD:
PRINTED BY STEPHEN AUSTIN AND SONS

To my two Daughters,

MARIA ELEANOR VERE,

AND

ANNA MARIA ELIZABETH,

THIS FEELING FOR THE TRUTH

IS

Dedicated.

And now my Summer-task is ended. Roll
  Up all my papers, and my volumes close :
From parts divergent I have sought a whole,
  Complete and perfect, as before me rose
      The variant Message, which from Heaven's abode
      Came down to earth to lead poor man to God.

Each Message but reveals th' unchanging plan
  Of Love and Kindness to poor Humankind,
And, like a sunflower, turns the heart of man
  Groping through darkness his soul's sun to find :
      No cavern is so dark, but through the night
      One ray streams in of God's eternal light.

As his forefathers did in Abraham's time,
  Still by the stream the Brahmin chaunts his prayers ;
The Buddhist asks for nothing, but sublime
  Emancipation from Life's dreary cares.
      Oh ! could no Angel earth's hard path have trod
      To whisper in his ear : " There is a God !"

Can we believe, that all-embracing Grace,
  Which o'er Creation's waters used to glide,
Chose out one puny, graceless, Jewish Race,
  And shut the gates of Hope on all beside :
      Let them indulge their passions and their crimes
      And raise up trophies to outlive all times ?

Búddha, Confucius, Plato, Socrates,
  Left words of gold, which no age can destroy ;
They please, when all things else have ceased to please :
  But of those holy men how great the joy,
      Had God's own Message by their soul been heard ;
      If one still voice their inward heart had stirred !

"Call nothing common and unclean" applies
  Not to the Future only, but the Past :
To one He gives, to others He denies ;
  According to His will man's lot is cast :
    He will not reap, where He has never sown,
    Or claim obedience, where He is not known.

Full many a heathen lived out holy days,
  Died for his altar, for his country strove ;
Spake hymns Heaven-prompted, full of prayer and praise,
  And words of Wisdom, Piety, and Love.
    Fell not Thy shadow, Lord ! on those behind,
    When on the Cross Thou suffered for mankind?

Poor little children die, who knew no spot,
  Unconscious of their life, and undefiled :
Can we suppose, that torture is their lot ?
  Were not the heathen Races like a child?
    Salvation is the goal of Heaven's great plan,
    And justifies the ways of God to man.

I hope through Him, who has the power to save,
  To be with Christ, which is far better—far.
To those, to whom the Holy Spirit gave
  To speak like Christ, oh ! can there be a bar ?
    For Socrates and Búddha if there be
    No place in Heaven, what place, alas ! for me?

Let us adore Thee in Thy fulness, Lord,
  With the Creator on Creation's day,
When Thou rejoiced with Him in full accord,
  And Morning-stars commenced their joyous way :
    And when on Calvary's mount the palm was won
    All was completed, and God's purpose done.

Eastbourne, Sept. 26, 1893.

CONTENTS.

		PAGE
1.	Title-page	v
2.	Dedication	vii
3.	Poem	ix
4.	Contents	xi
5.	Exordium	xiii
6.	Classification of Subject	xxiii
7.	Motive and Plan	1
	Cap. I. A Supernatural Power	15
	Cap. II. Worship of such a Power	35
	Cap. III. Manifestation of such a Power	74
	Cap. IV. Early Human Practices and Notions	92
	Cap. V. Records of Past Generations	112
	Cap. VI. Religiosity and Morals	144
	Cap. VII. Progress of the Human Race	156
8.	Concluding Remarks	163
9.	Poem	181
10.	Bibliography	183
11.	Index of Subjects, Phrases, Quotations, Illustrations	187
12.	Errata	195

EXORDIUM.

He was sitting in his Library, in the decline of life: independent in fortune, free from vulgar cares, he had throughout his life made Science, Absolute Science, his object. No coarse vice, no moral weakness, had troubled him: he had been spared that temptation: a sound constitution, and regular habits, had brought him through seventy years, unbroken in body or mind.

With the help of Astronomy, he had pierced the vault of Heaven, had numbered and weighed the stars, and called them all by their names. By the thread of Geology, he had forced his way into the hidden recesses of Mother-Earth, and had groped his way back to Chaos and beyond. He had drank deep of the sweet stores of Botany and Zoology, and had been foremost in the Study of Anthropology, and had recognised to the full the principle of Evolution, and Natural Selection. He had classified the Languages spoken in every part of the world, and traced their affiliation back to their different seed-plots. With Electricity he had spanned the round world, and dissatisfied with the revealed secrets of Nature, he was always peering through half-opened doors to catch some new Fact, or Idea. He had tried to calculate, how long this world had existed, and how much longer, in spite of the continual expenditure of heat, it would continue to exist. He had dropped his plummet into the deepest well, and had found no bottom.

There he sat, like a statue of Armed Science, waiting for More Light: no scoffing, no blasphemous word, had ever passed his lips: he had thought kindly, even pityingly, of all, deeming, them to be blind, or to be walking with intentionally closed eyes. He knew from experience what an exacting mistress Science was, and how easy it was to be deceived, and he extended to the vagaries of others the same large-hearted charity, which he gently, but unobtrusively, claimed for his own. No Philosopher was ever so free from dogmatism, so alien from the bitterness of controversy, so devoid of Egotism, as he was; so modest in his assertions, so ready to anticipate the objections of others, or himself to suggest objections for the purpose of exhausting the subject. Like the late Ernest Renan, he would listen to the speculations of others with attention, make a polite bow, and, commencing with, "Je suis tout avec vous, Monsieur," proceed politely in measured tones to tear the theory propounded to atoms.

It is a mistake to suppose, that men of Science attack Religion from pure malice, for it is to be feared, that they do not think of Religion at all: they are led on in spite of themselves in search of absolute tested Truth. The real contest is betwixt one phase of Science and another, betwixt the crude knowledge of yesterday and the less crude knowledge of to-day. The contest is merely the measure of the difficulty of exchanging obsolete notions for new and accurate ones. Our ancestors transmitted to us certain notions, which they honestly and piously entertained, but to which we cannot assent without considerable revision. The discovery by Copernicus of the rotation of the globe is an instance. It had nothing to do with man's belief in God, and yet at the time of the discovery it was deemed atheistic, and contrary to the Scriptures.

As in the newly-discovered ruins of an ancient city, students occupy themselves in digging, and sorting, everything, that the spade turned up, and speculating on its origin and object: so in the pages of ancient Manuscripts, he tried to look below the actual written words, and with the lens of Higher Criticism try to find out the motive, the environment, the materials available, and the antecedents, of the writer.

Among his large acquaintance he had never taken intimate counsel with any: he was not a thoughtless observer: he had known many, who all their life had been worldly, immoral, with no thought of ever turning to their Creator, careless of the future, unrepentant of the past, and yet Prosperity of every kind had accompanied them from the cradle to the grave. On the other hand, he knew of good men and women, whose life had been embittered by sorrow, suffering, want, and bereavement, the result of the errors of others. He read in the papers of hundreds being suffocated in a mine, drowned in a shipwreck, or crushed to death in a railway accident, of some bright angel of purity and goodness being drowned in a boat-accident.

He thought of the lines of the Poet Claudian, written 1400 years before, which were as true now as they were then :

> Sæpe mihi dubiam tenuit sententia mentem,
> Curarent Superi terras, an nullus inesset
> Rector, et incerto fluerent mortalia casu :
> Nam, cum dispositi quæsissem fœdera mundi,
> Præscriptosque maris fines, amnisque meatus,
> Et lucis, noctisque, vices : tunc omnia rebar
> Concilio firmata Dei :
> Sed cum res hominum tantâ caligine volvi
> Aspiciam, lætosque diu florere nocentes,
> Vexarique pios, rursus labefacta cadebat
> Religio.
> (CLAUDIAN, A.D. 400.)

The secret, which Claudian could not find out, is still unsolved. We, indeed, ex animo believe, that there is a God, who rules the affairs of men in the best, and wisest, and kindest way; but to the last three lines there is no reply. The old clergyman's saw, repeated in the ears of widows, and orphans, and bereaved ones, by the side of the death-bed of the loved one, does not help us.

Nothing remained on his memory, which was not positive Fact, or logical deductions from those Facts. As to the past, he admitted the existence of a great Building, or Institution, and allowed by a safe induction a period for its erection and development. As to History, he believed nothing, except so far as the statements made stood the test of his scientific evidential requirements. He had never cared to think of the future: with his favourite Poet Horace, he was content to say each day "Vixi": the future may be what it likes, but the Deity Himself cannot change the past. He knew, that by a physical law all must die, and that by the books of the Actuaries seventy was above the average of lives; but it was nothing to him.

To him it seemed quite reasonable, that in the course of centuries old things should pass away in the Education of the world in things spiritual, as well as in things material. Morality, and a rule of things absolutely right and absolutely wrong, can never change, but he thought, that the *aspect* of the relation of Man to God could change, and did change in proportion, as More Light was vouchsafed by the Creator to His poor creatures. This made him wonder, why such inapposite selections from the Hebrew Scriptures were read in Churches, such as the Priestly code, which had passed away, the immoralities of David and Solomon, the cruel massacres of defeated enemies, and of Gentile Priests, the conduct of Lot, and Jael, the slaughter of women and children; for what lessons of Faith, or Morals, or Charity, could be learnt from the reading of such fearful stories, the absolute truth of which it is a labour of Charity and Pity to doubt, to the uneducated or imperfectly experienced people of Great Britain, who are on such an entirely different platform of Ideas, Human and Divine.

He was one morning thinking of Wisdom, and he read the famous passage in the Proverbs descriptive of Ἡ ἁγίη Σοφία, for he was acquainted with all the Sacred Books of the Human Race, and was up to the level of the latest Exploration: there seemed to be a common resting-place in the conception of the Λόγος as expounded by Plato, Philo, and the Apostle John, for the Christian, the neo-Jewish, and neo-Platonic, Philosophy. He thought it out in his usual calm, earnest, thorough way, as he would have thought out the description of a new development of Electricity, or a new Region discovered in Geography, or a new Palæolithic specimen. There were no idols of the Den, of the Market-place, of the Theatre, or of the Temple, to obscure his vision: he was not afraid of logical consequences, or reasonable inductions from well-ascertained Facts: he was not afraid of finding, that he had been mistaken.

This threw him back on the fundamental conception that not to be born, or to die as soon as possible after birth, was the kindest lot. The lines of Theognis came to his mind:

Ἀρχὴν μὲν μὴ φῦναι ἐπιχθονίοισιν ἄριστον,
Μηδ᾽ ἐσιδεῖν αὐγὰς ὀξέος ἠελίου·
φύντας δ᾽ ὅπως ὤκιστα πύλας Ἀΐδαο περῆσαι,
καὶ κεῖσθαι πολλὴν γῆν ἐπαμησάμενον.

His thoughts then lifted him up to a high eminence, whence he could survey the cities of men, and their inhabitants: they looked like ants and ant-hills. Bodies Politic called States, and Bodies Ecclesiastic called Churches, assumed their relative importance, or rather want of importance, in the great progression of Man's destiny: History and the cause of things, Geography and the position of things, Logic and the reason of things, Wisdom and the object of things, appeared stretched before him. Rising to a still higher eminence, he stood on the lowest steps of the throne of Divine Knowledge, Ἡ ἁγίη Σοφία, and saw below him Creeds, Dogmas, Rituals, things which blind the wise, and hoodwink the unlearned: he saw through the tricks of a long succession of Priesthoods; through the hypocrisy of the respectable, and those, who sail easily with every wind; through the gross falsehood of the Dogmatist: all these appeared thick and murky, like the banks of clouds, which envelop the Lower Alps, but Truth shone out like the Sun above all. What is Truth? Pilate asked the question, but received no reply: the Latin anagram tells it:

"Quid est Veritas?"   "Vir est qui adest."

He was fond of dwelling upon the extreme opportuneness, both in time and place, of the appearance of Christ in the form of man: looking backwards or forwards in History to Abraham, 1900 B.C., and to the present Epoch, 1900 A.D., no Epoch, and no Locality, was so suitable per se for the enunciation of a worldwide dispensation as Palestine in Anno Domini.

Not only was the Hellenic genius at its zenith, and the Latin genius developing itself as a worthy rival of its elder sister, but beyond, in an unknown region beyond the Alps, was the great Teutonic Race, which had just found its way into Europe, and was standing ready to accept the new Religious conception, clothed in the bright languages of Greece and Rome, as the foundation of their spiritual and material existences. He laid stress on the mighty change in the whole frame and attitude of the Human mind in respect of Divine Things, which commenced from that date its march literally and actually over the whole world; the conception of a Kingdom of Heaven, a divine Society, the individuality of belief, and yet the universality, the extreme necessity to all, the exclusion of none, the reasonableness, the simplicity, and the impossibility of suggesting any other scheme of Salvation.

In the last few years many things had occupied his thoughts. A transition-period had arrived in Religious affairs: old bulwarks had been swept away. The inhabitants of the most distant regions of the world had begun to know each other. The spade of the excavator was exposing to view treasures never dreamt of in the shape of the documents of the past. New worlds of Science were opening round young intellects, to which Science was the necessity of life. He passed then under review:

I. The Geographical, Ethnical, and Linguistic, revelations.
II. The larger view of Historical Research.
III. The Comparative Study of the Religions of the world.
IV. The excavations in Egypt, Mesopotamia, Syria, and India.
V. The Higher Criticism of the Old Testament.
VI. The fearless, methodical, scientific, Spirit of Inquiry in every portion of the great Kosmos.
VII. A deeper moral consciousness of the relation of the Creator to all His poor creatures from the beginning of the ages until the present Epoch.

When he read the History of the ancient nations, and heard the bold assertions of his own countrymen as to the spiritual position of the great mass of mankind, who did not agree with them as to matters not of Science, but of belief, he wondered, and this day that he was meditating on the Wisdom, 'Η ἀγίη Σοφία, which had helped the Creator to create the world (Proverbs, viii, 22), he fell into a new train of thought, carefully keeping to Facts, and legitimate deductions, that it seemed a disparagement to the Wisdom of the Creator to imagine,

> I. That the vast mass of His creatures, in countless generations and untold Millions, were born, lived, and died, without the opportunity of finding the Truth in a matter deemed by themselves to be most essential to their welfare.
>
> II. That to one portion of the great world alone, and for a few centuries out of the great succession of years, the Truth was believed to have been revealed.
>
> III. That although for many centuries great Nations in Asia had laboured hard in the search for Divine Truth, all their stored-up wealth of knowledge was nothing worth, and in the eyes of the few, who asserted a monopoly of Divine things, they themselves and their ancestors were deemed to be as the beasts that perish. This seemed to him very strange, and in strong contrast with the words of Cicero, "De Naturâ Deorum," II, 66:

"Nemo vir magnus sine aliquo afflatu divino unquam fuit."

Such were his reflections, and looking forward into the vista of years, and backward to the fountains of Historic, and Religious, Knowledge, he from his own point of view wondered, whether future ages might not bring further development: the Jew thought his conception final; the Zoroastrian thought the same of his: only a few fragments remain of either: the Brahmanist, the Buddhist, and the Confucianist, still count their hundreds of Millions, and show no signs of moral, material, or intellectual, decay. From the Jew had sprung the Christian in his Millions; from the Christian and Jew united had sprung the followers of Islam; from Islam, new developments (notably the Bábi) were coming into existence, and the air was full of the rustling of leaves, and the rumbling of earthquakes: there was a sound of advancing conceptions, and new Faiths in germ, springing up from old roots; and the hand of the Intolerant Persecutor, which made such havoc of so-called Heresies in early centuries, was shortened for ever. So far the world had made a solid advance, and was ready for further advances.

He adopted the sentiments of the great and tolerant author of "Ecce Homo," p. 74, "that the path of Christian Truth is "overgrown with prejudices, and strewn with fallen theories and "rotten systems, which hide it from our view. It is quite as "hard to *think* rightly as to *act* rightly, or even *feel* rightly. "Men do not understand, or appreciate, the difficulty of "finding Truth." In fact some men do not think at all, and raise an inane cry against the thinker. He used to quote with approbation a sentence from the Review of "Ecce Homo" by Mr. Gladstone, on which all should humbly reflect: "The "astounding fact of the manifestation of the Lord of Glory "in the veil of Human flesh *may*, *and does*, stagger in some "minds the whole faculty of belief. Happy are those, who "do examine, and after full consideration believe, *but we cannot* "*condemn those, who do not*: 'Lord, help their unbelief.'" How different is the practice! "Receive it as a little child," shouts the Protestant. "Believe it because the Pope says so," cries the Jesuit. "Swallow it because it is in the Veda," cries the Brahmin. "Have 'Imám,' and read the Korán," says the Mahometan. "Believe nothing, if incapable of physical proof," suggests the Agnostic. "There is no God," says the fool. "If there is one, he cares not for man," says the modern Epicurean. "Prove all things by the help of the Holy Spirit, which is within you," murmurs the humble believer.

He used sometimes to say, that he had more in his intellectual structure of Erasmus than of Luther: his desire was to cut away abuses, and reform errors, rather than pull a fabric down, or destroy the strength of a great organization, which had come into existence for purposes of Religion, Morality, and Benevolence, by breaking it up into fragments, each fragment bitterly hostile to the others. The Encomium Moriæ, or "Praise of Folly," was ever his delight, and some of the sentiments of the great mediæval Prophet were adopted by him, such as, "the party, which has the fools at its back, has usually the majority of numbers"; "the best of mankind have been called heretics"; and "men, who have been themselves reformers, are the least tolerant, when a movement takes a form, which they dislike."

Strong in his convictions, that the present generation was heir of all the ages, that throughout all the ages one increasing purpose ran, and that the thoughts of men grew wider with the progress of the Sun; that Pythagoras, Socrates, Plato,

Zoroaster, the Hindu Sages, Búddha, and Kong-Fu-Tsee, would have done larger and better things, had they had deeper and wider experience; that man ought to profit by History, and not be a slave to it; that a so-called Church, appealing to ignorant people in dark ages, was the greatest enemy to the Manifestation of the Divinity, which is ever fresh and new in the person of Christ, he determined to collect, in a cold, unimpassioned, way, the Common Features of Religious Belief: certain things he seemed instinctively to loathe, such as Dogmatism, Priestcraft, Ritual, Liturgical recitations, and certain things to love (for Love must be the motive power), such as the humble prayer of the Publican, the cry of the penitent thief on the Cross, the words of Christ on the Cross, and the prayer for his murderers by Stephen.

He regarded an Establishment, supported by the favour of the State, and endowed with ancestral Revenues, for the benefit of *all* the population of a country, but in the lapse of years appropriated by a *portion only* of that population, as a great scandal, an evil inheritance from bad old times, when the lust of a monarch, or the caprice of a ruling faction, tried, as in the days of the Kings of Israel and Judah, to modify, restrict, or even forbid, the free worship of an ignorant people. The Hindu and Mahometan in British India are in a better plight than the Hebrews were in the times of the Kings, or the English in the time of Henry VIII and his two daughters: a hierarchy appointed by the caprice of those in power, the sale by public advertisement, or private contract, of the right to give Spiritual teaching, the retention in office of grossly immoral servants, the elevation of the Ecclesiastic from the humble position occupied by Christ (Mark, x, 43) of minister or "famulus" (Castellio's Latin version) to that of Rector, or Dominus, or Sacerdos, claiming the burial-ground as his freehold, in which he can feed his sheep, and the place of worship as a spot, in which he can indulge himself in any new Ecclesiastical vagaries of ornament, or practice, without any respect to the feelings of the congregation, who were sold into his hands for the term of his life by an alien impropriator, a capitular body, or a solicitor acting for a bankrupt, without giving the poor sheep an opportunity of objecting to his appointment, or getting rid of him as a bad shepherd.

From the wealth of his note-books, from the pigeon-holes of his well-stored memory, from the shelves of his classified book-case, from the pages of his beloved and well-marked books, from the carton-boxes, containing the accumulated cuttings from periodical literature, and extracts from favourite volumes, from letters full of sympathy and suggestions received from some few chosen ones, to whose judgment he had submitted portions, according to their experiences, of his rough drafts, he had completed these pages, and had paused to take breath, but before they had passed to the Press, he himself passed away.

After completing the last chapter, he fell asleep there:

> Sull' eterne pagine
> Cadde la stanca man.

He knows the Truth, and *the whole Truth*, now.
Socrates had two thousand three hundred years before uttered among his dying words:

> "Καλὸν τὸ ἆθλον, καὶ ἡ 'ελπὶς μεγάλη."

So by God's blessing may it prove to us all!

To another hand it has fallen to carry out his intentions. His Essay is, no doubt, not didactic, as the outcome of a master of a great subject, but tentative for the satisfaction of his own mind. The great teacher has made up his mind, and in the strength of those convictions makes an utterance ex cathedrâ: perhaps after the lapse of twenty years his edifice will fall to the ground: the humble inquirer feels his way as he goes along: as he advances in his task, his tone matures, or his opinions recede; they grow with the growth of his knowledge, or dwindle under the sudden manifestation of new facts: his work is one of self-instruction: he is slow to enunciate an opinion; but when he utters the words, "I am not sure," his venturing to doubt, and not to condemn at once, carries more conviction to his fellow-labourers than the offhand assertions of others, for he would not have doubted, if he had been sure one way or the other.

He had adopted to the letter the remarks of his deceased friend, Robertson Smith (Expositor, June, 1894, p. 472), that "all History was the expression of a living will: it was the "student's business to go fearlessly ahead in honest inquiry, "because every addition to our knowledge of Human History "is a further step towards understanding the purposes of God."

Comparisons are constantly made, and by very imperfectly informed writers, between the Christian and non-Christian Religions, the Romish and Protestant Churches, and always in favour of the particular Religion, Church, or denomination, to which the writer belongs:

> "Solos credit habendos
> Esse Deos, quos ipse colit."
> (JUVENAL, *Sat*. xv.)

But few care, or dare to ask themselves the question: how far does it in its present manifestation answer the Great Master's Ideal? what are the causes of its early success, sudden arrestation, and the decay of its powerful influence for good on any who profess to be Christians? Humanum est errare: all Human institutions are liable to decay: an honest man is not content with spying out the shortcomings of other Religious systems, but he inquires how far his own conception falls short of the great Ideal.

CLASSIFICATION OF THE SUBJECT.

	PAGE
Motives and Plan	1

CAP. I.	A SUPERNATURAL POWER	15

(1) Existence of such a Power 15
   A. Anthropomorphism 19
   B. Monolatry 20
   C. Monotheism 21
   D. Polytheism 24
(2) Place of Residence of such a Power . . 24
(3) Theophanies, Visions, Dreams, Good and Evil Spirits 25
(4) Primeval Revelation: was there any? . 30
(5) Substitution of Idols made by Men's Hands for an Impersonal Divinity . . . 31
(6) Fatherhood of God 33
(7) Threats of Worshippers uttered against their gods 34

CAP. II.	WORSHIP OF SUCH A POWER	35

(1) What is it? 35
(2) Primeval 40
(3) Ancestral 43
(4) Sacrifice 47
(5) Prayer 53
(6) Ritual 62
(7) Priestcraft, Witchcraft, Exorcism . . 66
(8) Ceremonial Cleanness, or Uncleanness . 68
(9) Fasting, Celibacy, Asceticism, Eremitism . 69
(10) Feasting, Day of Rest 71
(11) Esoteric, or Exoteric 71

CAP. III.	MANIFESTATION OF SUCH A POWER	74

(1) Miracles 74
(2) Prophecies, Auguries, Ordeals . . . 79
(3) National Sins and Punishments, Anger and Hostility of the Deity . . . 85
(4) Signs from Heaven 88
(5) Conception of Fate, Nemesis, Ἐρινύς . 90

(xxiv)

		PAGE
CAP. IV.	EARLY HUMAN PRACTICES AND NOTIONS	92

 (1) Disposal of Dead 92
 (2) Eschatology 94
 (3) Mutilation or Disfigurement of Body . 109
 (4) Strange and Abominable Customs . . 110

CAP. V. RECORDS OF PAST GENERATIONS . . 112

 (1) Written 112
  A. Necessity for Higher Criticism . 116
  B. Connection between Language and Religion 121
  C. Advantages derived from perusal of Sacred Books 122
  D. Description of Sacred Books . . 126
  E. Was there a Divine Afflatus? . . 130
  F. Blemishes in literary style of the Books 135
 (2) Oral: Tradition 139

CAP. VI. RELIGIOSITY AND MORALS . . . 144

 (1) Morality 144
 (2) Arm of the Flesh 147
 (3) Fanaticism 152
 (4) Superstition 152
 (5) Change of Belief 153

CAP. VII. PROGRESS OF HUMAN RACE . . . 156

 (1) Multiplication and Improved Culture under all forms of Religious Belief . . 156
 (2) Arts, Sculpture, Painting, Architecture, Drama 160

MOTIVES AND PLAN.

The object was to note the common features of that attitude of the Human Reason, which is called Religion, comprising (1) Customs, (2) Conceptions, (3) Dogma.

The elder world was separated into all but unapproachable sections: the same remark may be made with regard to barbarous tribes at this present Epoch: they borrowed from their neighbours little or nothing, and lent little.

During the lapse of ages no Nation, or tribe, has gone back in its Religious conceptions: there are signs of development everywhere, in ancient times from their own fountain of knowledge, in modern times from contact with other Nations. During the last century there has been a marked process of inter-comparison, amalgamation, the result of contact with Races in a higher state of civilization, and endowed with superior physical force: the dead silence of past centuries has been broken; the Intellect of the whole Human Race is waking up from torpor: it does not follow, that it will be to the advantage of the Human Race intellectually, or morally: no opinions are given: facts are recorded: Galileo's utterance applies, "E púr si muove."

The conduct of the Christian Missionary, Theologian, and Historian, as regards forms of Religious belief other than their own, has been shameful in the extreme:

"Damnant, quod non intelligunt":

they have not taken time to study the subject, they give no quarter to the worshipper, and cover the Worship with ridicule; and yet the homage rendered by the Soul to the Unseen, and Unknown, Power, that governs the world, is always worthy of respect; at least Paul thought so, when he addressed the Athenians on Mars' Hill, and Plato and Cicero were of the same opinion. The non-Christian educated classes return the abuse of their Christian assailants: the account of the Christian Religion by a Japanese, or Chinese, scholar after a visit to England would be a fair reply to a young Missionary's description of Mahometans published, I am ashamed to say, in the periodical of a Missionary Society.

Let that pass: but such people have failed to fathom the depths of the Religious element: they are unacquainted with Homer, and the Greek Tragedians; with Virgil, Horace, Seneca, and Juvenal: they knew nothing first-hand of the History, and existing practice, of the Brahmanical, Búddhist, and Mahometan, their forms of Worship, their national legends, and the Religious conception, which underlies them. A study of the non-Christian Religion is not without use in the study of the Christian Religion.

Before we judge the non-Christian world, whom we do not know, let us analyse the Christian world, whom we do know. They may be divided into the following classes :

I. Extremist: ritualist, if High; sensationalist, if Low.
II. Real and undemonstrative.
III. Nominal: (A) for form's sake, *i.e.* Baptism, Marriage, and Funeral ; (B) those who have cast off all belief, yet still cling to Worship for fashion's sake, and to Morality for the sake of their social position.
IV. Theists, Agnostics, Theosophists.
V. Census-Christians, utterly without any Religious feelings.

Owing to very strict, and strictly enforced, laws in civilized countries, crime against person and property is kept in check. Before we condemn others, let them be weighed in the same scales, and subjected to the same civil and criminal laws: in India, for instance, all atrocious crime is stamped out, under the stern principle, that nothing can be theologically right, which is morally wrong. Had Abraham attempted to kill Isaac in an Indian District, the police would have interfered. Had Ananias and Sapphira been disposed of in an Indian District, the local Magistrate would have arrested all concerned. Had Stephen been stoned in the streets of Banáras, the young man, who held his clothes, and any of the other murderers, would have expiated their crime on the gallows.

A comparative study of the Religions of Antiquity, a thing impossible until this century, has widened the horizon of our Ideas, and has so thoroughly established the Universality of a certain amount of Central Religious Truth, that, if we found the Decalogue set out in an Assyrian Tablet, or a newly-translated Book of the Búddhists, we should not think of literary larceny, but of a common inheritance.

Let me be bold: I believe in the innate goodness of man to a certain extent: he is the chef d'œuvre of the works of the great Creator: I pass my eyes down the great scroll of the Vegetable, and Animal, World, and find nothing after all so excellent as man, in spite of all his failings, weaknesses, and errors: of all the animals he is the only one, to whom the Grace of repentance for an evil act is given: his heart turns like a sunflower to the great Creator: when the Holy Spirit does penetrate its darkness, it becomes full of light. There is in the Genus Homo, and in him alone, the power of apprehending the Infinite, or, at least, trying to do so. Whatever may be said of the want of evidence, or the unreasonableness of asking for it, man alone has the faculty of seizing on, and believing in, an Unknown Power.

'Ανθρωπος is interpreted as "ὁ ἄνω ἄθρων."

It is neither civilization, nor Revelation, nor Wisdom, nor Morality, that does this: it is the man, and it is evidenced in the lowest, and most degraded, Savage, whom we are obliged to class as man, and who yet, so far, justifies our classification.

Far be it from me to say, or imply, one word against the Truth, the reality, the power, of the Christian Religion of the Nineteenth Century: without it life would be poor indeed: let me enumerate the features of that Religion:

I. The Monotheism of a Deity.
II. The necessity of personal Morality.
III. The admission of sinfulness, and need of Salvation by a Saviour.
IV. An indwelling Holy Spirit.
V. The conception of Future Rewards and Punishments.
VI. Love, not Fear, governing the relation of the Creator to His poor children.
VII. The worship of the Creator in spirit and truth.
VIII. Complete tolerance of the belief of others.
IX. Doing unto others what we should wish others to do unto us.
X. Obedience to, and an abiding Hope in, God, and Faith in Christ.
XI. Love to our neighbour without any exception.
XII. Equality of both sexes in this world and the next.

Ever and anon from the non-Christian world comes up some glimpse of the admission of some of these features, as will be evidenced in the following pages, but some are totally absent: none more so than tolerance of the opinion of others: it seems so strange, that the Kings of Judah should have thought themselves at liberty to change backwards and forwards the Religious Worship of their people, oscillating from Hezekiah to Manasseh, and from him to Josiah: the Hindu and the Græco-Roman were ever tolerant, and the same may be said of the Zoroastrian, Buddhist, and Confucian forms of belief; but the Christian and Mahometan have been intolerant to a frightful extent, using the Arm of the Flesh to torture and slay: Archdeacon Farrar justly remarks, that "God knows of no orthodoxy "but the Truth: the attempt to identify orthodoxy with pre- "conceived, and purely traditional, opinion is rooted in "cowardice, and has been prolific in casuistry and disaster." (Expositor, vol. ix, p. 11.)

Paul quoted one line only of the far-famed passage of Aratus from the Poem Φαινόμενα (300 B.C.):

ἐκ Διὸς ἀρχώμεσθα, τὸν οὐδέποτ' ἄνδρες ἐῶμεν
ἄῤῥητον· μεσταὶ δὲ Διὸς πᾶσαι μὲν ἀγυιαί,
πᾶσαι δ' ἀνθρώπων ἀγοραί· μεστὴ δὲ Θάλασσα,
καὶ λιμένες·· πάντη δὲ Διὸς κεχρήμεθα πάντες·
Τοῦ γὰρ καὶ γένος ἐσμέν.

Perhaps the sentiment contained in the last half-line was a quotation from a still older Poet, for we find it again in the Hymn to Jupiter by Cleanthes, who also lived in the third century B.C., and the solemn earnest beauty of these lines, which I quote below, have never been surpassed by any Asiatic or European writer of any period:

Κύδιστ' ἀθανάτων, πολυώνυμε παγκρατὲς αἰεί,
Ζεῦ, φύσεως ἀρχηγέ, νόμου μέτα πάντα κυβερνῶν,
χαῖρε. Σὲ γὰρ πάντεσσι θέμις θνητοῖσι προσαυδᾶν.
Ἐκ σοῦ γὰρ γένος ἐσμέν, ἦς μίμημα λαχόντες
Μοῦνοι, ὅσα ζώει τε καὶ ἕρπει θνήτ' ἐπὶ γαῖαν.
Τῷ σε καθυμνήσω, καὶ σὸν κράτος αἰὲν ἀείσω.
Σοὶ δὴ πᾶς ὅδε κόσμος ἑλισσόμενος περὶ γαῖαν
Πείθεται ᾗ κεν ἄγῃς, καὶ ἑκὼν ὑπὸ σεῖο κρατεῖται,
Οὐδέ τι γίγνεται ἔργον ἐπὶ χθονὶ σοῦ δίχα, δαῖμον,
Οὔτε κατ' αἰθέριον θεῖον πόλον, οὔτ' ἐνὶ πόντῳ,
Πλὴν ὁπόσα ῥέζουσι κακοὶ σφετέρῃσιν ἀνοίαις.

Paul was not like so many Missionaries of modern time, ignorant of the sacred books of the Heathen. The Hindu books are as great or greater than those of the Greeks. I could quote passages from them of the most lofty character.

Only a short time ago Cardinal Vaughan quoted the following passage from Xavier: "Who can sit complacent and self-satisfied at home, while *hell is being filled with the souls of the Heathen?*" This seems to be a very bold assumption with regard to the Heathen, and a Spaniard of a nation, red with the blood of Protestants and Jews, might be more reticent as to future punishment of awful sins.

It may be reverently admitted, even by those, to whom Christ is the beginning, centre, and end, of their lives, that the non-Christian world in present and past times is capable of receiving influence from God: the Lord hardened Pharaoh's heart, and He influenced the heart of Cyrus in favour of the Jews: "Non sine Diis" may be written on the History of mankind. Socrates, Búddha, Kong-Fu-Tsee, Zoroaster, the Hindu Sages, received a supernatural elevation of their moral and intellectual faculties: in fact, they were favoured through the fog around their generation to recognise the existence of Moral Truth, and to see God. It may be boldly said, that each one of us, who allows his thoughts to wander on Heaven's track, whether in the wakeful hours of the night, when he is alone with God, or in his solitary walks, when he is alone with the magnificence of God's Works, or when he is alone and wrapped up in thoughts of God, has deeper introspection of Truth, a sudden lifting up for a moment of his aspirations, for the Holy Spirit thus works, and in all times has worked, with the Human Soul: we must not presume to shorten the hand of God in His touch of His poor children of elder centuries, or heathen environment in modern times: if it were His will, by one word all mankind could be brought to Christ this very day. Remember Peter's words, Acts, x, 34, 35, "no respecter of persons," $\pi\rho o\sigma\omega\pi o\lambda\dot{\eta}\pi\tau\eta\varsigma$. Remember Paul's words at Athens and Lystra: he did not begin his message of a new Religion by denouncing the old, as so many foolish Missionaries do: "what ye *worship in ignorance* I set forth unto you."

The study of the Religion of barbarous tribes is even more important from the point of view of this essay than that of a civilized Nation. In the latter we have the lucubrations of high culture by men, who thought calmly and deeply, such men as Socrates and Búddha: there is more of man, and less of God. In the latter it is the unadulterated touch of God upon the intellect of poor, uneducated man: but for God it would not have existed. We may venture to say, that not Moses only, but Plato, and his like, were in their own degree $\pi a\iota\delta a\gamma\omega\gamma o\grave{\iota}$ $\epsilon\grave{\iota}\varsigma$ $\chi\rho\iota\sigma\tau\acute{o}\nu$.

Religious convictions, words, and practices, should never be laughed at: to do so indicates an irreligious mind: the exhibition of Idols brought home from Africa at Missionary Meetings, in order to raise a smile on the ignorant members of the lower second class, or Sunday-school children, is a disgrace. Place such objects away in Museums alongside of the Ark of the Covenant, and the seven-branched candlestick, and the Palladium, and the tripod of Delphi, and the Brazen Serpent, and the Two Tables of Stone, when they are found. Religion even in a mistaken form is one of the highest outcomes of the Human Race: we know what Atheism and Agnosticism mean. The feeling after God, if haply you could find him, ennobles the Human Race. A competent author, Max Müller (Science of Religion, p. 263), writes: "The intention of Religion, wherever we meet it, is holy;

"however imperfect and childish it may be, it always places the Human Soul in the presence of God: however imperfect and childish may be the conception of God, it always represents the highest ideal of perfection, which the Human Soul at the time being, with reference to its environment, can reach, and grasp. It places the Human Soul in the presence of its highest Ideal; it lifts it above the level of ordinary goodness, and produces at least a yearning after a higher and better life, a life in the light of God."

The messages conveyed by the different non-Christian Religions, if properly looked at, all converge in due time in the more complete message of the Gospel. We hardly sufficiently admit, how much mankind owes to Plato, and to the doctrines of Búddha. Both these epoch-making individuals lived centuries before Anno Domini, and left their mark upon Oriental, and Occidental, thought, never to be effaced. It is stated, and truly stated, that the Religion of Christ has been paganized, but in that Paganism there were Messages of Humanity, Brotherhood, Self-Sacrifice, zeal for the Souls of others than their own Race, general benevolence, which the Hebrew never knew, and knows not to this day: having broken his law before the Exile, he kept it on his return to Palestine according to his lights, and hugged himself as an inheritor of Promises; but he cared not a straw for the rest of the world, which might go in darkness for all that concerned him: he was cruel beyond the cruelty of other Nations: he left no single Monument of Art or Science: he made no single discovery to enlighten the world: in an epoch of Inscriptions on stone, and brick, metal, and papyri, he left nothing, but the one book of the Old Testament, and but for the Greek Translation made at Alexandria, he would have withheld that from the eyes of the Gentile, if he had been able: he perished out of his own land eighteen centuries ago, while the lordly Races of Eastern Asia have maintained their tenets, and their Worship, to this day. It has been the fashion to exalt the Hebrew above other Nations, because of him came Christ after the flesh, and to him was committed the oracles of God; but the mighty Nations, and civilizations, of Greece, Rome, India, and China, were in all things, moral and material, infinitely superior to the insignificant Hebrew.

With regard to Búddha, much has been written, and some rash assertions made: if it be alleged, that any portion of the teaching of the New Testament was derived from the teaching of Búddha, a direct negative may be emphatically given on the grounds of the absence of contact; but with regard to Socrates and Plato, bearing in mind the existence of Jewish colonies at Alexandria, and everywhere, the reply must be made with hesitation: no assertion is made, but a negative cannot be

recorded on the ground of want of possible contact. I quote the following expressions of opinion:
"Plato was regarded by the Early Fathers in the light of "another Apostle of the Gentiles. Justin Martyr, Jerome, "Lactantius, all speak of him as the wisest and greatest of "philosophers. Augustine calls him his converter, and thanks "God, that he became acquainted with Plato first, and the Gospel "afterwards. Eusebius declared, that he, alone of all the Greeks, "had attained the Porch of Truth. It is easy to understand the "grounds of this feeling. Passages from his dialogues might be "multiplied to prove that close similarity, which exists between "them and the Scriptures, especially the Pentateuch. The "picture of the ideal Socrates, preaching Justice and Temperance, "and opposing the self-assertion of the Pharisee of his age; "the humility of the earnest inquirer, and soberness of Truth; "his declaration at his trial, that he will obey God rather than "men, and fear not those, who are only able to kill the body; the "description of the just man persecuted, scourged, tortured, "and finally impaled: such passages serve to explain the prayer "of Erasmus, who added to the invocation of the Saints in his "library, 'Sancte Socrates, ora pro nobis,' and the belief of so "many of the Fathers that Plato, like St. John the Baptist, was "a forerunner of Christ.

"Again:
"(1) The faith in the Immortality of the Soul,
"(2) The pollution of Sin,
"(3) The likeness of Virtue to God,
"(4) The idea of a word sown in the heart,
"(5) The parable of the Cave, and the Light of the Upper World,

"might be quoted to show the foreshadowing of Christianity so "often traced to Plato.

"Add to this the remark, that men should persevere in search "of the Truth, taking the best of Human words to bear them up, "as on a raft, through the stormy waters of life; but their voyage "on this frail bark would be perilous, unless they might hope to "meet with some securer stay, some Word of God, it might be. "Augustine thought that Plato might have listened to Jeremiah "in Egypt." (Plato: Clifton Collins, p. 193.)

Cardinal Wiseman remarks in Callista, p. 227: "Religion could "not be without hope. To worship a being, who did not speak "to us, recognise us, love us, was not Religion; it might be "a duty, or a merit, but the instinctive notion of Religion is the "Soul's response to a God, who has taken notice of the Soul: "it was a living intercourse, or a mere name."

In the lately discovered monuments of Egypt and Assyria we

can see the ancient monarchs offering tribute to their tutelar deities, Amen Ra, or Ashur: can we think that Religion was not to them a positive fact?

Bishop Westcott writes: "As each Nation contributes some-"thing to the Fulness of the Life of Humanity, and something to "the knowledge of Man's powers, so is it with the manifestation "of Religious belief and aspirations. The Religious History "of the World is the Soul of History. The natural voice of "humanity proclaims with no uncertain sound, that God hath "made himself known in various ways at various times." (Gospel of Life, p. 109.)

"Noble principles are found in the teaching of all Religious "systems; that God is the author of all Truth, and all right "impulses even in heathen minds, is readily admitted." (Ellinwod's Oriental Religion, p. 224.)

The early Greek Fathers, especially Justin Martyr and Clement of Alexandria, realized the fact, that there was a work *for* and *of* God going on during the apparent isolation of the heathen from that narrow Hebrew Region, in which the Spirit had revealed Him. Justin says, that the Truths in the utterance of Heathen Poetry and Philosophy are due to the fact, that a seed of the Word is inborn (ἔμφυτον) in every Race of man. Those, who grasped the Truth according to the portion of the seed in them, just as Christians, lived according to the knowledge and contemplation of the whole Word, that is to say Christ; in fact, that Socrates, Heraclitus, and those like them, and Abraham, and Elias, were Christians before Christ in the flesh, though Christ indeed was πρωτότοκος τῆς κτίσεως. (Gospel of Life, pp. 116, 117.)

It is indeed a Godless, and non-Christian, conception to hold, that all the Nations of the world, who have not embraced the Religion of Christ, are outcasts, *forgotten by God*. Are they not rather waiting their appointed time?

I quote extracts from the pages of a well-known writer, from whom I differ in many things, yet agree in this (Max Müller's "Science of Religion," 1873, p. 224):

"We admire the temples of the ancient Rome in Egypt, "Babylonia, Greece, and Italy: can we call the Deities, to whom "they were consecrated, mere idols and images, and class such "men as Pericles, Phidias, Socrates, Plato, Cicero, Marcus "Aurelius, as worshippers of stocks and stones? Neither "Art, nor Poetry, nor Philosophy could have been possible "without Religion. If we believe, that there is a God, who "created Heaven and earth, and ruleth all by His unceasing "Providence, we cannot believe, that Millions of Human "beings were in the time of their ignorance so utterly "abandoned, that their Religion was a falsehood, their whole "life a mockery, their Worship a farce."

And there were such men as Socrates, Epictétus, Séneca, Plato, Gaútama Búddha, and Kong-Fu-Tsee.

Justin Martyr remarks (Apol. ii, 83, "Survivals in Christianity," p. 50) that "men of every Race, that Socrates and others, were Christians because they lived according to Reason, which is the Divine Word immanent in the world."

I quote the opinion of another writer on the subject : "The great Religious conceptions of the world, with the "exception of Judaism and Christianity, have hitherto been "treated by Historians and Theologians with the greatest "unfairness. Every act in the lives of their founders, which "showed, that they were but men, has been eagerly seized "upon, and judged without mercy: many of their doctrines "have been distorted: acts of Worship, merely because they "differed from the preconceptions of the writer, have been "held up to ridicule and contempt. The consequence has "been, that Christianity has *been torn away from the sacred* "*context of the History of the World.* The History of the non- "Christian Religious conceptions represent to man the Divine "Education of the Human Race."

Philo writes: "Goodness and kindness were the final causes of all Creation." It is no new idea to claim for the poor heathen sonship of God : Mutianus Rufus, a Canon of Gotha before the Reformation, wrote: Quid alium est verus Christianus, verus Dei filius quam, ut Paulus dicit, " Sapientia Dei," quæ non solim adfuit Judæis in angustâ Syriæ regione, sed Græcis, et Italis, et Germanis, quamquam vario ritu Religionem observarentur. (Hibbert Lecture : Beard—*Reformation*, p. 50.)

Read the following quotation from a Review thirty years old: " The Apostolic age bears witness, such as no other age has " borne, to the depth and vitality of those Religious Truths, " which rest on the greatest realities of the Universe. They " have been buried for centuries under a hard incrustation " of Human Dogmatism, till the deep life beating within is " scarcely perceptible any longer. Christianity will then re- " sume its Apostolic fervour, when, going back to the original " fountain of Faith in the Human Soul, and, renouncing the " fruitless controversies about forms of opinions, which derive " their value from intellectual needs of different minds, it shall " throw itself once more without distrust and reservation on " that Eternal Religion of the heart and conscience, which is " the utterance of God's Spirit within us, which Christ once " acted in the narrow circle of Palestinian life, and which His " followers, believing in the perpetuity of heavenly life, have " been striving for nearly 2000 years to spread over the world."

Dean Stanley writes: "The thoughts of man have grown

"wider: we have learnt, that Religion can be degraded, when
"it loses the vivifying and elevating contact of every-day life.
"Ecclesiastical degradation means Spiritual decay: the chief
"object of Religion is to teach us the right way of living
"the true life of man." (Lectures, 1867, p. xvi.)

Archbishop Trench, in his Hulsean Lecture, 1846, p. 136, writes: "I would fain show, that it would be a grievous
"deficiency, if our Christian faith as concerns the whole
"ancient world, except the Jewish, stood in relation to nothing,
"which men had hitherto thought, or felt, or hoped, or
"believed; rested on no broader historic basis than the Jewish
"Religion would supply. It will be profitable to enquire,
"whether we may not contemplate the relations of the
"absolute Truth to the ancient Religions of the world under
"an aspect, in which we shall cease altogether from regarding
"with suspicion these apparent anticipations of good things
"given us in Christ; in which, instead of being secretly
"embarrassed by them, and hardly knowing exactly how to
"deal with, or where to range them, we shall joyfully accept
"these presentiments of the Truth, so far as they are satis-
"factorily made out, as enhancing the greatness and the glory
"of the Truth itself; and as being, so far as they are allowed
"to have any weight, confirmations of it."

Archbishop Benson, at Exeter Hall, Nov., 1893, spoke thus:
"No doubt there is scarcely a Religion, in which you cannot
"trace something that is above Humanity; but how does our
"Lord, and how did His Apostles, treat that Fact? Have they
"not made it plain, that all notions of God in the past, attained
"by the light of Nature, as we call it, by the Spirit of God, that
"is, stirring and lighting every man that cometh into the world,
"were all a preparation for that complete Religion, which
"it takes Humanity long ages to prepare for. Why, the very
"fact, that He died for all men is sufficient to establish the right
"of all men to know the Fact. If a great inheritance is left
"to a man, is it not a matter of common honesty, that he should
"be informed, that this inheritance is his? It is the very
"nature of the way, in which God has given us this knowledge,
"that man should only know it through man. He does not
"reveal it in lightnings upon the skies, but reveals it from man
"to man, from lip to lip. That is the only way, in which
"man could possibly know that, which it is the right of every
"man to know, because this Fact of Christ is theirs."

Mr. Lefroy, of the Delhi Mission, 1894, is very bold, and reflects the feeling of all, who think deeply and lovingly of the poor heathen in past and present times: "We hold, that
"there is no Nation in the world, which has been omitted from
"the Providence and discipline of God, no Nation, in which

" He has left Himself without a witness finding its expression,
" however distorted or perverted, in their creed and thoughts,
" no Nation therefore which cannot find in Christ, not the
" destruction, but the fulfilment and completion of all that
" is best and truest in the past."

Bishop Westcott writes: " It seems, as if a careful examination
" of the Religious teaching of representative Masters of the West
" would help towards a better understanding of the Christian
" Creed." (Religious Thoughts in the West, 1891 : Preface.)

A mistaken burst of occasional piety on the part of the Hebrews, with long intervals of gross Idolatry, and a steady refusal of Christians to look into the matter, free from prejudice and fanaticism, has until this generation led them to condemn all the Religious conceptions of the elder world, and declare, that the beliefs and Worship of the non-Christian world at the present day, is nothing but a master-work of Satan. Considering that the population of the world is 1400 Millions, and that only one-third are even *nominal* Christians, it would seem, that the strong man is out of possession of his own house, and that the hand of the Ruler of the Universe is shortened. Can this be so? What are the Facts? The early Nations were essentially pious, feeling after their great Creator, if haply they could find Him ; if they were Agnostics, they were unwillingly so from lack of knowledge, and not from a perverted superfluity of knowledge. A congenital Instinct had been granted to Man to utter articulate sounds, and turn to his great Creator even as the sunflower turns to the sun. " Self, the World, God," indicates the relation, which man occupied to his fellow-men, and the great Unknown : Language in the one case, and Religion in the other, was the mode of communication. The Egyptian, Indo-Iranian, Græco-Latin, Kelt-Teuton-Slav, recognised, and bowed to the Power of Nature, the Strong One, whose might was felt to be irresistible, constant, unchanging, and orderly, in its operation, yet full of pity, tender mercy, and benevolence ; providing for their wants by the luxuriant abundance of the Earth and the Water. They had no doubt of the presence of an eternal and active Intelligence, whom they tried in their weak, foolish, way to conciliate.

I quote the sentiments of an accomplished writer : "As we
" study, we begin to see, what ought never to have been
" doubted, that there is no Religion without God, and, as
" Augustine of Hippo expresses it, there is no false Religion,
" which does not contain some elements of Truth." We may return the compliment, that there is no form of the One True Religion, which has not some false elements clinging to it, the remanet of the conception, out of which it was developed.

It is bold to state, and dangerous to weak, narrow, minds to hear the statement, that our Heavenly Father has manifested Himself to His poor children at all times and in all places in the mode, in which He knew that the state of the intellectual culture of each exalted them to comprehend. Rightly or wrongly (I think wrongly), the first work of the modern Missionary of the Nineteenth Century is supposed to be to teach his converts, or inquirers, to read and write, to give them a cheap surface-Education, and introduce them to printed literature; it is assumed, that the oral teaching of the Master, and His Apostles, and of the early centuries, would not enable the neo-Christian to advance: this shows that to the modern notion Culture precedes, or accompanies, the Christian Faith. Culture is the outcome of Peace, Wealth, orderly government, tolerance, and justice between man and man. This is possible in the Nineteenth Century: was it within the comprehension of the elder world? How intolerant were the kings of Israel and Judah! What shall be said of the Hebrew people down to the assassination of Stephen? It is clear, that admitting fully that the Religion of the Hebrews was specially ordained by God for that petty Nation, which was never destined to rise beyond the position of a Slave-Nation, in a very low state of Culture, passing from the bondage of the Egyptians into that of the Philistines, Assyrians, and Babylonians, and afterwards of the Persians, Greeks, and Romans, until their utter extinction as a Nation, and the supercession of their Religion by a later conception, that later conception was suited to a state of Society much higher advanced in the scale of Culture, and calculated, by its freedom from all local ties, when the wall of separation of one Nation from another was dashed down, with its sweet reasonableness, and holy elasticity, to dominate the Globe, though that event seems now entirely out of all Human calculation, and, owing to the vast annual increase of the non-Christian population, at the rate of twelve Millions annually, to be utterly out of all reasonable expectation.

Nor was the dispensation to the Jews ever intended, as far as can be judged from the words of Isaiah and the other Prophets, or permitted, to be permanent. The Religious conceptions of the Zoroastrian, Hindu, Búddhist, and Confucianist have existed for nearly three thousand years, but the Mosaic dispensation at the best only lasted fourteen hundred years, and in B.C. 397 Malachi, the last of the Prophets, uttered the following words:

"I will be great among the Heathen, says the Lord; in every place incense shall be offered in My name from the rising to the going down of the Sun." The introduction of the term "incense" precludes the application of the words to the Christian Religion, where, except in degraded forms of Worship, incense has no place either in precept or practice. Viewed in that light, the scorn, and want of sympathy, with which the modern Missionary treats the pious non-Christian worshipper of his ancestral Faith, is a cause of surprise: it arises from the Egotism, and Albocracy, of the modern Teuton and Latin Races, and not from the precepts of the Holy Religion, which they are commissioned to convey.

More appalling, and confounding all expectations, is the new crop of Religious conceptions, of error, which stand in the way of Conversion to Christianity, much more spiritual than the older conceptions, and accompanied by the highest Morality: the Aria-Somáj, the Brahmo-Somáj, Theosophism, Mormonism, the Hau-Hau of New Zealand, Agnosticism, Unitarianism. In the early centuries of Christianity, there were the worshippers of Isis, and the Great Mother, Mithraism, Manichæism, but they were hunted down, and extirpated, by the Christians. Such unchristian violence cannot be used now: the majority of the new conceptions of the Nineteenth Century put forth the desire to worship a pure God, to live a pure life, to consider all men as brothers: this platform represents a mighty advance of the conception of Religion in its broadest sense, but on non-Christian lines.

We must be prepared for one thing: all Religious conceptions are made for man, all mankind, free from all degrading necessities, such as circumcision, tattooing, caste-marks, and connection with Idolatrous survivals, such as the Arabian Kaaba-Stone: History tells us, that when a world-wide conception impinges on different Races, on different rounds of Culture, with different historical and political environment, it does not lose its originality, but adapts itself: the different Churches of Asia, North Africa, and Europe, differed materially in their external form: the great sin of the Church of Rome was the desire to introduce uniformity, and submission to a so-called Vice-Regent of God, an erring man, aided by a most corrupt, self-seeking, Council: it has notably failed: it would be folly on the part of any Protestant Church to attempt to act in this way. The Negro Churches of West Africa, the Churches in South India, South Africa, the Extreme Orient, and Oceania, will never submit to such a domination.

The following great Truths have been worked out, and it cannot be denied, that the ancient Religious conceptions, which preceded the great Anno Domini, contributed to the great store, of which the Nineteenth Century is heir:

    I. The Unity of God.
    II. The Spirituality of Religion.
    III. The Substitution of Prayer for Sacrifice.

IV. The Highest Conception of Morality.
V. The great gift of Self-Sacrifice.
VI. The Hope of Immortality, or, in other words, the Sound of Glory ringing in our ears.

The unique characteristics of the Religion of Christ, being based on Faith, lie outside the orbit of this Essay, which accepts nothing incapable of scientific proof, or reasonable deductions from ascertained facts.

CAP. I. A SUPERNATURAL POWER.

1. Existence of such a Power.
   A. Anthropomorphism.
   B. Monolatry.
   C. Monotheism.
   D. Polytheism.
2. Place of Residence of such a Power.
3. Theophanies, Visions, Dreams, Good and Evil Spirits.
4. Primeval Revelation: was there any?
5. Substitution of Idols made by men's hands for an impersonal Divinity.
6. Fatherhood of God.
7. Threats of worshippers uttered against their gods.

1. EXISTENCE OF SUCH A POWER.

It may with great confidence be asserted, that no Race of men, however degraded, has been found, who have not a more or less distinct conception of a Power greater than themselves, whether for good, or for evil, whom it is their interest to conciliate, and their duty to obey.

Bishop Philip Brooke writes thus: "The Messenger of "Christianity finds some consciousness of the fact, that the "world belongs to God, wherever he goes. No land is so dark, "that there is not some such light there. No brutal savagedom "so savage, that in some breast of nobler sort, or it may be, "kept only in some fantastic rite, whose spiritual meaning has "long been lost, there is not uttered some craving for the true "nobility of servantship to God. It cannot be explained "away."

Peter, the Apostle, admits the fact: "In every Nation he, that feareth Him, and worketh righteousness, is accepted with Him." (Acts, x, 35.)

Paul, the Apostle, remarked: "Who in times past suffered all Nations to walk in their own ways." "He left not Himself without witness." (Acts, xiv, 16, 17.)

Bishop Westcott remarks in his Gospel of Life (1874, p. 19):
" Christianity assumes as its foundation :
"(1) The existence of an Infinite Personal God.
"(2) The existence of a finite Human will.
" This antithesis is assumed, and not proved. No arguments
" can establish it. It is a primary intuition, not a deduction ;
" it is capable of illustration from what we observe around
" us : but, if either proposition be denied, no reasoning can
" establish it."

The Latin Poets teem with quotations, indicating that the existence of God is recognised, that He controls the affairs of men, that it is wise to obey God, that it is impious to deny Him or oppose Him : it may be summed up in the apophthegm :

" Nihil humanarum rerum sine numine geritur,
   Nihil Diis invitis fieri potest." (Bible-Echoes, p. 189.)
" Divinâ prudentiâ agitur mundus."

What was inexorable Fate with the Græco-Latin Races, "Μοῖρα," "necessitas"? What in very truth was "Karma" with the Búddhist, though he declared that there was no God ? "Fata negant": "Sic volucre Parcæ," say Virgil and Horace, when in despair on the subject of undeserved affliction, or unmerited prosperity. Homer writes, Iliad, I, 5, Διὸς δ' ἐτελείετο βουλή. The Indian mind reached to a lower depth : it admits the guilt of the sufferer in past life as all the cause of his trouble ; he anticipates the reward of the innocent in the next life.

Herodotus was essentially a Religious man : speaking of the rumour, which ran through the Greek Army at Mycale, on the morning of the battle, of a victory gained the same day at Platæa, he says : " Many things prove to me, that the gods take a part in the affairs of men," and yet, about 450 B.C., the gods, under the influence of Philosophy, were departing from their Grecian temples : it is reported, that Herodotus was present in the Theatre of Bacchus at some of the great dramas, and he would then have heard the Divine Voice in some one of the great utterances of the actors, or the chorus. He must have felt οὔτεν ἄνευ τῶν Θεῶν ; but what those gods were he did not venture to speculate : he was too wide a traveller, and too deep a thinker, for that.

The Idea of God may be shrouded in darkness, but it is there : Professor Legge writes, that the Idea of one God, and one only God, existed among the Chinese from the earliest time, though it has been doubted by some writers, and is certainly obscured by the degraded conceptions of later ages. Nature was conceived to be a manipulation of a great Power, and peopled with Spirits in subordination to Him.

We must recollect, that the name, by which the Great Power is known, is unimportant. By many names men knew Him: Jehovah, Jove, Lord, Shaddai, Elohim, Allah, Mahéswara, Bóg, Deus, Θεός, Khuda, Gott : in China they cannot get beyond the word, which represents the Heavens. The character attributed to Him is of the prime importance. All other names are but the shadow of the reality. The Fatherhood of God stands confessed in the words of Homer, Ζεῦ πάτερ; of Virgil, " Hominum pater atque Deorum."

Hear Bishop Selwyn the younger: " In all ages, and in all " Races, men have felt after this great Truth : God has not left " Himself without a witness, and the Human heart, led by that " witness, whether internal or external, has always stretched out " its hands (it may be unconsciously) towards the Fatherhood " of God. The teaching of Christ is its very highest revelation : " 'Our Father, which art in Heaven.' In place of all the " countless Spirits, which they believe in, we tell them of the " one great omnipotent God, who made the world : when they " have grasped this truth in some measure, we tell them in the " name of Christ, that God is our Father, and that His name " is Love." (Ramsden Sermons, Cambridge.)

Driver remarks, on pp. 302, 303 of his Introduction to the Old Testament, that the fact, that God has pity on all Nations, is taught in the Book of Jonah; and the last verse of that Book indicates, that God has pity on the cattle also, as well as ignorant men.

Those, who have studied the great dramas of the Greek Tragedians, must feel that they are in the presence of those Deities, whom the Athenians worshipped. The Tragedians would not dare place in their mouths words unworthy of them. Truth, Purity, Retribution for sin, obedience to the Divine Will : these are the watchwords: the audience accepted with reverence the oracles of their God, the words of the 'Deus ex machinâ.' Their view of life is stern and severe: individual, family, Nation : their moral is always good : sorrow follows sin : vengeance will certainly find out the offender, though a long time is allowed to elapse: with the same measure, that a man metes, it will be measured to him again: suffering is the only road to true happiness, if it comes in the path of Duty. The Hindu sages elaborated the Idea still more fully. In the grand Epics of Homer and Virgil the Immortals above are as fully occupied in planning, and contriving, as the poor mortals below. Another view of the subject is presented in the utterances of Isaiah, Jeremiah, and Ezekiel: it is taken for granted, that they were commissioned by Jehovah to make certain utterances : the mode, in which the message came to them, is not stated: the word of the Lord, "dabar Yahveh," came to them.

The question, of course, arises to thoughtful minds: are we in the Nineteenth Century A.D. further off from God than these Prophets in the sixth century B.C.? The Deity no longer appears in Human form: the age of myths and legends has passed: Prophecy, Miracles, Theophanies, Signs from Heaven, are no longer in harmony with the Human intellect: but God is very nigh unto us, for all that, for all that: He is in our midst, when we assemble, and our bodies are the temples of the Holy Spirit. The old machinery, and manner of speaking, have passed away.

In the Egyptian papyri and Inscriptions we read of such a Power (Hibbert Lecture: Renouf, p. 25):

(1) To whom no temple is raised.
(2) Who was not graven on stone.
(3) Whose shrine was never found in painted figures.
(4) Who had neither ministrants nor offerings.
(5) Whose abode was unknown.

But that Power was practically in the course of centuries lost sight of. We meet in the Texts such phrases as this: (1) the Self-existing one, (2) the Self-becoming one, (3) the One, the One of Ones, (4) the One without a Second, (5) the beginners of becoming from the first, (6) the One, who made all things, but was not made.

I read the following Inscription on a Temple of Neith, at Said in Egypt (Sacred Anthology, p. 65):

"I am that, which has been, which is, which will be, and no one has yet lifted the veil, which covers me."

"Nuk pa nuk: I am that I am." (Hibbert Lecture: Renouf.)

Some think, that Αθήνη is a transposition of Neith. (Rawlinson's Herodotus, II, ph. 106, 107.)

Dr. Ginsburg writes, that the Moabites felt towards Chemosh the same feelings as the Hebrews to Yahveh, attributing to His anger their defeats, to His favour their victories: this phrase is retained in some modern prayers as the husk of an Idea, which has long died, but it was a very present Idea in the ancient world.

Religion is the one universal feature in the History of mankind, and the annals of no country introduce us to Atheism, or Agnosticism: quite the contrary: we find the existence of a Religion and a God, patent everywhere.

The Azteks of Mexico recognised the existence of a Supreme Creator, and Lord of the Universe. (Prescott, I, p. 52.)

The Idea of a Divinity is indeed the solution of the perplexity of existence: it comes by intuition, not by observation, and gradually develops; it does not require Science, or Philosophy, to point out the Deity; in the elements, in the environment, on Earth, in Heaven, *He is there*, and no place can be pointed out, where he is not. By introspection the lowest savage works out the syllogism of self, the world, or the rest of mankind, except himself, and something outside the world, and self, but which controls all, and is God.

A. Anthropomorphism.

Nothing strikes the reader more painfully than this feature in the Old Testament: of course, it stands out as, or even more, conspicuously in other forms of Religious conception. Moses goes so far as to arrange, that the Deity should only exhibit "his hinder parts": but throughout we hear of the Deity having ears, limbs, even weaknesses such as anger, infirmities such as hate, love, hardness of heart, wrath, even revenge; vacillation of purpose, repentance (Driver, O.T. p. 114): this cannot be explained by any reason such as the vagueness of Oriental expressions, or poetical license, or mistaken translation: Elijah twits the Priests of Baal, that their gods could not hear. Even down to the present epoch, Anthropomorphism has not been got rid of.

In other Religious conceptions, the gods were actually men with lusts and passions, partialities and prejudices. With rare exceptions Idols are made in Human form entirely, as Rama, and Krishna; or partially as Ganésa, with the head of an elephant, and Diana of Ephesus, a hideous monster.

The Idea of the Deity making a covenant with His poor creatures is a Human conception, and even now in Christian prayer we have such expressions as "let your ears be open to the prayers of your servant; your protecting hand, your observant eye": of course it means nothing beyond this, that man cannot form a conception of the Deity except through the known feature of poor Human Nature. The Asiatic makes his god a dark brown. The African makes his god black; the European naturally adopts a white colour.

Anthropomorphism seems to be an essential of all early Religion. Man in his earliest stage worshipped stocks and stones in their natural form: this was called Fetichism. As he arrived at the conviction, that he himself was the centre of animal existence; as he found no other animal equal to him in strength and cunning, in articulate speech, in the power of leaving tokens behind by marks on the sand, and broken twigs

in the forest, so that others coming after him could understand
his message; as he became dimly conscious of the possession
of five senses, and the gift of accumulating experience, he
could no longer worship a brute beast (though, strange to say,
the highly-cultured Egyptians did so), and he could invest the
Deity, the creation of his intellect, and Religious instinct, with
no form of higher dignity than the one, which he himself
possessed: the eye, the ear, the mouth, the nose, the hand.
Then the shapeless stone assumed the rough Idea of the
Human form: the Old Testament tells us that "that form was
in God's own Image."

B. *Monolatry.*

Many narrow-minded religionists, even to this day, get an
idea, that God is *their* God, *their peculiar* God, who manages
their affairs, who cares for *them*: this is their Faith, a selfish form
of Faith: a Protestant would scarcely admit, that it is the same
God, who is Father of His Roman Catholic children, and of the
non-Christian world: the Jews had the same conception; they
were before the time of Josiah, not Monotheists, but " Mono-
latrists," or, as some call it, " Enotheists": Yahveh was their
God, and looked after them: they had heard, that other tribes
had Baal, Rimmon, Chemosh, Ashtoreth: they did not deny
this: but their God was God of all gods, who had power to
influence Gentile Monarchs, such as Cyrus and Darius, in the
interest of His people (*i.e.* themselves). Gradually they came
out of this fog: we hear no more of the God of Abraham, Isaac,
and Jacob, except for purposes of argument as regards a Future
State; but Nehemiah is represented as praying at Shushan
to the God of Heaven, the same title, which Cyrus had given
Him (II Chron. xxxvi, 23).

Do Christians reflect on this? God is not the God of the
Christians only. Christ did not die for the Christians only, but
for the whole world. It would be questioning God's wisdom and
justice to assert, that the great people of India and China were
condemned to everlasting punishment, because they knew not the
God and Saviour, who had never been preached to them. Nor
can we attribute to the machinations of Satan the existences of
the great Religions of China, India, Persia, Mesopotamia, Egypt,
Greece, and Rome: the first verse of the Epistle to the Hebrews
teaches another lesson. God was not left without a witness
even in the childhood of the world, and it is the mark of an
arrogant, degraded, unchristian, spirit, to denounce the Religious
weaknesses of Nations, who never had the chance of being
Christians.

When we reflect calmly on the Features of the great Book-

Religions, and the mass of non-Christian Ideas and customs absorbed into itself by so-called Christianity, which is so far from the Gospel taught in Palestine, and preached by the Apostles, when we consider the loathsome sins of sinners in Christian cities, such as London, we may as well pause, for as far as concerns the masses Christianity has miserably failed: and who are we, the most drunken Nation in Europe, to throw dirt upon the Mahometan, and the ancient conceptions of India and China, whom the Lord of the world has permitted to exist for three thousand years? had it pleased Him, they might have passed away like the beautiful conceptions of Greece and Rome.

In the fourth volume of Renan's posthumous work, 1893 (p. 131), appears the following:

"The Deutero-Isaiah had held out a prospect to all Nations to enter Jerusalem: Ezra and his successors closed the door. Jehovah became again the peculiar property, and the exclusive right, of the Hebrews; their own particular Deity reappeared, a very Egoistical Deity, according to their views, very perverse and hostile to all the Human Race, except His Chosen People, very unjust to all the rest of His poor children. The Thora, as introduced by Ezra, was merely a scheme to bribe Jehovah by strict observance of certain rituals to get certain good things at His disposal: the caprice of this particular Deity had to be satisfied by services of hymns, by compliments to His Glory, and in return for the pleasure provided for Him He would give all the good things of the world: and much was to be done by His influencing the hearts of the men of this world, who held the physical force of Empire, on whom He was supposed to have a direct influence, though they were not His people."

If anyone doubts the Monolatrism of the Hebrews, let him consider the title "God of all gods"; and Psalm lxxxvi, 8, 10:

"Among the gods there is none like unto Thee, O Lord; there is not one that can do as Thou doest."

"Thou art God alone."

Whatever was the date of this Psalm the utterances are not those of one, who is a Monotheist, to whose mind the existence of any other gods would be an absurdity.

C. *Monotheism.*

Just at the same time that it was brought home to Isaiah, that the God hitherto called God of Israel was the only God, and that there was none but Him, the same line of reasoning led him to perceive that, if that point were conceded, He must be the God of all Mankind, Gentile as well as Jew: that word Gentile came into existence in Isaiah's time: the elder Hebrew had no thought beyond his own Nation, and a contemptuous hatred to all outside.

There was another result of Monotheism, a faint conception of the Perfection of the Deity: the Human mind, when it arrived at the first Idea, passed on to the further conception, that one so Powerful must be the Ideal of Perfection as regards Human qualities, the very essence of Righteousness, the very type of Sympathy, the impersonation of Law, Justice, Love, and Pity. According to the Ideal thus formed of their Divinity would be the permanence of their Faith, and the desire to develop, and grow into His Likeness. From this conception developed the Idea of a Future State, not such as is painted by Homer, but one of Rewards and Punishments: the Indian Sages got over this ethical difficulty by the conception of the transmigration of Souls to a higher or lower sphere according to the tenour of the life spent.

What grander description of the Infinite Deity can be cited than this quotation from the great Sanskrit Poem, Raghuvansa, by Kalidása, the greatest of the Indian Bards?

" He sat, that awful Deity, in state:
" His throne encircling heavenly armies wait;
" Around His head celestial rays were shed;
" Beneath His feet His conquered foes were spread;
" To Him the trembling gods their homage brought:
" Incomprehensible in word or thought.

" O Thou, whom threefold might and splendour veil,
" Maker, Preserver, and Destroyer, hail!
" Thy gaze surveys this world from clime to clime,
" Thyself immeasurable in space, or time:
" To no corrupt desires, no passions prone,
" Unconquered Conqueror, infinite, unknown.
" Though in one form Thou veil'st Thy might divine,
" Still at Thy pleasure every form is Thine:
" Pure crystals thus prismatic hues assume,
" As varying lights, and varying tints, illume.
" Men think Thee absent: Thou art ever near,
" Pitying those sorrows, which Thou ne'er can'st fear.
" Unsordid penance Thou alone can'st pay:
" Unchanged, unchanging, old without decay.
" Thou knowest all things: who Thy praise can state?
" Createdst all things, Thyself uncreate:

" The world obeys Thy uncontrolled behest
" In whatsoever form Thou stand'st confessed.
" Though Human wisdom many roads can see,
" That lead to happiness, all verge in Thee:
" So Ganga's waves from many a distant snow
" Unite, and to one mighty ocean flow.
" They, who on Thee have fixed their steadfast mind,
" And to Thy power themselves, their all, consigned,
" Free from desire Thou lead'st them to that bourne,
" Where all must go, whence none can e'er return.
" Though of Thy might before man's wondering eyes
" The earth, the universe, in witness rise,
" Still by no human skill, no mortal mind,
" Can Thy infinity be e'er defined.
" As the bright pearls surpass the ocean bed,
" The sun the light by wandering planets shed,
" So far Thy real form's celestial ray
" Exceeds the homage, which weak mortals pay:
" And, if to bid Thy awful grandeur hail,
" Our feeble voices in their tribute fail,
" 'Tis not the number of Thy praises cease,
" But that our power, alas! knows no increase."

(ROBERT N. CUST:
Poems of many years and places, 1842.)

So in the Egyptian system Amen Ra is more a spiritual conception than a material reality. In Homer Zeus is Lord of all. More than this: beyond the conception of one great Power was the great Idea of the Avatára, the Immanuel, the Son of God, sent to redeem man in Human form. One of the fiercest apophthegms of the Mahometan is, " Men will tell any lie; they even say that God can have a son." Yet History tells us, that in the annals of the two greatest Races of mankind, the Græco-Roman and the Indian, this was an accepted article of Faith long before the great Anno Domini. The Roman Centurion, who had witnessed the awful scene of the Crucifixion, belonged no doubt to the Olympian Religion, and bore testimony that He, who had died on the Cross, was the Son of God; he could think of nothing higher, to which he could compare his dignity, his patience, his God-likeness, than to Hercules, Bacchus, or the Gemini. No ignorant Gentile, as he was, could have had any conception of the Logos, the Ἁγία Σοφία, the Second Person of the Trinity.

At the eve of the epoch of the great Anno Domini, we find Horace addressing the Emperor Augustus in the following line:

" Serus in cœlum redeas."

And Virgil, writing of the same Emperor:
"Namque erit ille mihi semper Deus."
Adrian's dying words are worth recording:
"Ut puto, Deus fio."
Caligula's instructions to his subjects ran thus:
"Dominus, et Deus, noster, sic fieri jubet."
(SUETONIUS, cap. xiii.)

In India I have known ignorant men trying to get something out of their English Ruler by gross flattery. I have myself been addressed in the shocking blasphemous way, "Hazúr Paraméshvar," "your Highness is the great God."

The words had lost their spiritual force; the Idea of the name, originally reserved to the Ruler of the Universe, had been degraded: the same fate has happened to the words κύριος, dominus, lord, Herr, in Europe; the sovereigns of the last two centuries have usurped the title of Majesty, formerly reserved to the Deity.

D. *Polytheism*.

As Monotheism was the elevation of the Idea of the great Power, so Polytheism was the frightful degradation, Those, who have lived in India, know it too well. In this direction Mahometanism, has done good service, and depraved forms of Christianity have done evil service by reintroducing the Worship of other persons except the Triune God, and a Hierarchy of Saints, male and female. It is sad to reflect that, as the Heathen world are gradually passing out of Polytheism, and Mahometanism, and all the other new conceptions keep at the greatest distance from it, the Souls of professedly Christians are filled with material objects of adoration and Worship.

To make the Idea of the Divine Power intelligible to the ignorant, minor Deities were introduced with limited powers as objects of fear and worship, demi-gods, demiurges, both in the Egyptian, Hellenic, and Hindu systems. Ra appears as the mid-day Sun, Atín-Ra as the Sun's disk, Harmakh as the rising Sun, Tum as the setting Sun. Triads appear in all these conceptions.

2. PLACE OF RESIDENCE OF SUCH A POWER.

In the Græco-Roman legends the Deity dwelt on Mount Olympus; in the Brahmanical legends on Mount Meru; in Assyria there was some locality fixed in a mountainous country: in the conception of Búddha and Kong-Fu-Tsee, nothing of the kind exists. The Jews thought of Yahveh as dwelling above the clouds in Heaven (Lamentations, iii. 50). Stephen's dying words conveyed this conception, and Paul seemed to share it. In the books of the Hebrews the Deity is conceived of as actually residing in the Temple at Jerusalem: Solomon asks the question, II Chronicles, vi, 18, "Will God in very deed dwell with men on the earth? Behold Heaven, and the Heaven of heavens, cannot contain Thee; how much less this house which I have built!" These words, attributed to Solomon, were no doubt recorded after the return from exile, when Monotheism was thoroughly established. This was hardly the case in the time of Solomon, for we read in I Kings, xi, 4, "that his heart was turned after other gods." The prophet Ezekiel had higher conceptions. The hill-tops were favourite places to worship the Deity: some of the most interesting shrines in India, such as Naini Devi, are at the top of high hills, with stone-steps ascending the hill-sides. The discovery of the rotation of the Globe, and of the nature of the interior of the Globe, has revolutionized the Idea: all allusions to geographical position have died away.

It is difficult to free the Religious mind, prone to superstition, from such notions: Christian Churches are still erected with certain reference to the East: I suppose that this bears reference to Jerusalem, which lies to the East of Europe: but the Orientation of Churches is also maintained in India, which is to the East of Jerusalem. So it is a mere superstition.

The Mahometans have fallen as low. In the life of Baba Nának, the founder of the Sikh sect of the Brahmanical Religion, it is recorded, that a Mahometan cried out to him: "Base Infidel, how darest thou turn thy feet towards the House of God?" alluding to Mekka in Arabia. Nanak replied, "Canst thou turn towards any spot on earth, where the House of God *is not?*"

Paul, the Apostle, echoing at Athens the words used by Stephen at Jerusalem, gave life to the doctrine, which has never been departed from since, that the Lord of Heaven and Earth dwelleth not in Temples made by hands, and he uttered these words, as he stood on Mars' Hill, right in front of the Parthenon, with the gigantic statue of Athéné looking down on him.

3. Theophanies, Visions, Dreams, Good and Evil Spirits.

Amidst an ignorant, credulous, excitable, population, without the corrective control of Public Opinion over the narrator, and opportunity to test statements, it was to be expected, that these strange phenomena would be recorded. The readiness to believe still exists. I have visited the chief great Roman Catholic Shrines to inform myself. The appearance of the Mother of Our Lord at two places in France, is asserted within the last quarter of a century. Under this head comes, Ghosts of the departed, Heavenly Voices, Heavenly Warnings, Heavenly leaders in Battle, Portents, Personal guidance, possession of an individual by an Evil Spirit: in fact, all the channels, by which an outward manifestation of the Deity in persons, or places, permanently or temporarily, is asserted.

It is an awful subject to tell falsehoods about, whether in Prose or Verse, but the Greek and Latin Authors made light of that moral obliquity. Virgil in the Æneid tells us, how the Deity Venus appeared to her reputed son Æneas; Homer tells us, how Athéné appeared repeatedly to Ulysses; Ovid tells us, how Jupiter appeared with Mercury to an old couple; and Livy, how in the hour of battle, Castor and Pollux appeared fighting for Rome. The conception of Angels, embodied attributes of God or Heavenly Messengers, developed itself, and naturally the conception of Evil Spirits followed, and the germ of both conceptions can clearly be traced back to Zoroaster. The word Satan or Shaitan, the ordinary word for the Devil to this day in Persian and cognate Languages, only appears four times in the Old Testament: (1) opposing the purification of Joshua, the High-Priest, in the Prophecy of Zechariah; (2) once in the Drama of Job; (3) once in the Chronicles, as tempting David to take a census of his Subjects; (4) once in the Psalms: the word Baalzebúb never appears in the Old Testament. In the New Testament their appearances are more frequent, and in the Roman Catholic legends, nothing is so common as the appearance of an angel, and even of Satan himself.

We read the following in *The Times* of 1893:

"As soon as a sufficient force could be collected, the Kongo
" Free-State despatched an Expedition against the Arabs in
" the Upper Kongo Region. The first battle was fought on
" the Lohmámi, and resulted in the rout of the Arabs, who
" explained their defeat as due to supernatural agency, alleging
" that in the thick of the fight a white woman was seen walking
" on the river, and that every man of the Arab forces, who
" looked upon her, fell dead."

Pass on to Visions by day, or to Dreams by night. Socrates is recorded to have seen in a dream a cygnet flying to him, and singing sweetly; next morning Plato was brought to him, and he considered the dream fulfilled. In Virgil's great Poem dreams are freely used. In the Old and New Testament we find the same phenomena: when Joseph told his dream, his brothers spoke of this dreamer in scorn; many hundred years later another Joseph considered, that he was warned of

God in a dream; and yet in this age, if anyone talked of regulating his conduct in consequence of a vision or a dream, he would be laughed at. The conception of personal spiritual communion with the Deity, and a sense of being guided by the Holy Spirit, have taken the place of material appearances. The fond and foolish conception of the appearance of Ghosts still holds its own with weak people.

Homer writes:

καὶ γάρ τ'ὄναρ ἐκ Διός ἐστιν.
(Iliad, I, 63.)

Again, we find "Dream" actually personified as a God. Jupiter thus addresses him:

βάσκ' ἴθι, οὖλε Ὄνειρε, θοὰς ἐπὶ νῆας Ἀχαιῶν
ἐλθὼν ἐς κλισίην Ἀγαμέμνονος Ἀτρείδαο.
(Iliad, II, 8–15.)

In the Odyssey we read further of the two gates through which dreams pass: Virgil repeats it (Æneid, VI. 893):

δοιαὶ γάρ τε πύλαι ἀμενηνῶν εἰσιν ὀνείρων
αἱ μὲν γὰρ κεράεσσι τετεύχαται, αἱ δ' ἐλέφαντι.

Those, that pass through the ivory gate, are false and deceive.
Those, that pass through the horn gate are true.
(XIX, 560, 568.)

In one Inscription of Nabonídus, King of Babylonia, it is mentioned, that he was summoned in a dream by Merodach to restore a ruined shrine. (Sayce's Monuments, p. 187.)

It is astounding to find a survival of dreams in a most unexpected quarter:

" That very morning he had received from Sherman the news
" of Johnston's impending surrender. Grant, as it happened,
" had just arrived in Washington, expressing great anxiety as
" to intelligence from Sherman. The President answered
" him in that singular vein of poetic mysticism, which,
" though constantly held in check by his strong common-
" sense, formed a remarkable element in his character. He
" assured Grant, that the news would come soon and come
" favourably, for he had last night had his usual dream, which
" preceded great events. The dream, like the heathen oracles,
" received a double and unexpected interpretation. Meantime,
" there was a Cabinet-meeting, where the treatment of the
" vanquished rebels was discussed. Lincoln spoke peremptorily
" in favour of clemency. No one need expect that he would take
" any part in hanging or killing those men, even the worst of

" them. Frighten them out of the country, open the gates,
" let down the bars, scare them off, he said, throwing up his
" hands, as if scaring sheep. Enough lives have been sacrificed.
" We must extinguish our resentments, if we expect harmony
" and union. That evening he was murdered. Superstition was
" blended with his strong common-sense; he had faith in dreams
" and omens, and was so far a fatalist, that he sincerely believed
" in his destiny. If he were the predestined instrument, he
" would be privileged to complete the work."

With regard to Spirits, a competent authority (Tiele, p. 9) remarks, that Animism is a primitive philosophy, which rules the whole life of natural man: it is the belief in the existence of Spirits, some of whom are powerful, and on some man is dependent, and of some he is afraid, and hence they acquired the rank of Divine beings, and became objects of Worship. These Spirits are conceived to move through space, either of their own accord, or under some spell, which implies compulsion. They appear to men: this is Spiritism; or take up their abode in some object, living or lifeless, and this object is endowed with certain powers, and is an object of Worship, or employed to protect individuals, or communities: this is Fetichism. Sacrifices are offered to the Spirits of the dead, even Human Sacrifices.

It is proved, as an anthropological fact, in all parts of the world, that men in their primeval state believed, that man had a Soul, which continued to exist after death for a longer or shorter time, and could return to the earth and influence for good or evil the affairs of the living: this conception lies at the root of Ancestor-Worship.

Angelology was one of the Hebrew conceptions of a late date, and certainly sprang from contact with Zoroastrianism during the Babylonian exile. It is reasonable to suppose, that all such conceptions, which became the common property of the Zoroastrian and Jewish Religions, are survivals of the common Belief-store, or Legend-germ, of Mankind: the more ignorant, degraded, and politically dependent that a population becomes, the more readily it accepts lies, innocent lies, yet dangerous perversions of a central Truth. At the time of Christ the Sadducees had their eyes more open than their ritualistic neighbours the Pharisees: the populace was always ready to be deceived, and was deceived; it swallowed open-mouthed any marvel. Thus grew the legend of Angels: the Book of Tobit is a mere Hebrew Haggadah, or pious fairy story: the idea of men being possessed with devils was a purely Palestinian conception: no contemporary Latin or Greek Historian notices such possessions. European Christianity never accepted such a condition of mankind in Europe: no miracle was ever performed by the Apostles in Europe: the disease of devil-possession is not alluded to in the Gospel of St. John, written at Ephesus after the fall of Jerusalem. No Religious movement ever gets a permanent start without follies and excesses: we see it in the Salvation-Army of modern time: it is quite possible, that even in the cold, cynical, incredulous, atmosphere of London we shall have a crop of Visions and Evil Spirits: the soil is being well manured for such a crop: all sensational forms of Religion are liable to such weaknesses.

In Mahometan times the world had advanced beyond the intellectual level of the first century A.D.: Angels could only make a spiritual appearance. A Súfi called out to God, "The desire of God has seized me: I yearn to see Thee." The answer came directly to his heart, "Be content with My name." So long as this is the channel of communication, we may rejoice, that the Holy Spirit holds converse with men. It is possible, that in the Old Testament this was meant, when it is so constantly stated that "God said," "God spake," and it is to be regretted, that it was not so expressed. (Max Müller: Gifford Lectures, 1893, p. 340.)

As a remarkable instance of Heavenly Voices, I may mention the Emperor Adrian's written Memorandum on the Statue of Memnon at Luxor: "Ego Hadrianus divinam vocem audivi." He indeed heard the sound of the wind through the stones: since the Statue has been repaired the sound has disappeared. The people of Lycaonia are recorded in the Acts, xiv, 11 to have at once imagined, that Paul and Barnabas were Jupiter and Mercury in disguise, and the inevitable Sacrifice of animals commenced.

In Isaiah, viii, 19, we read: "And when they shall say unto "you, Seek unto them, that have familiar Spirits, and unto "wizards that peep and that mutter, should not a people seek "unto their God."

In Luke, xiii, 16: "The woman, whom Satan hath bound these eighteen years (with a spirit of infirmity)."

In the Synoptic Gospels we read of possession by evil Spirits. The conception can be traced back to Hesiod of Heavenly Spiritual Beings, who fill the unseen world, and can influence the lot of men. The same strain of thought appears in Thales, who defines Demons as Spiritual existences. Pythagoras was of opinion, that these Spirits could be seen or felt. Heraclitus held that all things were full of Spirits, and Empedocles describes the wanderings through the Universe of a lost Soul: this calls to recollection the Chinese conception on this subject. Plato asserts, that some can read the minds of living men, are grieved by wrong-doing, appear to men in their sleep, are made known by voices and oracles, in health, sickness, and the dying hour. After the great oracles were silent, and the Philosophic Schools had discredited the previously accepted Cosmogony, still the idea of Spirits seems to have revived. Plutarch, A.D. 100, seems to admit their existence, and to assert, that they give oracles: it is a feature in the neo-Platonic system. In Acts, xvi, 16, we read of a damsel possessed of a spirit of Divination, who was a source of profit to her masters, and the Spirit, at the command of Paul, came out of her. This kind of occupation could have no relation to the cases alluded to in the Synoptic Gospels, as they were obviously cases of epilepsy, hysteria, or the hypnotism of that age.

4. PRIMEVAL REVELATION: WAS THERE ANY?

With regard to the Religious instinct congenital to Man, the theory of the existence of a Primitive Revelation, or a Primeval Tradition, has gained ground with many thinkers: it is absolutely unsupported by evidence, and generates new questions of insoluble difficulty. One author writes as follows:
"Throughout all the Heathen World there lie scattered the
" seeds of a Primeval Tradition, sometimes nearly obliterated
" by Fable, overlaid by Mythology, or absorbed by Philosophy,
" but still supplying elements of Truth. The germs of the
" Gospel existed, as they were communicated to men. Appeal
" should be made in reasoning to Primeval Truth; an appeal
" to common principles of belief will conduce to the acknow-
" ledgment of a Truth," but not as if it were a conception, which came into existence in Syria in Anno Domini, instead of being part of the great scheme of Creation. (Indian Missionary Manual, 1870, 2nd edition, p. 195.)

I freely admit that a Religious instinct was a part, and an indispensable part, of the Genus Homo, but it seems clear that, just as there was no one common seedplot of Languages, but distinct seedplots, so the Human Race, differentiated by white, black, yellow, red, and brown colours, and by bodily features of the most marked kind, did not proceed from a common pair, as was believed in the earlier centuries after Anno Domini. Before that date there is no evidence of any belief at all on the subject; at any rate, the Hebrew Race would never have admitted, that all mankind came from a common ancestor.

The writer of the above extract does not state the quarter, from which he derived the theory, that *throughout the Heathen World* the seed was scattered: of the tribes of Africa, Oceania, and North America, we have nothing but the vaguest tradition. The Book-Religions, and excavated Monuments, of the great Races of Asia, and Egypt, do not supply evidence; at any rate, I have failed to find it. It is a tremendous assumption to make, and implies, that there has been a continuous degradation of a Divine conception, instead of a gradual increase, and expansion, and elevation, and evolution, from century to century, which is my deliberate opinion. The existence of the Sacred Books of the East seems to indicate this, and the long procession of Law-givers, Philosophers, and Sages, always adding to the Store of Divine knowledge, Virtue, and 'Η ἁγία Σοφία, καὶ 'Η ἀρέτη, ended in the appearance of Christ in the Fulness of Time. The fact seems to be, that the Great Father imparted to all His poor children a Religious instinct, and a Religious faculty capable of development according to their physical environment, and metaphysical opportunities.

5. Substitution of Idols made by Men's Hands for an Impersonal Divinity.

This process insensibly takes place in an ignorant Community: they require something visible, tangible, realizable to the perception, and naturally the Idols assumed Human form, and, as Art advanced, the most beautiful Human forms, that could be conceived; but there is no reason to suppose, that the physical embodiment, which the Deity is supposed to have assumed for the convenience of his worshipper, should be a copy of his form: the εἴδωλον was not necessarily a simulacrum: originally a cairn, a rude stone pillar, a conical stone, a phallus, were the symbols, under which the Divinity was to be worshipped. The following sentiment is attributed to Apollonius of Tyana in the first century after Anno Domini: "The mind finds for itself something, which it delineates better than what any Art can do." We must all feel this: to the cultured mind the contemplation of a Statue or picture deplorably limits the conception, which had been previously formed, or which could be supplied by words.

At any rate, by the time of the Anno Domini the epoch of Worship of the Works of the hand of man had pretty well come to its end: such lines as those of Horace,

"Olim truncus eram ficulnus, inutile lignum"
(*Sat.* I, viii, 1),

speak for themselves.

These words appear in the Wisdom of Solomon, by an unknown Alexandrian Jew, probably a contemporary of Horace: "No man can make a god like unto himself: for he himself is better than the things, which he worships: for he lived once, but they never." The very latest Book of the Christian Canon gives, however, instance of the taste for animal symbolism, in the Lion, the Lamb, the Bull; and the allegory of the four Evangelists in the Eagle, the Angel, the Lion, and the Bull. No doubt there is some point in the retort of the Brahmin to the Christian Missionary, "You blame me for worshipping a Bull: why do you worship a Lamb? Are not both animals symbols?"

It is not necessarily a Worship of Idols. The Roman Catholic, as far as regards externals, acts in precisely the same way to his saints: he kisses the brass toe of St. Peter; he bows, and prays to, and presents offerings to, images of men, and women of ancient days: I carefully exclude all representations of the Persons of the Triune God. The Hindu distinctly denies, that he worships the stone object, but the Religious conception of which that object is the outward expression. Let us take the humble example of a female child with her doll: endowed with feelings, which hereafter may develop into motherhood, she looks on the doll as her companion, her great care, and object of her tenderest affection: she knows, that it is only wood and linen, and she knows that the bystanders know this also, yet she feels for it, if it falls to the ground, or is ill-used: she is voluntarily deceived: the day comes suddenly, when the cloud is lifted up from her eyes, and with no sense of shame she puts it away in her cabinet. It has no longer a charm for her, but she is tolerant, if her younger sisters find in it the same pleasure, which she did.

So with the barbarian: he is man in his childhood: he accepts the Idea, more than the fact, that the Anthropomorphic object is the Deity: if necessary, he will call in the artificer to repair it or paint it, but he has invested it in his mind with his very best gifts: its eyes look on his wants; its ears listen to his prayers; its nose smells his sacrifice; its touch heals his ailments: his simple untrained intellect cannot conceive of a Deity, which fills all space, governs the world, and yet is neither visible, nor tangible: he claims no such power for his Deity, who belongs to his tribe alone.

Then comes the question of Polytheism, or many Deities with equal power; or Monism, where there is one Deity, who is the Chief God among many gods; or Monolatrism, where each tribe has one god, will worship no other, still admits that other tribes have their own god; and lastly Monotheism, where there is one only God, Lord of the Universe: the Jews did not arrive at this last stage till the time of Isaiah. Yahveh was only the God of Israel to them: this was Monolatry: the Polytheistic Greeks admitted, that there was a power greater than that of Zeus, the overruling Fates: here we touch ground with Monism.

6. FATHERHOOD OF GOD.

Wherever the traveller penetrates, he finds out by what name the local Deity is known, whether he is a person, or impersonal, what Idea is conveyed with the name, whether he is merely a tribal Deity, or God of the whole world, whether the existence of other gods is admitted as a fact. Man everywhere, and in every age, requires, that there should be personal relations betwixt him and his Deity: where otherwise would he find a solution of the perplexities of existence? The Idea of a Deity possesses him by intuition, or observation: it gradually develops: it does not require Science, or Philosophy, to find out the Deity: *He is there*, in the elements, or in the environment.

The difference betwixt the primeval, and later, conception of the relation of Man to the Deity is five-fold, and necessarily affects the Anthropomorphic Idea:

(1) The Deity is perfectly good: there is no envy of man in Him: His relation is that of a Father to all His poor children on Earth.
(2) Each individual has a personal relation with the Deity.
(3) An Idea of what is actually good and bad is formed, and outward prosperity is no longer the chief good, and outward adversity the chief evil.
(4) There is a consciousness of social progress to higher levels of goodness and wisdom.
(5) The conception of a future life becomes paramount: the inequalities of Human life will there be set right, and there will be a compensation for individual suffering.

Carlyle, in his "Hero-Worship," remarks that Idol is εἴδωλον, a thing seen, a symbol: it is not a god, but a symbol: one may question, whether even one of the most benighted mortals took it for more than a symbol; whether he ever thought that the poor Image, which his own hand had made, was a god, but that a god was emblemed by it, that a god was in it in some way or other. But in process of time, as the Worship grew to be ancestral, some portion of the community began to believe, that there was something special in the Image. Take, for instance, the Madonna of the Pilár in Spain; the Virgin of Loretto in Italy; the figure of Jagarnath; the Lingam in India; the Kaaba-Stone in Arabia; the tomb of our Lord in Jerusalem. We know what happened to the Brazen Serpent: it was destroyed, because it was worshipped: then real Idolatry begins. The bitter attacks of Isaiah, and of Protestant Churches, come into existence then: no one supposes, that the Roman

Catholic worships the Crucifix, which happens to be on the Altar: that is only a symbol: but, when he has walked a thousand miles to kiss the great toe of St. Peter, he does worship: the enlightened Priest, whether Greek, Hindu, or Roman, may think, that it is only a symbol; the ignorant multitude think otherwise.

7. THREATS OF WORSHIPPERS UTTERED AGAINST THEIR GODS.

It is a strange degradation of the Idea, when the ignorant worshipper threatens his god, if he does not do what he, the worshipper, wants: the attempt to bribe him is common enough by an additional Sacrifice: we read in Virgil's Æneid:

"Multa tibi ante aram nostrâ cadet hostia dextrâ,"

or Horace's promise to his fountain of Bandusia:

"Cras donaberis hædo."

Clearly Horace and Virgil were getting in their notions beyond the epoch of Sacrifice.

CAP. II. WORSHIP OF SUCH A POWER.

1. What is it?
2. Primeval.
3. Ancestral.
4. Sacrifice.
5. Prayer.
6. Ritual.
7. Priestcraft, Witchcraft, Exorcism.
8. Ceremonial Cleanness, or Uncleanness.
9. Fasting, Celibacy, Asceticism, Eremitism.
10. Feasting, Days of Rest.
11. Esoteric, or Exoteric.

1. WHAT IS IT?

All Nations have some form of Worship: what is Worship? Survey mankind from China to Peru, and go back to the remotest ages, and you will not find a people, however low in culture, however restricted in local environment, who have not had a dim conception of a Power greater than themselves, to the behests of which they are compelled to bow, which they try to conciliate in their own rough way. The civilized Nations, who swayed the world before the great Anno Domini, present marked instances. The Amen Ra of the Egyptian Monarch, the Ashur of the Assyrian, the Jupiter Optimus Maximus of the Roman, the Divine Power of the Zúlu, the great Father and Spirit of the Red Indian, the Quetyalcoatl of the Mexican, were the genuine outcomes of the great motive of Religious Worship:

"Primus in orbe Deos fecit Timor."

The mode of Worship varies, being limited by the abundance, and variety, of resources. But the gigantic figures carved on the rocks in the solitary Easter Island in Oceania are as impressive to the spectator, and as suggestive of real Worship, as the stately Monuments at Abu Simbul, the solitary Memnon at Karnak, and the winged bulls at Nineveh.

With the majority of mankind, Worship of some kind makes up the sum total of Religion: can this be so? What is Religion, of what is it composed?

Is it a desire to save the Soul by Worship and dogma? Or a devotion to goodness, which is practical?

It would fill a volume to descant further on forms of Worship: they vary beyond conception: considered of the highest importance by one Nation, and laughed at as folly by their neighbours.

A writer thus expresses himself: "The History of Religion "is very curious: looked at dispassionately it has done very "little for mankind in general, save to prove one fundamental "Truth, which is more significant than any dogma: that Truth "is the need of all humanity to have something to worship: "from the highest to the lowest civilization that need has "made itself the exponent of external forms: it is the kernel "of all Religions." ("Mystery of Turkish Bath," p. 11.)

I give a quotation from the Agni Puràna, one of the Sanskrit Sacred Books of the Hindu: "That is the best Worship, "which is made without the expectation of the attainment of "any particular object; the worst is that, which is performed "for the accomplishment of a particular end."

The Worship may be spiritual, but it generally is carnal, and the tendency is year by year to become more so. Its object is presumed:

(1) To please the Deity, Demi-god, or Saint.
(2) To conciliate his, or her, favour.
(3) To remove his, or her, anger.
(4) To render thanks for past mercies attributed fondly to him, or her.
(5) To pray for future blessings.
(6) To persuade the Deity to destroy the enemies of the worshipper.

I designedly omit the details of Christian Worship of all kinds, except when illustrating phenomena of non-Christian Worship, and I take my examples from Pagan Greece and Rome in the past, the contemporary Worship of the Brahman, the Búddhist, the Jew, and the Barbarian of Africa, North and South America, and Oceania. I am tolerably familiar with them all.

Old Homer tells us how offerings were made to Athéné:

$$\iota\nu' \text{ } \accentset{,}{\alpha}\gamma\alpha\lambda\mu\alpha \text{ } \theta\epsilon\grave{\alpha} \text{ } \kappa\epsilon\chi\alpha\rho\acute{o}\iota\tau o \text{ } \iota\deltao\tilde{v}\sigma\alpha.$$

(*Odyssey*, III, 438.)

Cardinal Lavigerie has unconsciously, but happily, interpreted the sentiment in his Inscription to the Mother of Christ in her reputed home at Jerusalem, which the Pope has selected for her: " When the Virgin looks down from Heaven to the place " of her birth, her eyes will fall on the names of those, " who have subscribed so many francs to the repair of the " building."

Abraham was ready to offer up Isaac; Agamemnon actually offered his daughter Iphigenia, though Artemis interfered to save her; Jephthah sacrificed his daughter; children were passed through the fire to Molech in the city of Jerusalem just before the Exile, Jeremiah, xxxii, 35.

Asking for blessings, and returning thanks for them, trying to conciliate the Deity, if things go bad with the worshipper, calling for vengeance and slaughter of enemies, loading the altars with the flesh of plundered cattle, ornamenting the temple with the precious metals ravished from plundered houses, hanging up the trophies of war, and Standards of Regiments, in the place of Worship; going after new Deities, if the old one seemed slow to discharge his duties, and send seasonable rain, abundant harvests, and long periods of rest from war and invasion: such were the features pourtrayed in the Books of Kings and Chronicles of the Hebrew people, and are a fair sample of the rest of the world in the ages preceding the great Anno Domini.

But the mockery of Worship in the Nineteenth Century A.D. is still more marked : on every public occasion in every country of Europe a function is performed : Protestants, members of the Greek Church, of the Church of Rome, Mahometans, Turks, Atheists, Agnostics, and those, who care nothing for Religion, assemble to listen to Music and Anthems, and intoned prayers, a tribute to some departed Statesman, or to celebrate a Christening, a Confirmation, a Marriage, a Funeral, of some member of the Royal Family. What an awful burlesque on the true faith of Christ is such purely formal Christianity! we laugh at the Buddhist, and Chinese, but is this not much worse ? The silver jubilee of the King of Siam's reign was celebrated by a series of Religious services and State processions, in which the King took part. Great satisfaction was felt among the people, because the Diplomatic Corps was fully represented at an audience. It is presumed, that the sentiment of Religion exalts or degrades itself according to the comparative ignorance, or advancement in general culture, of the professors of that Religion; and unquestionably Religion, like all other movements of thought and belief, is subject to the Laws of Development: it cannot remain stationary without certainty of decay.

A craving for a spiritual unity with the Deity has inspired many Christians, and non-Christians, but this craving has never been so fully developed as in the Philosophic Schools of ancient India. So also in all external form of Worship, they showed the way.

The Roman Classical Authors admitted, that Greece, conquered in arms, ruled in intellect; so also Paganism, though conquered, clings to the skirts of, and defiles, Christian Worship. Archbishop Whateley boldly says, that the Roman Catholic system of Saints, Shrines, Processions, Priestcraft, is but a modern Paganism, and, if we look closer, we find that Church-Architecture, Church-vestments, Church-terminology, such as templum, sacerdos, hostia, altare, are Pagan: the initiated into the Greek mysteries were required to fast (Hibbert Lectures, 1888, p. 298: Hatch) before they drank the mystic liquor, or ate the mystic cake: Paganism, instead of being uprooted, was absorbed into the life of the Italian Church.

When you enter a Roman Catholic Church on the Continent, it seems, as if you passed into a different Epoch intellectually; old buildings, old altars, old tombs, Mass, music, worshippers: is it real? The pictures on the walls tell of the life of Jesus, but does this exhibition represent the Spirit of the Master? Does the majority of the worshippers understand what they are doing? What is the essential difference betwixt their cultus and that of Pagan Rome? How do the Priests of one cult differ from those of the other? When you meet them in the Sacristy, is it not obvious, that the whole thing is "opus operatum," and that no possible good can have accrued to the Soul of Priest, or People. Does not Westminster Abbey reflect some of these features? the chant of the singing men and boys, unconverted men and boys, giving out in high and low musical notes, without any sign of feeling, the great mysteries of the Incarnation, Resurrection, and Procession of the Holy Ghost, in the Creed. Each paragraph of that Creed is the outcome of deadly strife, and the certainty of it cannot be asserted with mathematical accuracy, and it is only understood by study and prayer; yet it slips off the tongue of a lad, whose only qualification is the possession of the gift of sweet sounds, and who possibly may have been singing for hire at a Cider-Cellar the previous evening.

St. George Mivart, in the "Nineteenth Century," Dec., 1892, p. 913, writes: "In a certain time the Paganism of Greece, "and Rome, was true as well as righteous, and Zeus and Athéné, "Ares and Aphrodité, were expressions of the Divine: the Pagan "rites and ceremonies were in a measure good, and the Pagan "Worship an acceptable service." This gives a measure of Worship.

A Missionary in South Africa writes: "We see that many acts "which, according to Western ideas, are far removed from the

" region of devotion and Worship, are in reality parts of a life,
" every act, word, and movement of which has a significance
" in a Religious sense. I have seen natives of Africa perform
" acts of devotion before the eyes of men, who declared that
" they had no idea of Worship nor of gods. When a native
" glances at the sun or moon, he prays; when he drops a small
" particle of food on the ground before he begins to eat, he
" offers an oblation; if he throws a tuft of grass, a bit of stick,
" or a stone out of his hut door in the morning before emerging
" himself, he has said matins." These remarks throw light
upon the very important question, whether all men possess what
we may call the Religious sense. I have always believed that
we have the best ethnological authority for saying, that no
savage tribe has ever been found wholly devoid of this Religious
sense.

Cardinal Wiseman, in a discourse on University-Education in
1852, p. 96, writes: " God's writing is on the wall, whether of
" the Indian fane, or the portico of Greece: He is with the
" Greek Dramatist in his denunciation of tyranny and injustice,
" and his auguries of Divine vengeance on crime. Even in the
" legends of popular Mythology He casts His shadow, and it is
" dimly discerned in the ode, in the epic, as in troubled waters,
" or fantastic dreams."

It must not be supposed that, because two doctrines, and two
practices, resemble each other in Nations, which never at any
period came into contact, they must have been derived one from
the other. Of course, a partisan of one will assert, that the other
party derived from him. The Romish Fathers, Huc and Gabet,
fondly thought, that the Búddhists of Tibet had borrowed much
of their ritual from the Church of Rome. The real truth is,
that the germs of Dogma and Practice were part of the original
outfit of the Human Race. The same power of reasoning,
which they all equally possessed, flowed in the same channel,
and under similar circumstances worked out the same phenomena.
We see this with our eyes in the monuments of Egypt and
Mesopotamia: an act of adoration to a Deity is being made:
call it, if you like, foolish, mistaken, Worship, yet it is the
outcome of a specific faith. Rabshakeh boasted to the people
of Jerusalem of what his King, and his King's god, had done:
it was no reply that the God of the Hebrews is supposed to have
made: it was clear that the same Ruler of the world was
worshipped by both, who influenced the Kings of all the round
world to do His will: all mankind were equally His poor
creatures, the objects of His Pity and Love, then, before Anno
Domini, as it is admitted, that they were after that date, and
the illusion of the chosen people had cleared away.

It must surprise, and even seem repulsive to, a Native of

China and India, when he first reads the Old Testament. A thoughtful Brahmin would say: "It is all very well for you "English, who were savages at the time of Anno Domini, "Sacrificers of Human beings, grossly ignorant, with no Re- "ligion, or Ritual, or Dogma, or Sacred Books, to welcome "the Missionary from Jerusalem with the good news; but we "Indians had had all these things for centuries: we worshipped "the Paramésvara, the Great Deity, to the best of our ability; "we built magnificent temples, wrote learned treatises, and "elaborated costly rituals; we did what we could, with a free "heart, feeling after God, if haply we could find Him; we did "it in our magnificent cities, amidst wealth, rank, power, and "numbers; and yet this miserable tribe of the Hebrews, who "occupied a country about the size of two out of our hundred "districts, and have left no memorial of Architecture, of In- "scriptions, or Statuary, no literature, but one collection of "sacred books, the largest part of which were put to paper at "a date subsequent to Zoroaster, Buddha, and Kong-Fu-Tsee, "talk about the Deity being their's only instead of being the "common Father of all mankind, and calling our ancestors "by insulting names, who had never even heard of the exist- "ence of this petty tribe, which has long ceased to exist as a "Nation, while we are still a Nation of two hundred Millions."

2. PRIMEVAL.

This branch of the subject has been very carefully studied in important volumes. There has been a certain order, according to which man has graduated, as it were, in his Worship: (A) the Tree; (B) the Phallus, or Lingam; (C) the Serpent; (D) the Fire; (E) the Sun and the Heavenly Host; (F) Animals; (G) Totemism; (H) Fetichism; (I) Hero-Worship. It is unnecessary to enter at large on these Subjects: the point before us is, that some of these forms are ubiquitous. In every country the narratives of travellers report grottos, stones, pillars, cairns, impressions of footmarks. The tree of Knowledge of Good and Evil appears in the Earliest Hebrew legends. The Phallus is believed to be the root-conception of the Obelisk: in India it is manifest, but there is no obscene motive: the multiplication of the animal from generation to generation is in itself a marvel, and this is the symbol of reproduction. The Serpent again appears in the Earliest Hebrew legends. When we come to Fire, in all its manifold appearances, we find a real object of Worship, a maker and preserver, and destroyer, a great blessing and a great curse, a good servant and a bad master, which comes into existence we know not how, and which disappears we know not whither, which destroys vast forests, and is itself quenched by water, which is the instrument of Sacrifice everywhere, which sometimes appears to fall from Heaven in the stroke of lightning, and sometimes appears from the hard rock as the Naphtha-spring. I was standing at the famous Naphtha-springs of Jowála Mukhi, in North India, when a Hindu, who had travelled many hundred leagues, arrived, and bowed before it, and turning to me said, in accents of deep devotion, "This indeed is God." He had felt after this, and had found Him, "Agni," the Fire, "a symbol of the Comforter and Destroyer."

The Worship of the Moon, and the Heavenly Host, in a clear Eastern night is excusable. The glory of the rising and setting Sun cannot be exceeded. In the beautiful Græco-Roman conceptions, Phœbus Apollo, and Artemis Diana, represented the Sun and the Moon. The god of the Moabite was named Chemosh, or Shumsh, the Sun; and Sampson means, "like the Sun." Astrology was an early weakness of the Human Race. To this very day, the days of the weeks are named after the Sun, the Moon, and the five Planets, Mercury, Mars, Venus, Jupiter, and Saturn, or Deities analogous to them.

The Gáyatri of the Brahman is impressive: "Let us adore "the Supremacy of the Divine Sun, the Deity, who illuminates "all, from whom all proceed, and are renovated, and to whom "all must return; whom we invoke to direct our intellect aright "in our progress towards His Holy Seat" (Sacred Anthology, p. 103). The great God of the Egyptians was Ra, the Sun.

Tree and Serpent-Worship have been the special Study of a very competent Scholar, the late James Fergusson, and his magnificent book tells its own story. Sayce, in his Higher Criticism and the Monuments, 1893, writes as follows (p. 182):
"All over Syria rags are hung up as offerings, nominally to "the Shaikh, after whom some tomb is named, but really to "the Spirit of the Tree, to whom Worship had been paid before "the days of Islam. Tree-Worship is of immense antiquity in "Semitic lands, but the Tree must be solitary and alone before "it could be deemed holy: the Tree, which stood in the midst "of the Babylonian Garden of Eden, and under whose shadowy "branches was the shrine of Tammuz, may have been a re-"flection of the Sacred Tree. In Genesis we read of the "Serpent and the Apple-Tree. Throughout India the traveller "comes across votive rags fastened on the branches of particular "trees."

We read in Deut. iv, 19: "The Sun, and the Moon, and "Stars, even all the Host of Heaven . . . . which the Lord "thy God hath divided [apportioned] unto all Nations under "the whole Heaven."

In the time of Justin Martyr it was believed by some, that God had allowed the Heathen to worship the heavenly bodies. (Speaker's Commentary.) Bishop Westcott quotes the passage with the following remark : " In two passages of Deuteronomy, " even false Religions are presented as part of the Divine " ordering of Humanity : even their Idolatries had a work to " do for Him, an office in the discipline of men." (Westcott : Gospel of Life, p. 114.)

We cannot doubt, that in those early days of man's History, when the artificial world, the creation of men's hands, Cities, Temples, etc., did not exist, the Kosmos, made by the hand of God, the starry Heavens, the vast Rivers peopled by fish, the impassable Forests occupied by animals in their freedom, went for much more; and the simple Souls of God's poor children had through them avenues leading up to God, obscured to us by the nearer horizon of our Arts and Sciences, Prejudices, and Religious conceptions, the creatures of Man's Intellect at particular epochs of his existence, modified but not effaced by the stream of time, as it flowed on. The Soul of the Heathen in its naked and untutored simplicity went straight up without the intermediates of Priests to the Throne of Grace and Goodness, like the lisping of the Children at the knees of their Parents. They knew not the Divine Name, but they knew the Hand, which gave.

There was a stage in the growth of Religious conceptions which is called by Tiele, a great authority, the "Therianthropic." Men began to worship Animals (θήρ), and then the chief of Animals, Man (ἄνθρωπος). In Totemism every tribe and city had its Totem, or sacred animal, to whom it offered some moderate Worship, and considered as in some way its blood-relation. This developed into actual Worship: in Egypt and in India we find notable examples: some animals were deemed sacred, such as the Cow in India, and are addressed by the ignorant herd in terms of respect, such as Mahadéo. The Bull and the Cat were the objects of Worship in Egypt : we read of the Calf in the Wilderness, the Calves at Bethel : in his Hibbert Lecture, Montefiore, himself a Hebrew, asserts, that Bulls were part of Hebrew Worship. The Brahmanical system teems with them, the Fish, the Tortoise, the Boar, the Man-Lion, the Elephant. Although this form of Worship died out gradually, and the worshipper would deny with scorn, that their Deities were ever represented by animals, still there is a survival. Some Deities retain a portion of an animal's body, such as Ganésa with the head of an elephant. In the Assyrian and Babylonian and Egyptian Monuments there is the figure of a man with the head of an animal, and winged Bulls with the head of a man: a stage lower certain animals are described as sacred to, and symbols of, certain Deities; formerly they were the Deities themselves. The higher development of Animal-Worship is evidenced in Hero-Worship, which is ubiquitous: it is difficult to draw the line betwixt Deities, when they are only Demi-gods and illustrious men: the Avatára of the Hindu evidences this: (1) the Tortoise, (2) the Fish, (3) the Boar, (4) the Man-Lion, (5) the Dwarf; then four Heroes.

In the Roman system there were Altars to Augustus in his lifetime:

"Præsenti tibi majores largimur honores."

(VIRGIL.)

In the same category come Hercules, Bacchus, Castor and Pollux, and finally all the Roman Emperors.

Those unfortunate objects of Worship, such as the Egyptian and Assyrian Deities, and the statue of Diana of the Ephesians, have found their way into Museums: objects, which were once of Worship, are now of pity, and even of derision.

The Saints of the Romish Church took the place of the dethroned Deities and Demi-gods: they were expressions of the same superstitious desire to conciliate something, or somebody, outside the conception of God; in many instances the same tradition is carried out with only change of name: there is a Church dedicated to St. Theodosius at Rome, which occupies the site of a Temple to Romulus, and discharges the same duty of protection of young children. In course of time the statues of Saints will follow the statues of the Demi-gods, and find their way to the Museums, as specimens of Art of the time, and of the degree of superstition of those, who employed the Art for that purpose, then of pity, and lastly of derision.

3. ANCESTRAL.

In the last chapter the forms of Worship were general; here they are individual. Appeals to the memory of deceased parents and ancestors belong to the tender associations of the Human Race, and within limits are holy: when a Religion is changed, there is much suffering: Hindu fathers threaten to destroy themselves, if their sons become Mahometan or Christian; a Roman Catholic Mother would deplore her child becoming a Protestant, and *vice versâ*. The Worship of Ancestors is one of the most prevalent features in all Nations and at all times. In China it is notorious: among the Romans there were the Dii Penates and Lares: this feeling has led to the Worship of shrines, tombs, relics: we read of the worship of Teraphim among the Hebrews; in Africa of Fetichism. Every one of these forms of Worship is based on a degraded superstition, always developing. Next comes the conception of the duty of Pilgrimage: Jerome, in the fourth century A.D., inveighed against this tendency, which was growing in his age: it is now one of the sins of the Church of Rome: of course Miracles soon grow out of such pilgrimages, and will continue to grow: it is the same with the Hindu, Mahometan, and Buddhist: the most certain cure of barrenness for a woman is to go on pilgrimage. The following notices are startling as occurring in London this very year:

"At St. Mary's Roman Catholic Church, in Cadogan-street,
" S.W., there have been during the last three days special
" devotions in honour of ' Blessed Thomas More,' through whose
" intercession a remarkable cure is said to have been effected. It
" appears that a lady who had been upon her bed for more than
" four years, and who had been unable for two years even to
" place her foot upon the ground, requested her friends to say
" prayers to the Chelsea-martyr on her behalf. This they
" willingly did. One night recently the lady in question suddenly
" displayed a disposition to rise from her bed, and to her own
" surprise, and that of her maid, she found herself perfectly able
" to walk across the road."

" On Saturday the body of Romanists known as 'The Guild
" of Our Lady of Ransom,' had their annual pilgrimage to the
" shrine of Thomas à Becket in Canterbury Cathedral. According
" to a daily contemporary, the proceedings in the Cathedral ' were
" characterized by great devotion,' the pilgrim being asked to
" pray earnestly, ' especially for the reconversion of this country
" to the faith, in defence of which the blissful martyr died.' "

No one can be present at an Indian place of pilgrimage, such as the Ganges, without feeling what a vast capacity of Religious enthusiasm the Hindu has, a capacity of Sacrifice to God of his all, for many do not live to return home; a readiness to bear hardships, long journeys, hunger, thirst, sickness, death: all for the love of the Deity. Does the European Missionary give the poor Pagan the credit of this? does he himself live up to the same ideal?

The Idea of the advantage of a Pilgrimage is common to all Religious conceptions.

" He who has controlled his own spirit and desires, who has
" knowledge, piety, and a good character, gathers fruit from
" a pilgrimage. Even in the sacred forest inflamed passions
" cause crime, and in the city self-control brings piety to dwell.
" The virtuous man's home is his desert of devotion." (Sacred Anthology, p. 140.)

A poor pilgrim followed the caravan to Mekka, but when she saw the others praying round the Kaaba, she cried out, " Oh! weak followers of the weak, thou hast travelled land and

" sea to seek in this far-off place the god, who had long ago
" come to thee." (Julaluddin : Sacred Anthology, p. 90.)
The pious Hindu traverses the length and breadth of India,
laying himself flat on the ground, making a mark in the earth
where his head lay, rising up, and placing his feet where his
head was, thus slowly advancing towards the place of pilgrimage
in days, months, and years.

In a paper on "Hausa Pilgrimages from the Western Sudán,"
the Rev. Charles H. Robinson said, that he had just returned
from a preliminary journey along part of the north border of
the Sahára, which had been made with a view to ascertain the
possibility of crossing the Great Sahára from Tripoli in order
to visit the Hausa States, which lay to the west of Lake
Tchad, and to the north of the Niger and river Binue. His
intercourse with Hausa-speaking natives in North Africa served
to reveal the enormous extent, to which the *pilgrimage* to Mekka
was affecting the life and habits of the people in the far interior. Many thousands of such pilgrims found their way
thence to Mekka, some by crossing the Great Sahara, and
going by sea from Tripoli, others by way of Wadai, Darfúr,
Khartúm, and Súakin.

Now that the Government of India has arranged with Messrs.
Cook, of Ludgate Circus, to conduct the Mahometan Pilgrimage,
we get more accurate statistics of this great Religious phenomenon.

The Mekka Pilgrim Traffic. "A brief account of last year's
" pilgrimage to Mekka is now published in Consul Richard's
" Report on the trade of Jeddah. As the principal day of the Haj
" fell on a Friday, it was anticipated, that the number of pilgrims
" would be very large, but the reality outstripped the most
" sanguine anticipations. At Jeddah and Yambo over 90,000
" landed: that is about double the average: and, in all, from
" 250,000 to 300,000 persons went to Mekka during the season,
" British India supplying the largest number. Cholera, it will
" be remembered, raged in the Mekka valley while the pilgrims
" were there, the daily number of deaths being at least 1,000,
" and, subsequently, the disease broke out at Jeddah, where they
" were waiting for embarkation, and from 500 to 600 deaths
" occurred daily. Mr. Richards says the official estimate of
" deaths of those, who travelled by sea, which was 9,577, was
" certainly below the mark, while no fewer than 15,000 of those
" who went to Mekka by land perished. Thus last year's Haj
" will be memorable for the extraordinary number of the faithful,
" who took part in its ceremonies, and for the ravages, which
" were far greater than any previous record. Indeed, to a great
" extent, this may be considered as an ordinary sequence of cause
" and effect, although, undoubtedly, the fact, that the simoon was

" blowing steadily and unintermittently for eleven days during the
" latter end of May, while the heat during the first ten days of
" June was unusually intense, contributed not a little to the
" development of conditions, under which the rapid spread of
" the disease was inevitable."

So deeply rooted in the Semitic mind is the belief in the Sanctity of Stones, that Mahomet allowed the Kaaba of Mekka, in Arabia, to remain as an object of Worship in his new Religion, thus separating his Religious conception from the Buddhist and Christian, inasmuch as they both belong to the world at large, and have no permanent tie to any particular country.

The disease of Relic-Worship breaks out in unexpected quarters. When the remains of Mr. Spurgeon were brought to England, the following is recorded in the paper of the day: " The coffin
" was enclosed in a packing-case, and on the arrival of the
" steamer was removed out of the case and deposited in the van
" attached to the train. The impulse, which leads men to treasure
" tangible objects connected with the notable dead, is strong even
" among those, who profess to rate low all material associations,
" and some of the spectators yesterday eagerly seized chips and
" fragments of cordage, as the coffin was removed."

Under this head of Relics must come the brazen serpent kept by the Hebrews, and very properly destroyed by King Hezekiah; the Romans had a Palladium. In many parts of the world there are stores of such relics: at Lahór we had the sleeping drawers of Mahomet; at Treves the Holy Coat: both in Christian Europe, and Mahometan, and Pagan, Asia and Africa, the Fetich is the lowest type. Among the people in the Kongo-basin crosses, and rosaries, left by the Romish Mission, who centuries ago occupied that Region, are still prized as Pagan Fetiches, showing how closely united are all false developments of the Religious Idea.

It is difficult to realize the feelings of a newly-converted member of the Church of Rome: all credit be given to him for selecting his own way of Salvation with all his heart, and no doubt he has found his Saviour. But suddenly the world is to him peopled with Spirits: the Apostles are, as it were, brought again to life; holy men and women of the Middle Ages, supposed to have been long in their graves, St. Francis, St. Teresa, and others, became objects of interest, and Worship, and of prayer. Conspicuous among them is the Mother of Christ, and her husband, Joseph, now placed by an audacious Bishop in charge of all the Missions to Africa: all these august personages are supposed to be cognizant of his thoughts, appear to him in his dreams, have power to interfere in his favour, and are powerful to save.

The ark of the Lord became a Palladium, and was taken into battle, and, in fact, was taken prisoner: it was a fair taunt in the mouth of the Philistines, that a Deity, which could not take care of His own Ark, could scarcely be a powerful Deity. In the Spanish wars to free Spain from the Mahometans, the black Virgin of the Pilár at Zaragossa was constantly at the head of the Spanish forces, and, according to them, brought victory.

I quote an esteemed authority about Spirits:

"In Oceania one ruling idea of Worship prevails, that the
" Spirits of the Dead are the rulers, and protectors of the living:
" the mysterious power called 'Mana,' abides with such after
" death, and a powerful man in the world will be a powerful
" Spirit after death in another world. It is conceived of
" as being of like passions with ourselves; it is conciliated
" to be a friend, yet it is deemed to be ever ready on the least
" offence to be malevolent, and against others it is invoked for
" every kind of injury: the element of dread superstition enters
" into all the transactions of life." (Bishop John Selwyn: Ramsden Sermons, May 21, 1893.)

" In the battle of life there is one thought, to obtain Spiritual
" help: preparing for the fight, the native eats the leaf of a tree,
" which he believes will fill him with the strength of the Spirit of
" the Sun : if he kill a man, he deems, that his arrow has been
" directed by the Mana, or Spirit, with which he is endowed."
(*Ibid.*)

" When we tell our converts of the power of the Spirit, which
" God gives through Christ, we tell them what their simple
" Faith at once understands." (*Ibid.*)

4. SACRIFICE.

I was standing a few years ago, one Sunday forenoon, in the gallery of the Cathedral of Aix-la-Chapelle, close to the tomb of the great Emperor Charlemagne, who died over one thousand years ago. As I looked on the performance of High Mass going on in the Chancel below me, and on the suspended Crucifix above, and the figures of the Saints around me ; as I smelt the smell of incense, listened to the Latin chants of unintelligent perfunctory Priests, and looked at the stupid bovine faces of the German boers, who occasionally threw in a formal response, I thought to myself, Can the Almighty accept such Worship ? God is a Spirit, and they, that worship Him, must worship in Spirit and Truth : both these ingredients were totally absent here : it was a mere function; a Royal levée ; a grand guard mounting ; a salute of so many guns from a warship : " Vox et præterea nihil."

My thoughts ascended to the beginning of recorded History, and wandered round the world. Man is no doubt a Religious animal, but his Religion is evidenced in a different way at a different epoch of Human existence, marking Progress. When the Lord turned the captivity of Job, he *prayed* for his friends, a Spiritual Worship, but the friends were ordered in expiation of their offences to "offer a Sacrifice of seven bullocks and seven rams at a burnt Sacrifice": it matters not, whether the book of Job is a drama, or actual History, for it represents the feelings of the writer and the readers, at the time of its being composed, whenever that was. No one in these last days would dream of sacrificing beasts in atonement for sin, not even the Hebrews of Houndsditch; and yet in all Pagan Annals of the past, and all narratives of Pagan customs in the present, Sacrifice in some form, and even Human Sacrifice, is found to be the chief lever for obtaining God's pardon, and protection. The abstract Idea is dead, but there are still survivals of antetypes, analogies, dedications, and mere verbiage of Ritual, where the ancient word is used to express a later conception, such as "the Sacrifice of God is a broken Spirit"; "we render our Souls and bodies a living Sacrifice"; and in one of the French translations of the New Testament the technical word ίερεύς is rendered by "Sacrifateur." The Jews in their Synagogues in London in this epoch pray, that the institution of Sacrifice may be restored; the enlightened Hebrews protest in vain against this Archaic conception. (Jewish Quarterly Review, Feb., 1893.)

This very year, January 7, I read in *The Graphic*, how a sheep was sacrificed by the Mahometan Rulers of Syria, on the occasion of the railway being commenced from Haifa to Damascus. Paul, in his Epistles to the Galatians, iii, 13, and Ephesians, v, 2, seems to borrow a Homeric Idea, and, sniffing the well-known smell in the Temple Court, writes of a "Sacrifice of sweet savour," though in a metaphorical sense. The enormous number of victims attributed to Solomon in the Chronicles on the opening of the Temple, must be a gross exaggeration, or a wicked, and frightful, cruelty to brute beasts. Homer tells us of hecatombs, but a hecatomb is as nothing compared to Hebrew annals. Of Human Sacrifice we have instances among the Druids of Britain, the Azteks of Mexico, the Polynesians of Oceania; among the Greeks the Sacrifice of Iphigenia, among the Hebrews the case of Abraham and Isaac, and Jephthah, and the passing children through the fire; in India it is only a quarter of a century back, that the practice was put down by force of arms among a non-Arian tribe in the Province of Bangál.

A terrible example of the remains of heathenism in Russia

is mentioned in the *Moscow Gazette* and other journals. A trial, in 1894, took place of a number of peasants living in a district of Kazan for killing one of their numbers as a Sacrifice to the idols of the Votjaks, a Finn Race, of whom considerable numbers continue to live in more or less uncivilized conditions along the Volga between the Viatka and Kama rivers.

The Sacrifice of female chastity, either in the ordinary way, or by connection with a stone lingam, is more disgusting, though less bloody.

Socrates' dying words were, "A cock to Æsculapius." In the Anthology we read:

" Rode, caper, vitem, tamen hinc, cum stabis ad aram,
    In tua quod spargi cornua possit, erit."

This shows how a vegetable libation of wine was coupled with the animal Sacrifice.

But presents were also offered, and I fear are still, to Demi-gods and Demi-goddesses, under the name of Saints and Saintesses. In Virgil we read how the poor Trojan women, in the agony of the siege, took a garment to offer to the goddess, who would not look at them. In how many a Romish Chapel altar-cloths, candlesticks, diamonds, are offered to saints, who, it is to be feared, have never evidenced their satisfaction to their worshippers.

Aristophanes exposes the gross conception, that the gods and goddesses actually consumed the food offered: in "The Birds" he describes, how a wall was run up in mid-Heaven, and the gods of Olympus were starved out. Homer tells us, how the gods used to go to dine with the blameless Ethiopians. In the Apocryphal Book "Bel and the Dragon" we read, how the priest ate the sacrifices, and made the people believe that the god ate it. No doubt the Hebrew Priest lived by the Altar: his salary was paid, therefore, in slaughtered beasts. This is clear from the story of the sons of Eli in I Samuel, ii.

The offering of Sacrifice is described as being of two kinds: (1) fruits of the earth, (2) animals, including Human beings; and with two objects: (1) hostia honorata, a token of love and gratitude, and (2) hostia piaculans, an atonement, a bribe to ward off evil, a price to purchase some gift (Enc. Brit. xxi, p. 132). Neither Greek philosopher, nor Jewish Rabbi, ever got clear of the Idea, that Sacrifice afforded some physical satisfaction to the Deity: if it did not actually feed him, he was at least gratified by the odour: this was the only intercourse betwixt the Deity and man: they shared the same feast: such Worship was closely National, for men of different tribes could not eat or drink together. The Idea of Sacrifice occupied an important place in early Christianity: it had been a fundamental element of both Jewish and Gentile Religions, and Christianity had to absorb and modify it. But already to many Jews, and Gentiles, the conception was dying out, and a new belief had sprung up, that the most appropriate offering to the Deity was that of a pure and humble heart, and that Prayer was the proper channel of communication. Among the ignorant the gross conception still survives: the people of the Panjáb only a few years ago believed, that the British Government, when commencing a public work of importance, had given orders secretly to collect children's heads, as a propitiatory Sacrifice to the River Deities. Unless they had still within themselves the fundamental Idea of Sacrifice of animals, they would not have attributed such a scheme to others. A rumour of such a kind would avail nothing in Europe.

Human Sacrifice disappeared by the substitution of animal Sacrifice. We read in II Kings, iii, 27, that Mesha, king of Moab, about 895 B.C., "took his eldest son, who should have reigned in his stead, and offered him on the wall for a burnt-offering." We must recollect, that this is the statement of a hostile narrator, but we find in II Kings, xxiii, 10, that in 625 B.C. the residents at Jerusalem made their sons, or daughters, pass through fire to Molech; and in II Kings, xxi, 6, and II Chronicles, xxiii, 6, we read that Manasseh, king of Judah, made his son, and children, pass through the fire: and this is the report of two National Chroniclers, who may be credited with knowledge. Animal Sacrifice disappeared under the influence of civilization, and in the case of Christians by the conviction, that Christ was the complete, and *final*, Sacrifice: the sacerdotal Sacrifice of bread and wine in its extreme view is but a remembrance of this one great Sacrifice, for that form of Worship has had its day. If by some turn of Fortune's wheel the Hebrew Race were to get possession of Jerusalem, and rebuild their temple, they would find insuperable obstacles to the reintroduction of a rite, which is out of date.

The Pagan Idea of Religion was a quid for a quô: "I sacrifice to the gods: the gods look after my welfare": the remnant of the Idea clings to the Worship of Saints. A bowl of milk was put out by the farmer's wife to conciliate Robin Goodfellow. A low view exists among some Christians: how can you expect God to look after you, if you never go to Church, and say your prayers? but Love, not Fear, should be the attraction to God: Faith and Hope lead up to Love: "Though He slay me, I will trust in Him." But the Sacrifice of Self, the readiness to lay Self on the Altar of God, in God's service, for the saving of Souls of fellow-creatures, that great and inestimable gift of Self-Sacrifice, still survives, and will last as long as Human hearts beat: the antetype has swallowed up the type. The Roman, who leapt into the yawning chasm to save his country, set the example: the Idea seems monstrous to slaughter, not the wild beast, but the domestic animals, such as oxen, sheep, goats, pigeons, and turtle-doves: it is possible that a lamb, which was the playmate of the children, would have its throat cut, as a Religious act, by the father. We do not read of a single Hebrew man or woman offering themselves as a bonâ-fide Sacrifice: instances occur of devotion to country like that of Judith, but as a rule devout men preferred offering a substitute, and one cannot blame them: so that there was no personal service, and it goes without saying, that the liberal Sacrifices of the great and powerful were violently supplied from the herds of the weak and poor. To surrender life for the welfare of another is the perfection of Human Virtue, Love stronger than Death. Scarcely for a righteous man before the great Anno Domini would a man die, however ready he was to slaughter innocent animals, and turn his place of Worship into a Butcher's Shambles.

The Hindu went further: he believed, that the power of Sacrifice was so great, that the gods could be compelled to do what the worshipper required. With the Greeks the use of the word ἔταμον, in connection with the completion of a contract, shows, that the death of one of God's creatures was considered necessary to ratify an agreement. No Divine Command is quoted as an authority for this institution: it is mentioned in connection with the two first of the Human Race that were born, and there is reason to believe, that the practice was universal, and the spirit of the word has survived to our time, though for centuries the practice has ceased.

"New treasures still of countless price,
God will provide for Sacrifice."
(KEBLE.)

To what a deep degradation the custom had fallen is evidenced by the assembled Greek leaders, at the advice of their Priest, not deeming it unworthy of themselves after due deliberation to sacrifice the life of a young girl: the conscience of mankind was improving, for within a few centuries before the great Anno Domini, Lucretius, the Poet, wrote his scathing condemnation: and we read that the Sect of the Essenes in the second century before Anno Domini declined to make bloody Sacrifice, and substituted vegetable offerings (Renan: Israel, vol. v, p. 66). Professor Robertson Smith, in his Burnett Lectures, Aberdeen, gives an elaborate exposition of the theory, that the original

Idea of Sacrifice was that of a meal partaken in common by the members of a particular tribe, and their tribal Deity. (Fundamental Institution of Semitic Religion, 1889.)

The gross view of Sacrifice no doubt was, that a bloody king, a dishonest official, a bad, libidinous, cruel man, could throw off in some such way the result of an evil life, and of all the misery, which was brought on his contemporaries, by a spell of ostentatious repentance, and the Sacrifice of innocent animals to conciliate a god, whom he had neglected, insulted, and offended all his life. The Hindu Moralist saw this; in the Vishnu Puránna I read:

"Holy acts of Sacrifice are performed by those, who are devoted to their own duties, whose conduct is right and free from blemish, who are good, and tread in good paths."

Séneca discovered that "the gods were not to be worshipped by victims, however costly and refulgent with gold, but to be honoured with a pious and upright heart."

The Hebrew Prophets and Psalmist had long before pointed this out:

"The Sacrifice of God is a broken Spirit."

"Make no more vain oblations: incense is an abomination to Me."

"I will have Mercy, and not Sacrifice."

Yet still up to the very last day of the existence of Jerusalem the daily Sacrifice, during the Roman siege, was performed, as if it were of vital importance to the State and the Religion. In the obliquity of their vision they seemed quite oblivious of the change of the drift of thought of mankind, or were determined to despise it. The Jews of the Dispersion could have had no Sacrifice, and learnt to do very well without it, as the Jews do at the present time.

All Human Institutions, even when divinely originated, have the term of their existence fixed; if allowed to exist beyond that, then they become anachronisms, because the Ideal of moral conceptions has risen above their level. It is quite unnecessary to condemn the practice in past ages, or to pass any opinion upon the possibility of its having satisfied the requirements of a people no longer existing. Sacrifice is certainly one of the Institutions, which the world has outgrown. The most ignorant peasant of the Nineteenth Century would smile at the Idea of Sacrificing a turtle-dove on the occasion of the Baptism of his child.

Libations are in some degree subsidiary to Sacrifice: when the gross conception of the Deity consuming the food and drink offered was outgrown, the former was consumed by fire, and the latter poured out on the ground. In Psalm l, 13, we have the following:

"Will I eat the flesh of bulls, or drink the blood of goats?"

But there is no other instance. In the Græco-Roman world it was exceedingly common. Dr. Legge tells us, that to this day in China libations are made, not in the sense of propitiation, or expiation of Sin, but as tributes of duty and gratitude, the Idea of substitution having never entered the Chinese mind. (Religion of China, p. 53.)

5. Prayer.

All mankind in past and present times, and in all Regions, have been ready to have recourse to Prayer of some sort or other: they have recognised, that there existed a Power greater than themselves, and they tried to get help from Him, flying to the Deity for help in doubt, creeping to Him in sorrow: their Prayers may have been most unworthy, but the fact remains, that they prayed; they believed that they would get something, and, moreover, in many cases they expressed thanks for mercies received in reply to Prayer.

Prayer was often an act of merchandise: adoration was offered to the Deity, His protection solicited and expected: if the Deity failed, the petitioner would go elsewhere: both Sacrifice and Prayer were commercial transactions: "do ut des"; Jacob make this very clear (Genesis, xxviii, 20-22): "If God will be "with me, and will keep me in this way that I go, and will give "me bread to eat, and raiment to put on .... then shall the "Lord be my God .... and of all that Thou shalt give me, "I will surely give the tenth unto Thee."

A universal Hindu Conference was held at Banáras, 1892, and a Report read on the subject of the deterioration of the Brahmanical Religion in its practice. One of the conclusions of the Report was, that all the Priests of the Temple should offer Prayer to the Supreme Power, so that their Religion might be saved from the state, to which it had sunk. A day for general Prayer was fixed. (G. Smith: Conversion of India, p. 220.)

We catch a glimpse of the Roman Soldier at the epoch of Anno Domini: he was not necessarily an Italian, or a European, but certainly a Gentile; but he is described as "a devout man, and one that feared God, with all his house, which gave much alms to the people, and prayed to God alway" (Acts, x, 2). No doubt many of the Jews, who opposed the new movement, were devout, almsgiving, and prayerful, very much as the Hindu, who are described in the preceding paragraph.

When a man in an Oriental country tries to get something out of one higher in position and power than himself, he approaches with flattery: all know it in India: officials are told that, they are the wisest, and the best: the petitioner would bribe, if he dared: he gets others more influential to intercede for him: this is the instinct, motif, and origin of Prayer. He clothes his Deity with all the tastes, weaknesses, of his own Race: he tries music, and litanies, and hymns, to conciliate Him, and sometimes has recourse to abuse, when he cannot get what he wants.

Threats were held out to the special Deity, warning him that he must do his duty, or take the consequences. An Egyptian woman in childbed identifies herself with the goddess Isis, calls on the other gods to assist her in her labour, and threatens the direst consequences to the whole world, if anything happens to her. Thus Prayer was superseded by menace. Porphyry, 270 A.D., mentions a case, and remarks on the madness of man, who thus threatens Powers, whom he deems to be so weak and feeble as to listen to threats. Analogous to this is the Spanish sailor, who flogs the Statue of St. Martin, if he does not supply the wind required.

In Brittany the customs of the population were primitive, and their Religion was a sort of Christianity grafted on the most evident Paganism. They worshipped innumerable Saints unknown to the Roman Calendar, and did not scruple to threaten these Divinities, when they wanted anything from them. A blacksmith, whose child was ill, stalked into the roadside Chapel where the statue of his favourite Saint stood, and, brandishing a red-hot horse-shoe, threatened to "shoe the saint," if the child did not recover.

The Tibetan Buddhist cuts out figures of horses in paper, and commits them to the wind with a view of carrying help, paper-help, to some traveller. The Poet Horace tells us of the owners of merchandise in home-returning vessels running down to the shore to appease the Storm-gods by their "miserable" Prayers and vows to save their profits from the storm. The Prayer of the British Missionary Society is for more money, and when the Lord of the Harvest, under which term Missionary Societies habitually address the Ruler of the World, grants it, then the cry is for more men to spend the money: at the same time, in France, the Lord of the Vineyard is petitioned by the owner to send abundant grapes, and of such quality as will make good intoxicating wine. I have known portions of an Indian District, in which directly contrary prayers are being made: the cultivators of the cotton-fields implore their particular local Deity to send rain, as their crop is grown in unirrigated soil, as a rain-crop: money is offered in the temple to conciliate the great Cloud-compeller. At the same time the cultivator of the sugar-cane, which is an irrigated crop, dependent on wells, prays that rain be not sent, as it will be as untimely as rain in hay-season in Europe. Rival Sovereigns at war are having "Te Deums" intoned in their several Cathedrals at the same hour on account of the same event.

It is clear that two sets of people may be praying for the very contrary result: the passengers of a ship in a storm were praying for safety, and vowing a portion of their merchandise to their Deity; the "wreckers" on a dangerous coast were supplicating their Deity to send them spoil, promising a share.

Throughout the great Sanskrit Epic of the Ramáyana, we have accounts of blessings exacted from the unwilling Deity by the force of Prayer. The opponents of the Bill proposed a few years ago to modify the existing custom, having the force of law, regarding infant-marriages in Hindu Families, held a Religious service at Kálighat, near Calcutta, in the year 1891, and offered Prayers and Sacrifices to the goddess Kali, to induce her to influence the Viceroy of India not to pass the Bill into law. Only in 1893 the Priests of Rome in Hungary distributed forms of printed Prayers to the Virgin Mary for ignorant fools to repeat to prevent the introduction by law of Civil Contract of Matrimony: it sounds ridiculous: the majority of mankind are fools. Hired mourners were called in to say Prayers after a death; hireling Priests are still called in to repeat Masses; vain repetitions are common in all countries: "Ave Maria"; "Ram Ram"; "Bismillah." The Prayer of the Buddhist is for nothing, and to nobody: it is merely the use of a form of words for the purpose of heaping up merit: the prayer-wheel was invented by the Tibetans, that the words, "Om Mani Pani hom" ("Oh the Beautiful Lotus!"), might be turned round by the hand.

Specimens of Prayers in use with the Brahmanical, the Zoroastrian, the Confucian, the Egyptian, the Mahometan, have been collected (Gifford Lectures, 1893, p. 22). They present a strange picture of the common infirmity of the Human Race:

"The kind Creator casts His pitying eyes
On the pale upturned faces, and *denies*."

Hear about the Jews in England:

" Most of the Jews of the poorer parts of London, when they
" wish to say their Prayer, go through a series of sounds, of the
" meaning of which they have not the slightest idea, and which,
" as they utter them, often have no meaning at all. Should
" anyone enter the room, as the Jew stands at his devotions,
" he is not at all disturbed; he merely turns round and talks to

"the visitor for a few minutes, and then returns to the per-
"functory repetition of sounds! Again, after a minute or so
"he renews his conversation, and once more returns to his
"Religious duties, and so on, until there is no one to talk to,
"or the Prayer is over. Stranger than all this, is the fact, that
"it is, humanly speaking, impossible to convince him, that all
"this is a mockery; so low is the Jewish estimate of the
"Divine Mind." (J. H. Scott, Rector of Spitalfields.)

Prayer is nowhere commanded as a duty in the Hebrew law, and Prayers were only prescribed at the Sacrifices on the day of Atonement, and the thanksgiving offering for firstfruits: it is probable that it always accompanied Sacrifice: we read in Genesis, iv, 26, that men began "to call upon the name of the Lord": in the century preceding Anno Domini there was an excess of formal Prayer among the Pharisees.

The Poet Juvenal, nineteen centuries back, had discovered the vanity of all this, and remarks that "Man is held dearer "by the Deity, than he is by the Man himself, and that the "Deity knows best what is really useful, or really detrimental, "to Mankind." I quote his magnificent lines, as a landmark in Human progress:

"Ut tamen et poscas aliquid, voveasque sacellis
"Exta, et candiduli divina tomacula porci:
"Orandum est, ut sit mens sana in corpore sano:
"Fortem posce animum, mortis terrore carentem,
"Qui spatium vitæ extrema inter munera ponat
"Naturæ, qui ferre queat quoscunque labores;
"Nesciat irasci, cupiat nihil: Semita certe
"Tranquillæ per virtutem patet unica vitæ."

(*Sat.* X, 346.)

To give an idea of the abuse of Prayer I quote the following, lately printed (Daughters of Syria, April, 1893): "We moved "to another village occupied by Druses in Mount Lebanon; "we lost nothing all the time, except one teaspoon, and we "prayed about it, and it was brought back. What a gracious "Master we have, so ready to undertake any little detail of our "daily life!" This shows how very slightly the Religious conception has advanced since the days of the Hebrews.

The approach to the Deity in Prayer has been at all times either collective or private, either real or formal. We know what the teaching of Christ was, but it has made little effect in modern Christian Churches. We have a form of words, very often in a language totally unknown to the one who prays; in words familiar as regards sound, but the meaning of which is quite unknown. Prayers are offered for things, which the worshipper cares not for, a mere common form, such as the Deity influencing the heart of the Sovereign, or asking for Peace within their own borders, when the Nation is attacking weaker tribes in Asia or Africa all round without any provocation. Then, again, Music in many Churches crushes the prayer, or the words are taken out of the mouth of the congregation by unconverted young men and boys in white surplices, who happen to be gifted with the power of sweet sounds; or it is intoned in a non-natural way by a trained Clerk in Orders. When civilized Nations act in the present day in such manner, how can we wonder at the conduct of the Priests of Baal on Mount Carmel? They at least had Faith, though in a wrong person, and they gave their lives for that Faith, and were as much Martyrs, as any recorded in History.

The Roman Catholic, the Ritualist, the Evangelical, the Hindu, Buddhist, Mahometan, are using the same weapons each after their own method to confound each other. The stereotyped form of an Evangelical Meeting is to utter Prayer, that things may turn out in the way that those who pray wish: "insanum vulgus vult fieri quod vult": that the Papists may be confounded, the Ritualists be put to flight, and the vacant see be not filled up with another High Church wolf; that all men be brought to the Truth (*i.e.* the Truth as held by the Meeting); that the Indo-Chinese Opium-Trade be stopped, the Slave-dealer be shot down, U-ganda and Ma-Shona-land be annexed to Great Britain; that the Missionary's wife be safely delivered of her tenth child, that suitable candidates come forward for vacant posts, and that the Lord of the Harvest send bread to feed these extra mouths, and support their large families of children; that the followers of the false prophet may be routed; that the real meaning of Faith, as interpreted in the Church Missionary Society's *Intelligencer*, Sept., 1893, p. 711, be practically and unfalteringly evidenced by contributions increased to meet a standard of expenditure, such as no cautious Christian can possibly approve of.

Within a few streets we have a procession of the Guards of the League of the Cross, carrying a banner of "Our Lady of Ransom," and singing such hymns as:

"Oh! when shall we gaze on
 "*Her* Glory restored?
"Oh! when will poor England
 "Return to *Her* Lord?
"Behold in St. Paul's
 "The sweet Mother replaced,
"And Westminster now with
 "*Her* image is graced."

The Procession passed by a side street, in which there stands a Jewish Synagogue, where Prayers are still offered for the Restitution of the Sacrifice of Animals, where male babies have their persons cruelly mutilated, and animals are killed for consumption in a manner believed by many to be calculated to put them to unnecessary torture for the purpose of maintaining the husk of an Idea of a few thousands, who have missed step in the spiritual progress of Religious conceptions.

I remember how in Paris thousands of women thronged the Cathedral of Notre Dame, praying all night, that the Empress Eugenie might be delivered of a son: were their Prayers heard? Did any advantage to the Nation at large, or to those women in particular, come of it?

The Poet Milton, in one of his beautiful odes, describes a noble Christian lady as "calling the heathen goddess Lucína to her throes." The Amir Dost Mahómed of Kábul, while a prisoner in North India, was offering his regular Prayer in due form, when he overheard two Christians, sitting near him, conversing, and stating some facts about a horse: the Dost turned round and said in Persian, "Darogh ast" ("it is a lie"), and then went on with his Arabic Prayers, not one word of which he understood any better than an Italian peasant does of a Latin Litany. When the Khedive went to pay his respects to the Sultan at Constantinople, the Court Circular notes, how they went together to the weekly Prayers. The great Reformer of the Panjáb, Baba Nanak, enlarges on the subject of Prayer, and tells one of his enquirers, that his Prayer was nothing, as he was thinking all the time of his horses. The idea of Prayer entertained by the Jews is illustrated by the fact, that in the Song of the Three Children, all the elements, seasons, the animate, the inanimate, world, are represented as offering praise to the Deity with much the same spiritual force as poor ignorant men.

I have brought together these instances from different countries, and ages, to illustrate how far the conception, or practice, of Prayer has departed from the Sermon on the Mount, and the Epistle of James, v, 16, and it is difficult to say, whether the privilege of approaching the Deity in the humble accents of Praise, Confession of Sin, and Prayer, has been more painfully abused by heathen Monarchs, or sensational self-satisfied individuals, and coteries, in the middle classes of Great Britain.

When we consider the words of the Hymns of the Pagan world, such as the Hymns to Amen Ra (Records of the Past), the Hymns of the early Veda, and portions of the Bhágavad-Gita, passages in Homer and Virgil, and the Athenian Tragedians, we cannot but remark with how strong a uniformity of language the feelings of the Human heart find utterance, when under the pressure of trouble, or the conviction of sin :

"ἑκών, ἑκών, ἥμαρτον· οὐκ ἀρνήσομαι."

It is not a monopoly of the Hebrew Scriptures, though a beautiful feature in them.

Not only is Prayer available to ask for spiritual or material blessings for the one, who may offer Prayer, but malignant Prayers are offered to injure others : thus we read that Elias made Prayer, that there should be no rain for 3½ years (ἐπὶ τῆς γῆς) in the land. It may mean the Kingdom of Israel, or all the world over, and was a dreadful request to make by an erring Human creature. In China one man, the Sovereign of China, though of an alien Race from his subjects, is the only person permitted to present to the Lord of the Universe the National offerings of Reverence, Gratitude, and Prayer. In India such duties devolve on the Father of each family just as much as labouring to procure their daily food. I once asked a young Hindu what kind of Prayers he offered : he replied, " None, as that was his father's business." I have sat in Hindu, and Sikh, temples, trying to fathom the motive of the singsong chanting of the Purána, or the Granth, which my acquired knowledge enabled me to follow better than Priest or People, but to the assembled masses they were sounds, and they ejaculated Ram Ram, or Wa Guru, in return at intervals. In Japan petitioners write their petitions on paper, or have it written by the Priest ; they then put it into their mouths, and chew it to a paste, and spit it at the image of the Deity: if well aimed, and if the paper sticks, it is a good omen, that the Prayer is heard (Cobbold's Religion in Japan, S.P.C.K.). Homer tells us how Ulysses retired to a solitary place away from his companions to pray to the Immortal Gods for their guidance on his way home ; this shows that the conceptions of the Poet at least were in the right direction. There is an amazing freshness in the outpourings to their Creator of some of those far-off and despised Pagans; they did not speak to cliques, or use conventional tags, to suit the exacting ears of their fellow-creatures. Even the Azteks addressed God in their Prayer, as "the Power, " in whom they lived, omnipotent, omniscient, giver of all gifts, " without whom man is nothing ; a Power, which is invisible, " incorporeal, of perfect perfection, and purity, under whose " wings repose and sure defence can be found " (Prescott : Mexico, I, p. 52).

This is the Prayer of the Zoroastrians as recorded in the Zend-Avesta :

" We worship the pure, the Lord of purity ; we worship the

" Universe of the true Spirit, visible, invisible, and all that " sustains the welfare of the good Creator. We praise all good " thoughts, all good works, all good deeds, which are and will " be, and keep pure all that is good. We worship the Wise " One, who formed and furthered the Spirit of Earth: we " worship with our bodies, and our Souls."

Think of the Te Deums, and State Religious Services, which took place after events, such as the Battle of Inkermann, 1854, which both the Russians and Anglo-French claimed as a victory. I remember the story of a pious Lady, interested in Houses for the Poor, getting the late Lord Shaftesbury, myself, and others to a Prayer-meeting, and proposing that we should pray to God to influence the heart of a certain Royal Princess not to place High Churchmen on the Committee of Management. Lord Shaftesbury remonstrated: the request was too strong even for him, and he made a compromise by agreeing to call on the Princess, and influence her by Human argument, instead of making use of the spiritual engine, proposed by the Evangelical convener of the meeting.

The practice of the Búddhists in Tibet to set a prayer-wheel going by placing it in a mill-stream, which turns round and round the four sacred words, is often alluded to with derision: it is forgotten, that the worshippers are on the lowest round of intellectual culture: their motive was good; their liturgical apparatus was imperfect: but in the scale of measures taken by poor man to approach the Infinite, is the Tibetan wheel so far below the Litanies and Collects in a foreign tongue, the " Dominus Vobiscum " of the Romish, and " Gospodi Pomeloi " of the Russian, Church, the " fabricated " prayer of the higher cultured Búddhist (Williams: Búddhist, p. 154). On the other extreme, we come on the "agonizing in Prayer" at Keswick, 1893 (Sunday at Home, Sept., 1893), the " Passionate Prayer " of some Poems, the claiming of a sick child of God in answer to Prayer by the Church Missionary Society's Missionaries on the Niger, the specific Prayer of the simple-hearted man, who prayed for £500 per annum, *paid quarterly*; the suggestion of the Missionary Committee-man, that all the organized Deputation-system should be dispensed with, and that " the Secretaries should just go into the closet, shut to the door, and pray for the exact sum required for the year's expenses." To some aged people the repetition of Prayer is a mere opus operatum: I have travelled with old Priests of Rome in the train, and watched them working hard to read their breviary amidst distracting conversation, and gladly putting the book into their pocket, and looking out at the scenery. This very year, 1894, we find an Archbishop praising an aged clergyman, not for the number of Souls saved, or comforted, during an incumbency extending far beyond any profitable use, but for another reason: "It was my happiness " in my former Diocese to have among my clergy one aged " man more than 90, who never failed to say his daily office " within his Church, even when there was no Congregation, " or, as he happily expressed it, 'nobody but the Angels.'" Would not these last have been present with him in his own humble extempore ejaculations of penitence, prayer, and praise, within his own chamber, without surplice, or scarf?

Nothing is so soul-depressing as to think out this serious subject. The servants in a great Nobleman's house are assembled in a great Hall, jerked away from their domestic, or menial, duties, by the clang of a bell: the groom leaves his horse only partially rubbed down, the housemaid leaves her pail on the stairs, the cook leaves her cooking in danger of being spoiled, the ladies of the house drop the cosmetics and the paint-box, the young men hurry down buttoning their waistcoats: a miserable form of words is read by a Chaplain, who has ridden over from the next village, a chapter from the Bible is run through, and the party disperse: opus operatum.

It is a sad truth, that the uneducated community is little, in spiritual matters, above the beasts that perish; a portion of the community has rarely any policy for themselves in anything, they are totally devoid of personal originality. A Sanskrit Poet describes this class as "gatanagátika," plodding on in the steps of those that go before. They trust to their own particular Newspaper for their politics; to their lawyer for the safety of their property; to their doctor for the well-being of their vile bodies; and their particular minister for the safety of their Immortal Souls. Many leave this latter detail quite out of the sphere of their thoughts.

Cardinal Vaughan, when he founded St. Joseph's Foreign Mission Society with a College at Mill Hill, Hampstead, in 1868, wrote as follows, and his address has been republished in 1894: "The contribution of your Prayers is asked: this is a " gift, which all are rich enough to make, and it is a gift of " value, for I can assert, that every measure taken towards the " establishment of this College has succeeded, when it has " been supported, and furthered, by the Prayers of holy Souls: " had I been inclined to doubt the value of Prayer, I should be " worse than blind to doubt of its efficacy, after what I have " witnessed of its power these past years" Now similar Prayers go up week by week, day by day, from the Evangelical Section of the Church, notably the Church Missionary Society, in whose periodicals the Church of Rome, which Cardinal Vaughan represents, is denounced. From U-Ganda, during the last two or three years, two conflicting streams of Prayer, one in French, one in English, have been offered to the Throne of Grace, accompanied by the dying cries of women and children, slaughtered in an inter-Christian struggle to carry the Gospel to the Natives of Central Africa. It must indeed make the Angels weep. In December, 1894, we read how Cardinal Vaughan has moved the Archbishop of Toledo to set the prayer-wheel going in Spain, for the conversion of Great Britain to the Pope: "Fiat experimentum in corpore vili."

6. RITUAL.

The Religious Idea soon passed in all ages and places into empty Ritual: it is one of the great sins of all Religions. The Church of Rome delights in Temples, Bells, Music, Incense, Processions, artful devices of the senses to deceive the vulgar: then come Places of Refuge, or Sanctuaries for fugitive criminals; Penance, or what the Hindu calls "tapas," Expiation, Fasting, invoking blessing on animals, on slaves, about to be exported from Africa to America (see *Graphic*, Aug. 19, 1893, p. 232), and a mass of folly.

The following speaks for itself: Dates of the consecration of divers rites and institutions of the Romish Church: (1) holy water, A.D. 120; (2) penance, A.D. 157; (3) monkhood, A.D. 348; (4) Latin Mass, A.D. 394; (5) extreme unction, A.D. 550; (6) invocation of Virgin and Saints, A.D. 715; (7) kissing the Pope's toe, A.D. 809; (8) canonization of Saints, A.D. 993; (9) baptizing of bells, A.D. 1000; (10) celibacy of priests, A.D. 1015; (11) indulgences, A.D. 1119; (12) Papal dispensations, A.D. 1200; (13) elevation of the Host, A.D. 1200; (14) the Inquisition, A.D. 1204; (15) auricular confession, A.D. 1215; (16) dogma of the Immaculate Conception, A.D. 1853; (17) infallibility of the Pope, A.D. 1870.

The Hindu, and the Græco-Roman Priests, were the precursors of, and the latter were the great examples to, the Christian Churches. Bishop Westcott remarks (Cambridge Companion to the Bible, 1893, p. 21), in his Essay on the Sacred Books of pre-Christian Religions, that "Ritual in each case has finally overpowered the stirrings after a personal, and spiritual, fellowship with God," and without that Religion is a mere farce. It was all very well for a Roman in the Augustine age to pour out a libation to the gods: even the last words of Socrates, "A cock to the god Æsculapius," sounds sad to our ears: how far more ennobling were the two dying sentences of Stephen, commending his Spirit to his Saviour, and craving pardon for his murderers! we seem to feel sure, that Socrates had this feeling, but was unable to express it: he had not learnt the terminology.

What rational opinion can be formed of the decoration of Churches beyond what is necessary for the convenient assembly of worshippers, or a table at one end being called an altar, and decorated with flowers, vessels, crosses, and crucifixes? When we read of the Pan Athenaic procession at Athens, and stand in the ruined Temples at Pompeii, we cannot but feel, how very Pagan are the so-called imitations of more advanced, and more intelligent, ages: the very words "consecration of a brick and mortar fabric" and "sacrilege" as applied to metal vessels being stolen, have a Pagan smack about them. The Church consists of the Souls of the congregation, brought together in a decent suitable building set apart for the purpose, but always liable to return to secular uses. In India the Roman Catholic Church does not consecrate the building, but the altar, which it can remove. What misery and loss of life have been caused by the tendency of the followers of one Religious conception, or of the Sect of one, to appropriate the buildings of another Sect. We deem it, or at least many of us, an insult to Christianity, that so many Christian Churches have been turned into Mahometan Mosques, such as Sta. Sophia at Constantinople, and the great Church at Damascus, itself once a Pagan Temple; but how many places of Worship have Christians exultingly, and out of malice, annexed! In India the Mahometans annexed Hindu Temples, and in times of reaction the Hindu annexed Mahometan Mosques, and fights took place about bricks and mortar: the site of the Temple of Solomon is still occupied by a Mahometan Mosque. Even in London we have the sight of processions of members of the Church of Rome filing into Westminster Abbey to worship at the tomb of Edward the Confessor; and in Edinburgh the still more strange sight of a Presbyterian congregation occupying the Cathedral of St. Giles, so unsuitable to their simple form. Instances of such appropriation occur all over the Northern part of Europe.

And as regards Ritual, I have visited Troitska, one of the most sacred shrines of the Greek Church, near Moscow. Notwithstanding my considerable experience of the Ritualism of that Church, I was at a loss to follow the meaning of all the symbolism, but I have often stood in a Hindu Temple watching similar Ritual, and I felt that some of my old friends the Pujári Brahmins of Banáras would be quite at home, and in full sympathy, with the bowings and genuflexions, and manipulations, and the Gospodi Pomeloi of the Russian Papa. There is a strong family likeness in all manifestations of Human folly, and extravagant action.

In 1885 a sermon was preached by the lamented Dr. Hatch of Oxford, whose Bampton-Lectures let in so much light into the origin of Ritual. One sentiment was remarkable: "All "scientific Truths had been denounced by Christians, as "Heresy, and the consequence was that, as knowledge "advanced, those, whose eyes were opened, regarded the "Religion, as presented to them, as a Cave of Adullam, in "which the collective weaknesses of mankind had taken "refuge, and that real Christianity had passed into a world of "shadows. That faith in Jesus, which had conquered the "world by its own innate Truth and greatness, was a simple "Creed, and that, which linked Christians together, was a "simple Brotherhood."

The consequence of the tendency to ornament places of Worship with spoils taken from other countries, and other places of Worship, renders so-called Sacrilege a common offence: the plunder of sacred vessels, the robbery of jewels and treasures from Sacristies, are loudly complained of: but why are they there? the spoil of plundered towns was dedicated to a Deity, who had uttered the words, "Thou shalt not steal": men and women were murdered in the name of Him, who had written, "Thou shalt not commit murder": the lands and houses and vineyards of others were coveted, and taken possession of by violence under the asserted guidance of Him, who had written, "Thou shalt not covet thy neighbour's house, nor anything that is his." Attila and Genghiz Khan could not be worse than were the Hebrews, and the Christian Kings of the Middle Ages.

With regard to Penance, a strange Idea has occupied the minds of ancient men, that physical pain purges away moral evil. This has led to Asceticism in India, whereby a power was obtained over the Deity, who was driven to practise unworthy tricks to break the power of the Ascete. Penance is one of the strange errors of the Romish Church.

If Ritual be kept within its legitimate limits, it matters not: it is then but a desire to protect the Essence of Religion, and to keep the thoughts from wandering, while engaged in Worship. This is what is sometimes called a warm Service, as opposed to the cold, haughty, attitude of the Mahometan, who so many times a day bandies words with his Creator, like a Sentry reports to his Commanding Officer. But those, the externals of whose Worship is like the rind of the fruit, should be reminded, that the Ritual of the Christian is but a copy of Jewish and Pagan Originals. It is evident, that the Ritual of Moses owed much to the Egyptian and Babylonian, or in other words to the common germ of such developments, which is part of the outfit of the Human Race. In course of time the Christian borrowed from the Jewish, and the Roman, and Greek, Paganism around him. No sooner did Christianity become Religio licita, than the same tendencies, which had displayed themselves in the Pagans of South Europe, began to appear; the notion prevailed, that in order to captivate the multitude, all Worship of the Deity needed to be surrounded with pomp and outward show. The humble Christian Minister assumed the dress and name of Sacerdos, and wore fine clothes. The upper room, or the humble conventicle, was supplanted by the Basilica, which rivalled the grandest of heathen temples; processions, gold and silver ornaments, incense, lighted tapers, and a grand Ritual, recalled the ceremonial of the old gods of Rome. It never occurred to that superstitious age, or to the present enlightened one, that all this outward glory, however suitable to the centuries before Anno Domini, and the Religious conceptions of that Epoch, were totally repugnant to the new and spiritual conception. The early Christians in their humble dwellings, and places of Worship, did approach the Lord in Prayer, living as He did in his earthly pilgrimage, but the allurements of the flesh now obstruct, and render difficult, the approach to Him in humility, Spirit, and Truth.

Could they have read clearer the page of History, and understood the march of Human events, they might have acted differently. The Palestinian Jew in the century preceding Anno Domini, had fallen to the lowest level of empty Ritual. The destruction of the Temple, and the cessation of the Mosaic form of Worship, were at hand. In the meantime the Jew of the Diasporá was supplying the leaven of progress to all the Races and Nations, with whom he came into contact. He had no Temple, no Priesthood, no Ritual, but he had a high Ideal, and he was unconsciously preparing a platform in every city of West Asia, North Africa, and Europe, on which the new Religious conception could rest: the Kingdom of Israel, and the old Jerusalem, were ready to disappear; the shadow of the Kingdom of God, and the new Jerusalem, fell on the slide of the great Lantern of the Universe. Moses was read in every Synagogue every Sabbath: a few years later Christ was to be read also, for it may roughly be said that, where there was a Synagogue, there would soon be a Church: Primitive Christianity sprang up in a soil prepared by two or three centuries of Hebrew culture. The Jew of the Diasporá, deprived of means of access to the outward centre of his hereditary worship, arrived at the conviction, that his call was to serve God in a pure manner, and observe the principles of his Religion, since he was hopelessly debarred from the Ritual. The Christian Church absorbed too much Paganism in its essence to keep clear of Ritual. With Ritual came dancing, music, ceremonies attending the initiation, the feast of love, and the funeral, noise made by bells, tam-tams, gongs. I have, in India, heard the followers of three different Religious conceptions, striving who could make the most noise. The dancing of the Corybantes has, in these last years, been renewed by the Salvation-Army in the streets of London, as it is by the Dervishes in the Mosques of Constantinople. On the paintings on the walls of Egyptian tombs of vast antiquity we find, that the fools of that epoch were doing just the same thing as the fools of this epoch, and as David did before the Ark, rousing the derision of at least one of the spectators.

The end is not yet: in *The Times* of 1894, I read how "the " anniversary of the execution of the so-called Manchester-" martyrs was celebrated in several of the principal towns of " Ireland. There were processions, speeches, some approach " to Religious ceremonies, and much decoration of Fenian " graves." This recalls the processions in honour of the martyrs of Kérbela, Hosan, and Hosein, in Mahometan countries, and of Tammuz, in Syria, and of many a Saint in the Church of Rome, notably the body of Xavier at Goa in West India.

The counting of beads is a form of Ritual, which the Christian Churches share with the Pagan. The Hindu repeats his "Ram Ram," and the Roman Catholic his "Ave Maria," with equal profit to his Soul. Every Tibetan has his Rosary of 108 beads, that he may keep up the reckoning of his good words, which to him supply the place of good deeds; to this day they place efficacy in vain repetitions.

Singularly enough sometimes the followers of one conception in their intense ignorance practise the Ritual-tricks of a totally distinct conception; the lower class Marátha Hindu, who have themselves rebelled against priestly domination very recently, not only respect, but participate in, Mahometan Religious customs in Poona. For instance, the majority of *tazia* (paper and wood representations of the tomb of the two grandsons of Mahomet) in the annual festival of the Mohurrum are made by the Marátha. The tomb of a saint, Shah Dawal, near Poona, is worshipped by the Marátha, who take goats, etc., as a Sacrifice to the saint every week.

7. PRIESTCRAFT, WITCHCRAFT, EXORCISM.

Certain phenomena have been the bane of all Religious conceptions, whether they appear in the degraded form of the Shaman in Central Asia, or the Medicine-man in North America. Islam is entirely free, at least, from Priestcraft, or the lofty type of the Hindu Brahman, the Hebrew Priest, or the Roman Catholic Cardinal. The instinct of these last leads them to strive to keep the office either as hereditary, or as a close corporation; to strive to keep all knowledge, secular or Religious, in their hands; to keep the laity in subjection by trickery, by cajolery, by intimidation, by threatenings of future punishment. Their best and their worst characteristics co-operated to work out their purpose, and indeed they had to secure the means of living in some way, especially after the cessation of animal sacrifices diminished the supply of food ready to be consumed by themselves and their families.

Sacerdotal pretensions have been, and continue to be, one of the greatest social curses, that the world ever knew. Far from encouraging Morality, or developing the Religious Idea, it has generally the contrary effect; and the enforcement of a spiritual tyranny, such as Priests delight to exert, has a decidedly immoral influence, destroying the independence of the individual Soul before the Deity.

The exercise, or pretence to exercise, Magical Arts; the conceptions of Charms against the Evil Eye, Drawing of Lots, Witchcraft, Incantation, are found everywhere. Sometimes these powers are claimed by the regular Priesthood; sometimes by a rival set of impostors, who are denounced by the Priests, as the Priests are by them.

The Hebrew Chroniclers notice an Ephod, which was consulted by the Priests, on the occasion of there being a doubt as to a policy to be assumed; in fact, Abiathar, when Nob was destroyed, went off with a view of helping David (I Samuel, xxx, 7). On the other hand, Magical Arts, consulting of familiar spirits, were forbidden. Saul asked counsel of a familiar spirit, and the form of Samuel appeared to him, and he inquired not of the Lord, therefore he slew him (I Chronicles, x, 14).

Bishop John Selwyn writes: "In many islands no one of "importance is deemed to die a natural death; a cause of his "illness must be sought, and that is Witchcraft; recourse is "had to Divination in some form or another. The innocent "inhabitant of some neighbouring village is pitched upon, as "the offender, and is pursued with unrelenting hate." (Ramsden Sermon, May 21, 1893.)

We find notice of the father of Khama, who was not only the Chief, but the Sorcerer of his tribe, and in the last capacity he had to study his Divination, and repeat his Incantations, as often as Ma-Tabéle inroads threatened.

We read in the Book of Numbers, how Balaam was sent for by the king of the tribe to launch curses on the Hebrews, as they approached his country. In fact, the practice in ancient time was universal.

With regard to Priesthoods, there is none in China. The official class do what is required, and the Emperor himself offers the Solstitial Service, not as Priest, but as King. Some Religious conceptions have tried to exist without a clergy, a class set apart for teaching, ministering, performing social rites such as matrimony, funerals, initiations, but it has been found, that a Ministry of some kind is as necessary to a Religious Worship, as a Schoolmaster to a School, or a Gardener to a Garden.

The names of the forms of deception may be extended so as to include Amulets, Sortilages, Omens, Ghosts, Philtres, hidden forms of words such as Kabála, and Palmistry, which is still practised in England, and is punishable as an attempt to deceive Her Majesty's subjects. Some of these deceptions rose even to the rank of Sciences, such as Astrology, Divination, in times past.

8. Ceremonial Cleanness, or Uncleanness.

The distinction of clean and unclean can scarcely be defined, or understood, in the Nineteenth Century, but it was the characteristic of all priesthoods over the ancient world, and rested in its origin on gross superstitions, the reason of which is forgotten, though the practice remains. Religion thus hardens down into ceremonial: some animals may be eaten, some may not; dead bodies, even of loved ones, were not to be touched; Caste grew from this in India, restricting matrimony, and commensality. A very dirty man may be deemed ceremonially clean, while a very clean man may be voted ceremonially unclean. Drinking water in vessels, touching articles, comes under that head: I remember the Hindu driver of a Post-Office-cart refusing to blow a bugle, which had been blown by a Mahometan. On one occasion there was a trouble in the city of Banáras, and I arrested some half a hundred, tied them all together with a rope, and sent them to the gaol: it was hot weather, but a Brahman refused to drink water, because there was a Christian prisoner tied by the same rope, about ten men off him: he was left to his thirst: the Greeks had it strongly ἕκας ἕκας ὅστις ἄλιτρος. The division of the animal world into clean and unclean for reasons quite unintelligible, such as cloven feet, or chewing the cud, must be a survival of Totemism: it prevailed among the Babylonians and Assyrians as well as among the Hebrews. All Religions on some pretence or another forbid some article of food: the Hebrews and Mahometans, for no obvious reason, forbid the eating of swine's flesh; the Hindu forbad the eating of cow's flesh, and eggs; the Sikhs forbad tobacco: and there is generally a corresponding indulgence in something else; for instance, tobacco being forbidden, the Sikhs take to opium. One of the main objections to the crusade against opium in India is, that the people deprived of their drug will take to alcoholics of some sort, imported from Europe.

9. FASTING, CELIBACY, ASCETICISM, EREMITISM.

Under this head we find the same features everywhere, as ridiculous, as useless for all spiritual advancement, engendering Pharisaic pride, and laying aside the very objects of Human existence: the more degraded the Religious conception, the more we hear of abstaining from certain meats, or all meats, forbidding matrimony, abandoning the ways of ordinary life, and retiring as hermits into deserts or forests to spend life in absolute uselessness, or to cluster in Monasteries in obedience to self-imposed vows, pretending to higher sanctity, neglecting the ordinary duties of men and women. There must be a fascination for such things in certain minds: we find instances of it among the Essenes, the hermits of Upper Egypt, the Brahmanical Brahmacharya, and Sanyási, and Yogi, the Buddhist, the Jew, the Greek, Romish and Armenian, Coptic, and Syriac, Monasteries. Such practices might have been tolerable, and useful, in times of confusion, and unrule: they are intolerable now. The Mahometans keep the Ramzán fast with great regularity, and really put up with a great deal of suffering ; the Roman Catholics have their jour maigre, but, as plenty of fish and eggs is allowed, it is a mere name. We hear of English Bishops dispensing by circular letters with fasts in Lent, which seems in modern days to be taking unnecessary trouble. Fasting is a mere survival: it may be very well for the glutton, or one who fares sumptuously, but for the spare liver, and advocate of temperance, it ranks among the works of supererogation ; to the labouring man it would mean inability to work : the wheels of the engine will not revolve, the fire in the hearth will go out, if there be no supply of fuel; the railway-engine, without supply of water, will cease to work: to go without food with a view of supplying the pressing need of a poorer brother is the real fast.

An Oxford correspondent of *The Times* "carries back the " practice of fasting-communion to the time of St. Basil " (A.D. 380).

" But whence was a custom, apparently so alien to the circum-
" stances of the original institution, imported into the Christian
" Church ? Probably, like so many other novelties of Ritual and
" doctrine, introduced into the Catholic Church in the third,
" fourth, and fifth centuries, from a Pagan source.

" The initiated in the Greek mysteries at Eleusis, before they
" were allowed to drink of the mystic κυκεών and eat of the
" sacred cakes, were required to fast for a day (Hatch's Hibbert-
" Lectures, 1888, p. 298).

" It was not till the conquered Paganism had begun to take
" such dire revenge by imposing much of its own philosophy
" and its own ritual on the victorious Church, that the necessity
" of fasting-communion was taught by the Fathers.

" Were it not for the difficulty in these days of delicate
" organizations and diminishing endurance, of combining this
" practice, probably Pagan in its origin, with a late celebration
" of the Eucharist, it is plain, from the correspondence in public
" newspapers, that we should hear of no objections to evening
" communions."

We hear of a Mahometan in Egypt in 1894 venturing to preach against Fasting in the Ramzán, as not being prescribed by the Korán: it led to a fanatical outburst: the man was taken to the Kazi, and received thirty strokes of the kurbash: this seems an act of great intolerance: the real offence of the man was his attempting to wound the feelings of others by his conduct and words; this no doubt was a punishable offence: at any rate, Fasting should be voluntary. The Jew still practises Fasting.

" Tuesday evening marked the beginning of the great Re-
" ligious day of the year in the Jewish Calendar, the Day of
" Atonement, and several thousands of English, German, Polish,
" and Russian, Jews attended at the Great Assembly Hall, Mile
" End Road, for its celebration. The day began at sunset, and
" the first service began at half-past five. The Fast is observed
" from dusk to dusk, and no adult Jew or Jewess is allowed to
" take any food or drink whatever during that period of time."

Penance to expiate sins committed comes under this category: putting on sackcloth and a sad face. A remarkable case is mentioned in Jonah, iii, 5: The people of Nineveh, Assyrians, seem to have known all about the way of conciliating an offended Deity. The king sat in ashes, and even the cattle, poor creatures! were covered with sackcloth, and put upon reduced diet. With the Hindu we read that the penance of the body was to be chaste, of the mouth to speak always truth and kindness, of the thoughts to control Self, purify the Soul, to be silent, and disposed to benevolence.

Búddha was seven years practising extreme asceticism; he then reflected, that the extreme mortification of the body did not bring him into the path of Perfect Knowledge. It struck him, that a guitar too lightly strained gave a harsh sound, one not strained enough gave no resonance, while a string moderately strained gave forth sweet sounds ; so he determined to practise moderate asceticism : he sate in contemplation under a tree, and ate food collected as alms sufficient to support life : thus he arrived at True Knowledge, subduing of the Passions, Precepts of the eight-fold Noble Path leading to the supreme God.

10. Feasting, Day of Rest.

Here all the old world, and great part of the modern world, are on common ground, and wish to keep a day of Rest, or Feasts, sometimes guided in their dates by the Revolution of the Sun, sometimes of the Moon. Among the Semites the day of Rest, called " Sabbath," can be traced through the Phenicians to the Akkadians (Tiele, p. 84); with the Jews it was deemed to be primeval, and the last day of the week, Saturday; with the Christians the first day of the week, Sunday; and with the Mahometans the last day but one of the week, Friday.

We read in Greek and Latin Poets of the Feasts, which the Seasons brought round, connected with their Deities. In India there are special periods, extending over days and weeks. Paul (Gal. iv, 17) alludes to the observance by the Jews and neo-Christians of days, months, and years ; the Roman Catholic Calendar is made up of days set apart, some to feasting, some to fasting. There is a great and universal superstition as regards times, places, persons, and seasons, which the Human Race will never outlive, and which they transfer from one Religion to another. Some days are lucky, some unlucky : the Harvest Home with its decorations is but a remnant of Paganism ; the gifts of the Earth have a beauty about them, but, when a pig's head is offered at the Communion-Table, the boundary seems to be passed, and yet herds of swine are as much means of honest livelihood, and support of families, as the more picturesque barn of corn, and vineyard.

11. Esoteric, or Exoteric.

I quote the words of a learned writer : " Last of the higher " polytheisms, we may name that of Greece. Here, as " elsewhere, we have an *esoteric* as well as an *exoteric* form of " Religion, the former being ultimately embodied in what are " known as the 'mysteries.' These, whatever they may at " times have degenerated into, were, in their first intention, " attempts to lead the Soul higher, 'the highest effort of " Paganism to realize sacramental communion with Deity.' " Thus, while many of the rites of the public Religion in

"Greece were gross and degrading, this higher teaching rose to a far nobler level."

We seem to see the first germ of this two-fold exhibition of the same conception in Mark, iv, 11, 34: "Unto you it is given to know the mystery of the kingdom of God, but unto them that are without, all these things are done in parables"; "But without a parable spake He not unto them; and when they were alone, He expounded all things to His disciples."

The Church of Rome in the dark ages made full use of this principle: "It concentrated Church-Authority and power in "the hands of the Clergy: but there was something worse and "more deadly: it developed the Idea, that the Religion of the "understanding, and of the head, was the prerogative of the "few, that a Ritual of devotion, born of ignorance, was the duty "incumbent on the many. Such a Church was not a Christian "Church, but it ought to have some Christians in it." (The Rev. Thomas Smith: Modern Missions, p. 238.)

But even in our own Protestant Churches, what do the School-children understand of the Catechism, to which they reply, and the prayers which they repeat? Let it pass: their childhood excuses them: they are being trained. What do the fathers and mothers of families, and the hard-working adults, know of the mysteries of Christianity? They are simple, if received into a simple heart, but when a rind of Human cares, vices, and desires, is formed round that heart, how can they understand? What are the feelings of a rustic congregation looking at the new painted window in memory of the Squire's wife? can they recognise in the bright blue, or red, or yellow, figures in the glass the Saviour of the world, the carpenter of Nazareth, who walked through Galilee as a humble peasant with no home, and nothing of the world's greatness? What authority have we to suppose, that there will be crowns of gold, or sceptres, or splendid robes in the next world, though the Author of the Revelation seems to hint at it?

Is there not, therefore, an esoteric and exoteric Doctrine to this day? a hazy conception on the part of the ignorant and uncultured? I quote the words of a competent student, if not master, of this subject:

"To expect that Religion can ever be placed beyond the "reach of scientific treatment, or of honest criticism, shows an "utter misapprehension of the signs of the times, and the "nature of the conception: it would after all be no more than "setting up the private judgment of some against the private "judgment of others: if the unalienable rights of private "judgment of all were recognised, the character of Religious "Controversy would be changed. Restriction provokes resent-"ment, and embitters all discussions.

"Religious intolerance is in some respects worse now than formerly: the Indians recognised, that the Religion of the young can never be quite the same as the Religion of the old, as diversity of class, tastes, education, culture, occupation, and training, must produce divergence in Religious thought. The ignoring of this simple fact leads to hypocrisy on the one side, and dogmatism on the other.

"I know how strong a feeling there is against anything like a Religion *for the few* different from the Religion *for the many*. An esoteric Religion seems to be one, that cannot show itself, that is afraid of the light, that is, in fact, dishonest: but far from being dishonest the distinction between a higher and lower form of Religion is actually the only honest recognition of the realities of life. To a philosophic man Religion is a Spiritual Love of God, and the joy of his full consciousness of the Spirit of God within him: but what meaning can such words convey to Millions of Human beings? They nevertheless want a Religion, a positive authoritative, revealed Religion, to teach them, that there is a God, and that His commands must be obeyed without questioning."

CAP. III. MANIFESTATION OF SUCH A POWER.

1. Miracles.
2. Prophecies, Auguries, Ordeals.
3. National Sins and Punishments, Anger and Hostility of the Deity.
4. Signs from Heaven.
5. Conception of Fate, Nemesis, 'Ερινύς.

1. MIRACLES.

In every country in the world down to the end of the Nineteenth Century there has been a fond belief in Miracles. It is so notorious, that no words are required. I have visited the Romish Shrines of Lourdes, Zaragossa, Treves, Loretto, Rome, Turin, Monte Serráto, near Barcelona, Einsiedeln, in Switzerland, and have no doubt, that it is believed, that the Mother of Christ can work Miracles, and does so: it is significant, that in Northern Europe, where the population is of a colder temperament, and of relatively higher culture, no such manifestations are notified; of course, in the elder days before the great Anno Domini they were the common stock of every Religious conception. The belief was very strong among the Hebrews; no instance of a Miracle performed by a Gentile occurs in the New Testament, and the belief in them, only faint in the Greek and Roman Church, is actually non-existent in the Protestant Churches; the unhappy Asiatic and African Churches, which suffered so much under the Mahometans for so many years, were never saved, or comforted, by miraculous interference, though such help would have been at that time most acceptable and opportune. Moreover, the Romish Church, notwithstanding that it pretends to have such extraordinary powers in reserve, never fails to lean on the Arm of the Flesh of an Earthly Power. As a fact, the Saints never do supply material help in the Mission-Field: a superstitious population of half-an-half Christians is required to start a Miracle-performing shrine; not one exists in the British Dominions. Neither

Búddhist, Confucianist, nor Zoroastrian, make any pretence to miraculous power, and no instance of a Brahmanical Miracle in India has occurred in the memory of man, or at least in my experience; the ordinary stock-forms, of raising from the dead, healing the sick, providing food, helping believers to drive off hostile invaders, are totally unknown. When an event has happened a very long time ago, a very long way off, the important point for the Philosophic Historian is to find out, whether it ever happened at all, or whether it was believed to have happened by any, who had evidence to the fact, and a faculty of recording it. We must recollect, that a great many Miracles are reported to have taken place with a view of injuring other people: a Court of Law would soon dispose of such cases. Whatever fanatics may say, a Miracle could not co-exist with a Public Press.

Mahomet, to his credit, never pretended to possess the power; he considered the Korán to be a Miracle, and as a literary work it is of the highest merit: we cannot undertake to say by what process Mahomet composed it, or received it when composed; we can only deal with it as we find it in Manuscript. Gautama Búddha never claimed the power.

We come face to face with Miracles in all the Sacred Books of the East: they were believed by honest, decent men of their time, and were not put into circulation from corrupt motives. We try to explain them by mistake of the copyist, or some philological interpretation, or by allegory, or by a dense misunderstanding of actual facts; but it is all in vain. I must painfully admit, that this idiosyncrasy belongs to all early Religious conceptions, and venture to assert that, unless atheists, cynics, agnostics, and a fearless public opinion and public Press, existed, they would come into existence again. It would be urged by the Missionary, (1) that a great mass of mankind has to be converted; (2) that judicious Miracles would greatly assist the process; (3) that God loves mankind as much now as ever, and does not wish any to perish; (4) that God's power is not limited; (5) that fervent Prayer, and our Saviour's Promises, can do much. Let us have evidence enough to satisfy a Common Jury.

The Birth of Búddha is surrounded with Miracles, 600 B.C.: all Nature was moved, the trees bowed down to him; as a newborn child he behaved in a manner totally unusual.

Stones bearing the impress of man's feet are shown at Ajódya (Awadh) in India, at Hasan-Abdal, and on the Mount of Olives. Rocks struck have given place to fountains at Hasan-Abdal. Heavenly Leaders are reported to have suddenly appeared in battle to help a particular cause. Pestilences have been sent to destroy the armies of enemies. All this is the common stock of ignorant National Legends. Such kind of things are never reported now.

It has been severely remarked, that Miracles have been the bane of all forms of Religious conceptions; if once admitted for a season, their possibility is calculated upon, and the vulgar mind expects them to continue. The Church of Rome is always logical: here is a notice under date September, 1890: " The feast of the Nativity of the Virgin was celebrated to day " by the issue of four decrees, declaring that due examination " has confirmed the virtues of four deceased monks, and " established the authenticity of Miracles, attributed to those " personages: they are accordingly beatified." And so on to the end of time.

There is no monopoly with Christians: in their ignorance, they think that they only are thaumaturges, but "in the " sixteenth century war was still waged on equal terms with ". the Mahometans. Both believed, that they were fighting for " the cause of God; both invoked His assistance. The " Turkish Admiral managed to *lull the wind*, which favoured " the Christian sails. Cardinal Ximenes, at the capture of " Oran, managed by his prayers to *stay the course of the Sun*, " until the Soldiers of the Cross were avenged of their Moorish " enemies. Houris were lent out of Heaven waving green " kerchiefs to lure the Ghazi to his martyrdom. St. James on " his white horse was seen in mid-air by pious eyes, leading " the charge of the Champions of the Cross."

The Khalífa Abdullah, successor of the Madhi at Khartûm, promised his troops the divine help of the beatified Mahdi, and a certain victory. This is just what the Papist Missionaries in Africa do to this day. A French Missionary writes to the Missions Catholiques from U-Ganda, that his brother Missionaries, who have died, have helped him by going among the people. Now the Madhi, the Khalífa, and the Papist Priests, were all holy, good men, constant in prayer, and ready to sacrifice their lives in their cause, yet they lent themselves to a lie. In the hands of dead Wahábi have been found sealed Arabic papers, promising them a happy Paradise, with a Pearl for a dwelling, and Houris to attend on them, if they fell fighting the battle of Islam.

What shall be said of the Book of Tobit? We read of an evil Spirit, whose name is recognised in Zoroastrian legends, who repeatedly killed the bridegroom of a girl on the wedding night, and by the miraculous interference of the Archangel Raphael, and the smell of a burning fish, fled away to the River Euphrates. The Æneid of Virgil is full of Miracles, and interference of the Deity, spoken of historically, and to support the argument of his Poem, not from any desire of lucre and power: it is a fair measure of the intellectual status of the educated classes at a period just anterior to the great Anno Domini. The monstrous miraculous vision, which Constantine is supposed to have seen in the Heavens, marks the degradation of thought three hundred years later: this, no doubt, is so entire a fabrication, that Cardinal Newman, who swallowed so much, could not accept it. In the Middle Ages it became the fashion to give a material character to mere visions and dreams of holy men; and a Miracle is reported, where nothing had occurred. The Miracles at shrines are monstrous. At Zaragossa I found that one man, who had his leg cut off by a scythe, through the intercession of the Madonna of the Pilár had it fastened on again, leaving only a red line as the mark of the adhesion.

Mr. Huxley remarks (Essays on Controverted Questions, 1892) "that no one is entitled to say à priori that:

" (1) A miraculous event is impossible,
" (2) Prayer for some ordinary change in the ordinary course of Nature cannot possibly avail,

" because such a supposition is obviously contradicted by
" analogies furnished by every-day experience. But the
" arguments à posteriori against (1) Miracles, (2) efficacy of
" Prayer, are conclusive: the lack of evidence is fatal. The
" effect of Prayer, however, within the supplicator's mind is a
" very different question. Scientific Faith takes us no further
" than the Prayer, which Ajax offered, but that petition is
" continually granted."

Miraculous stories drift from country to country. A spider spins his web over the mouth of the cave in which Mahomet was concealed: the thing is not impossible for the spider to do, but the impulse or motive of the spider is not proved. The same story is told in the life of Felix of Nola, with the moral: where Christ is with us, a spider's web becomes a wall to us; where Christ is not, a wall is a spider's web.

Miracles are asserted to have been performed of a malevolent character: in the Catholic Missions, Jan., 1892, an English paper, it is clearly stated, that many of those, who opposed the Romish Missionaries, died soon afterwards: the inference is obvious: to make such an assertion marks an unchristian heart. Miracles are reported in connection with Apollonius of Tyana, who died about 97 A.D., and was not a Christian.

A thoughtful writer remarks, that " Miracles form part of the
" furniture of all Religions in a particular stage of develop-
" ment: given a certain habit of thought, a certain crisis of
" spiritual urgency, a Miracle is sure to make its appearance, in
" the same way as hysterical excitement accompanies fanati-
" cism, whether Cybelic, or Bacchic. It is much more a form

"of popular belief than of conscious importance; it is the people's way of acknowledging the presence of God, while the devotee of Science recognises Him in inexorable Law, and unbroken Order." (Hibbert-Lectures, 1883, p. 365.)

It is asserted in a general way, that the Miraculous Power is dead, and that Prophecy is silent: we will not argue whether these two mysterious Agencies are more dead and silent now than they were in ages that are past, and a stage of culture, or rather non-culture, that can hardly be realized. The Jewish type of the Phenomenon exists no more. But we live in a period of real world-Miracles, for God still displays His power by His acts, and in a period of world-Prophecy, for God still speaks to our consciences, and in our little span of life we can see traces of His insurpassable Wisdom. How little the Hebrew knew of His Miraculous Power in ordering the affairs of the Human Race, of His Wisdom in planning and maintaining the great Kosmos, of His Love to the Bodies and Souls of His poor children, compared to what we know now, when our Bodies are temples of His Holy Spirit, and our lives in the very presence of Christ, the object of our gratitude and hope. The great Creator has allowed mankind by His so-called Science to pierce, generation after generation, deeper and deeper into the secrets of His Great Creation, and maintenance of the great round world, and find out some new element of His Power previously unrevealed, track the course of a Planet, which has been revolving for myriads of years, but has only come within our limited form of vision during the present century, and develop some phase of His Almighty Plan, which has remained concealed from the Beginning. The Interpretation of Nature is the unveiling of God.

Nor is the discovery of the untruthfulness of legends of Miracles a new feature; there always were some, who were not deceived. Livy, who died just before Anno Domini, writes thus:

"Romæ aut circa urbem, multa eâ hyeme prodigia facta, quod evenire solet; motis in religionem animis multa et nunciata, et temeré credita sunt."

Belief in Miracles ceases, when Education, and the knowledge of the laws of Nature, become diffused through a population, and whatever may have been the case in former centuries, they are now the outcome of a deliberate fraud. If at any period of their long existence the Hebrew Race were in need of Prophecy and Miracles, it is now, and yet none is vouchsafed.

In 1843 I was present on the occasion of the liquefaction of the blood of St. Januarius in the Cathedral of Naples: by favour of the Clergy I got very near the ostensorium, and saw the dark lump gradually melt into red blood: it was a trick worthy of a Conjuror, and very well exhibited. In Brittany they are less liberal to strangers. There was an arch-saint in the place, St. Yves, who was patron of the town, and who, if prayed to with fervour, would obligingly kill a man's enemy for him within a twelvemonth by sudden illness. This good saint, or rather his wooden presentment, stretched out his arms once a year to bless the people of Tréguier, but it was indispensable to the acccomplishment of this Miracle that the whole congregation should fix their gaze on the ground. If a single unbeliever raised his eyes to see, if the arms were really lifted, the saint, "justly incensed by such a want of faith, would refuse to perform," and, of course, the unbeliever had to face the wrath of his infuriated fellow-townsmen, who had been defrauded of their blessing.

2. PROPHECIES, AUGURIES, ORDEALS.

This is a well-known feature of past ages and former Religions: as a fact, the Idea has died out: the public Press, and public Conscience, would not tolerate the existence of a Prophecy, which was not properly fulfilled, and in the plain sense of the word, and as was intended by the Prophet. In Virgil's Æneid there are two very pretty Prophecies in the early books, which are fulfilled in the later: there must be no doubt now as to the date, on which the Prophecy was promulgated: those, recorded by Virgil, and in other books, are Prophecies after the event. Shakespeare allows himself to predict, that Queen Elizabeth would die unmarried: his play of Henry VIII was written after her death: it is a mere license of Poetry. Seneca made a lucky Prophecy as to the discovery of America; the Poet Horace predicted that his charming poetry would be read hereafter all over the world; the Mother of Christ predicted that all Nations would call her blessed; Isaiah predicted, that the knowledge of the Lord would cover the Earth as the waters cover the Sea: all these utterances have become strictly true: they were looking into a dim and remote future, and there can be no doubt about the material fulfilment of their predictions, except as to a small part of the round world.

But attempts have been made in all ages, and countries, to ascertain the near and impending future, and Religion generally has been the machine made use of: we come into contact with a miscellaneous horde: Soothsayers, inquirers of God, Augurs, Diviners, Watchers of the course of Birds, Vaticinators, Examiners of entrails of Animals, Interpreters of Omens, Interpreters of Dreams, Professional Cursers, Professional Blessers, Tellers of Lucky Days, Fortune-tellers by the palm of the hand, Oracles, such as Delphi, Dodona, Astrologers, Finders out of Lucky Days. The words "liars, and deceivers of mankind," may apply to all such, and they have totally disappeared, and it is difficult to understand, how the Hebrew Nation could have lent itself to such practices seriously after their experience of the scene, which took place in the presence of Ahab, and Jehoshaphat (II Chronicles, xviii, 21, 22). The Augurs were exposed in a memorable passage of Cicero: the Oracles, after being very dubious and facing both ways, at last became dumb: if any Sovereign were to ask to have his dreams interpreted, he would be overwhelmed with ridicule: Professors of Palmistry are sent to prison: Lucky Days, and Omens, are only spoken of as a kind of joke.

The practice of "inquiring of the Lord," either directly, or by an ephod, is painfully frequent in the Hebrew Historical Books: it indicates the low state of intellectual culture of that Nation: it is difficult to say by what channel the answer came: as it is stated now, it reads as if Saul had a telephonic communication: it is noteworthy that Hezekiah and Josiah had no such communications. The first line of Newton's hymn does not come under this category: "I asked the Lord," etc.: this refers to a spiritual communication betwixt the Soul of a man and his Creator on a matter affecting his Soul, not regarding mundane matters.

The magnificent prophecy of Virgil in the Æneid regarding the birth and early death of young Marcellus, indicates the liberty, which Poets were allowed to take with Truth, and how highly such efforts were commended. The same Poet would make us believe, that Æneas was supported in his troubles by the sure word of Prophecy. He puts words also in the mouth of Dido, predicting the triumphant career of the Carthaginian General, Hannibal, as avenging her wrongs: it is very charming to read, and it gives us an idea of the feelings on that subject of the elder world. Horace puts similar hopeful words in the mouth of Teucer, when seeking a new country. but all this was long after the fact: the principle may be laid down, that, unless you are sure of the date of the death of the Prophet, and its authenticity, it is nothing worth. The uncertainty of the date of the Book of Daniel, now relegated to the time of the Maccabees, destroys his prophetic reputation.

The new Pythagoreans, a school totally independent of the Hebrews, though coming into existence in Alexandria, thirsted for Prophecies, Oracles, and Signs, and thus gave an expression to the longing prevalent in the Western World, just before Anno Domini, for a supernatural revelation of the Divine Will. The Fourth Eclogue of Virgil is but one evidence of a fact, which we must take count of, for it is patent. Tacitus,

Suetonius, and Josephus, record that there was a wide-spread belief that some one coming from the East would rule the world: they considered the prediction fulfilled in the return of the General Vespasian from Jerusalem to be made Emperor: they attributed the rebellion of the Jews to their misinterpretation of this rumour in the appearance of their promised Messiah. The Christians took, and still take, a third view. At the time of the Mutinies, 1857, there was current a Prophecy that a king, named Dulíp, would conquer Delhi: as a fact, the Sikh soldiers did help materially the conquest: I myself had heard of this rumour before the Mutinies. From time to time, through the length and breadth of British India, a particular Prophetic Message is announced, more especially in times of political trouble. Jordánus, a Monk of the order of the Dominicans, reports in his book, Mirabilia Descripta, 1430 A.D., the Prophecy current among the people of India, that the Latins would subjugate the world. Prophecy, in fact, represents an apprehension. There was nothing foreign to the feelings of the age, or of reasonable probability, in the facts recorded in the Acts of the Apostles: (1) that a famine should be predicted, is a fact of annual occurrence in India, as common as that the hay-crop has failed in England; (2) that a man in the circumstances of Paul should run the chance of imprisonment, after what he had been doing in Asia Minor and Greece, required no great strength of Prophecy. In the time of the great upheaval of Religious conceptions, when Mithra, Serápis, Bona Dea, were all mingling in the confusion, Divination of all kinds was to be expected. Tertullian tells us, that his world was crowded with Oracles, second sight-seers, fortune-tellers. At an earlier period Plato doubted, and Aristotle remarked, that it was not easy to despise, such predictions, or to believe in them. Cicero has left his opinion in his Essay, "De Divinatione." Porphyry thought, that the only sure Religion was in direct communication from the gods, and wrote a book on the Philosophy to be drawn from Oracles. There was always on the lips of men the Prophecy, and in the hearts of men, a firm belief, that God was wont to warn beforehand, when great misfortunes were to happen to a City or Nation. This marks the great intellectual gulf between the Past and the Present.

In a fragment of Euripides we read:

Μάντις ἄριστος, ὅστις εἰκάζει καλῶς.
"He is the best prophet who guesses best."
(*Ramage*, p. 158.)

We read how the King of Israel blamed a Prophet for always prophesying things unfavourable to him; he must have believed, that the Prophet could say what he liked.

Assur-bani-pal, in one of his Inscriptions after the conquest of Babylon, writes : " In accordance with Prophecies, I cleared " the mercy-seats of their temples; I purified their chief places " of Prayer; I appeased their gods with penitential Psalms ; I " restored their daily Sacrifice." (Sayce : Monuments, p. 460.) Orpheus thus describes the Prophet :

" Τά τ' ἐόντα,
ὅσσατε πρόσθεν ἔην, ὅσα τ' ἔσσεται ὕστερον αὖθις,"

which centuries later Virgil rendered (Æn. iv, 392):

" Novit namque omnia vatis,
" Quæ sint, quæ fuerint, quæ mox ventura trahantur."

The Editors of Newspapers, the occupiers of Pulpits and Missionary platforms, are often exceedingly prophetic without the restraining qualifications of a Vatis, an accurate knowledge of the present, and any knowledge of the past.

In the *Expository Times* of 1894 appeared a paper entitled " Hebrew Prophecy and Modern Criticism," and a critic has recorded the following remarks on this paper: " Why it has " this important character will best appear from a summary of " its contents, which we will give as accurately as possible. " Starting from the fact, that this is an age of unparalleled " mental activity, indicated by the increasing demand for " education, and the changed character of it in itself, he passes " on to the consideration of the effects, which this of necessity " must have on Theology. *We must, therefore, translate the thought* " *of Religion into the best thought of our day*. It follows that " theological methods are undergoing complete change. This " is evident both in apologetics, and the exegesis of prophetic " writings. The old method was, first, to *assume* a certain " number of facts about the Bible, and then to study it *with* " *this understanding*; the modern does not necessarily accept, " or reject, any of these assumptions, but it does not allow " them to prejudice the study of Scripture. Thus it becomes " of obvious importance, that we should ascertain, in what " ways Biblical criticism affects our view of the character of " Prophecy, and its value as a branch of Religious evidences. " It would appear that 'the tendency of modern exegesis " obviously affects the argument from Prophecy in two impor- " tant respects: (1) It often shows, that what were previously " considered to be predictions of future events fulfilled within " the period of Jewish history, were in all *probability no predic-* " *tions at all*. (2) It makes it equally clear, that what were " believed to be simple predictions of a distant future, have " their most natural explanation in the historical events *of their* " *own time*.' "

The Apolline Oracle of Delphi was a mighty Power, ever on the side of Morality, bringing home to men's minds the notion of Right and Wrong, of Reward and Punishment: its predictions as to futurity were couched in ambiguous language; its opinion as to Right and Wrong was unhesitating. Thoughtful men, calling themselves Christians of the Nineteenth Century, must be cautious ere they laugh at the Greek Oracles, which lasted so many centuries, and died from their own exhaustion, not from foreign conquest: they had lived through all the Greek Epochs, from the most barbarous, and elementary, to the most polished forms of Human development; they had no life in themselves, and died. The Christian Historian, who refers their power to illusion, or imposture, forges a weapon against his own Religious conception. He, who believes in an all-wise Providence, and the efficacy of Prayer, must recollect, that in doing so he accepts the principle, which formed the basis of ancient Divination. We each and all believe, that our bodies are temples of the Holy Spirit, and that we lend ourselves to the influence of that Spirit in answer to Prayer in the discharge of our every-day duties, and in the vicissitudes of life: we believe that an answer is conveyed to us: the Oracles did no more.

"The last utterance of the Pythian Priestess was a kind
" of whisper of desolation in reply to the inquiry of the
" Emperor Julian: the last fragment of Greek Poetry, which
" has moved the hearts of men, the last Greek hexameters,
" which retain the ancient cadence, the majestic melancholy
" flow :

" εἴπατε τῷ βασιλῆι, χαμαὶ πέσε δαίδαλος αὐλά·
" οὐκέτι Φοῖβος ἔχει καλύβαν, οὐμάντιδα δάφνην,
" οὐ παγὰν λαλέουσαν· ἀπέσβετο καὶ λάλον ὕδωρ."

(*Myers' Essays*, p. 101.)

What is a miraculous vision? "A mistaking of subjective impression for outward revelation." Voices are rarely, if ever, heard by two persons: the Holy Spirit still speaks to the Soul in words, which cannot be uttered.

We read in Homer (Iliad, II, 93; Odyssey, III, 215) of a voice, or rumour, which runs Heaven-sent through multitudes of men, and is deemed the voice of Jupiter: ὄσσα, φήμη, κληδών, ὀμφή (Myers' Essays, p. 13).

The Etruscans had three ways of discovering the will of the gods: (1) thunder and lightning, (2) the flight of birds, which they believed was under Divine guidance, and for a purpose, (3) examination of the entrails of animals offered in Sacrifice. The interpretation of these signs rested with a body of arrogant men, who pretended to have an intimate acquaintance with the

(84)

Will of Heaven, and decrees of Fate (Canon Rawlinson's Religion of Ancient World, p. 192). We find a survival of this arrogant presumption of knowledge of God's dealings in Missionary Society Reports, where such phrases occur as "their work being owned by God"; "God's manifest guidance." The theory of Augury was this: the Stoics held that the gods, out of their goodness, had impressed on the nature of things certain marks, and notices of future events; such as on entrails of beasts, the flight of birds, thunder, and other celestial signs, which by long observation, and the experience of ages, were reduced to an art, and applied to the events, which were signified by it. Cicero was of opinion, that the original institution of Augury was from a persuasion of its divinity, and that, though by the advancement of knowledge, that opinion was outgrown, still it ought to be retained for the sake of its use to the Republic. This is the sin of many modern forms and institutions; they are retained, because they are useful, though known to be false.

The Augurs were possessed especially of the sacred lore connected with birds, who gave omens in three ways: flight, note, manner of eating their food: they had a system of interpretation for all phenomena: nothing could be done by the Roman State without consulting them. The right of consulting the will of the gods belonged to the Kings, and in republican days to the Consuls or Magistrates: they controlled the operation: the Augurs were referred to for the interpretation (Middleton: Cicero, p. 506). So long as this control was maintained by a strong Government, order could be preserved: we see the contrary in the petty Kingdom of Judah, where the Prophet became an incendiary: no Government could have been carried on under the conditions described in the Prophecies of Isaiah and Jeremiah: we have only to imagine Preachers, or itinerant Prophets, going about, and uttering denunciations of the Powers that be, and asserting Divine knowledge: we can see what a change had come over men's minds at the Epoch of the Anno Domini, when Paul recommends submission to Civil Authority: how were the poor people to know whether the Prophets were true or false? Jeremiah (x, 24, 25), though admitting that Jehovah was Lord of the world, could not understand why He was so kind to the Gentiles: he calls out to Jehovah to "pour out His fury on the heathen, that know Thee not, and the families that call not on Thy name": yet all were God's poor children, living by His favour, who hateth nothing that He hath made: in fact, the violent fanatical Journals of modern time are the only analogues of the utterances of the Prophets, who rendered all Civil Government impossible, and brought on the ruin of Judea.

In private life we have still in the Nineteenth Century

revivals of Superstition: unlucky days, bad omens, banshee-cries, tea-leaves in cups, thirteen at dinner: such was it at Rome also. The beautiful lines of Tibullus occur to me:

" Oh! quoties ingressus iter, mihi tristia dixi
" Offensum in portâ signa dedisse pedem.
* * * * * * *
" Delia non usquam, quæ me quam mittat ab urbe
" Dicitur ante omnes consuluisse Deos."

In Xenophon's Anabasis, III, 2–9, we read how "πταρνύται τις," "somebody sneezed." Xenophon was a pupil of Socrates, and yet he expresses an opinion, that it was a favourable augury from Jupiter. In India, when a person in power sneezes, his attendants snap their fingers; in England a sneeze is generally accompanied by the exclamation of "God bless you!"

Ordeals are a further development of the same notions: they prevail in Africa still to discover witches in a cruel and abominable form; in India, in an innocent form, to discover petty thefts, such as chewing of rice, throwing of mud, passing the hand over a table covered with ink.

I read in Maspero's Dawn of Civilization, p. 267, the following, as regards the Egyptian belief:

" Sometimes in the dark the Statues in the Temples raised
" their voices, and announced their will, or made gestures:
" when they were consulted, and made no sign, this meant
" disapprobation; if they bowed their heads once or twice, this
" showed, that they approved: no State-affair was settled
" without consulting them." In fact, the crafty Rulers made this excuse to get time for deliberation on any matters.

3. National Sins and Punishments, Anger and Hostility of the Deity.

This feeling is clearly evidenced in the Religions of the elder world. The individuality of man face to face with his Creator was not apprehended; men were thought of as flocks of sheep, differentiated by colour of skin, Language, shape of skull and body, and political institutions, but answerable collectively for each other, and one generation for former generations. The Mahometan has gone to the other extreme, and deals with his Creator as an individual: the whole world may perish, but he will be saved by his Faith. There are Christian Sects, who practise the same unchristian Individualism. A Plymouth Sister, being asked, whether she thought, that she and her sister were the only persons, who by God's mercy would be saved, at once replied, that she was not sure of her sister's salvation.

The Latin Poet Horace plaintively remarks:

"Delicta majorum immeritus lues,
"Romane, donec templa refeceris,
"Aedesque labentes Deorum";

and the general feeling of Pagan Rome was, that the Empire was being ruined by the neglect of the Worship of the Roman gods, who had made her great. It is notorious how salient a feature this was in the Jewish History. Ahab's grandchildren had to suffer for his sins: our fathers sinned; we were punished. Manasseh's sins were not purged even by his own death, but the consequences were carried on to his son Josiah. The poor sheep had three days pestilence because David made a census of his little tribe, and no punishment seems to follow our Indian census of 287 Millions. Ezekiel tried to soften down the hardness of the original decree, that children should suffer for the sins of their parents; Plutarch, Isocrates, Solon, and Herodotus, seem to echo the same sentiments. The compiler of the Chronicles, who lived some time after the return from the Captivity, seems to have outgrown this feeling to a certain extent; the solidarity of Sinners is no longer a dogma.

Even in Great Britain, at the end of the Nineteenth Century, with a House of Commons comprising Atheists, Mahometans, Parsi, men devoid of any Religious element, by the side of a confused body of Religious Sectarians, we hear the cuckoo-cry of National Sins. Sometimes the Indo-Chinese Opium-Trade is so described, while the drunkenness of our population, and the unblushing profligacy of our streets, the slaughter of poor African barbarians in the interest of Missions, Commerce in Alcoholic Liquors, Colonization, and unblushing annexation, is omitted. What National Sin can be greater than the slaughter, confiscation of private property, and political annexation, in Ma-Tabéleland in South Africa by a Chartered Company for the sake of gold-dust in 1894?

Montefiore, in his Hibbert-Lecture on the Origin and Growth of Religion of the Ancient Hebrews, remarks, p. 515:

"The feeling of commercial integrity was consistent, and even
" co-existent, with a sense of Human responsibility as towards
" God; but the same word was used by the Hebrews to express
" both iniquity and its penalty. When they and Israel were
" afflicted, they tended to feel sinful; when they and Israel
" were prosperous, they tended to feel righteous."

Another feature, which was universal, was the anger of the

Deity. Virgil tells us how Juno persistently persecuted Æneas, the supposed founder of the Roman Race. The Poet expresses a pious astonishment:

"tantæne animis cælestibus iræ!"

Apollo sent disease into the Greek camp, because the daughter of one of his priests had been carried off by Achilles. He took umbrage, because the followers of Ulysses captured some of his cattle, and killed them. So-called sacrilege was severely punished, even though the offender had erred without knowledge: worse than Anger, Envy is imputed to the Deity: Niobe's children were killed, only because the mother's pride of them offended Apollo and Diana. Can it be possible, that sensible people, who were far advanced beyond barbarism, could have believed such things? It marks a frightful degradation of the Religious Idea to attribute Disease or Death to the anger or jealousy of the Deity, and not to His Loving Wisdom; still more shocking is it, that Historians should impute to the Deity's interference the death of the enemies of the party, which they support. Lucretius soars above these idle notions (Book I, v. 61):

"Ipsa suis pollens opibus, nihil indiga nostri,
Nec bene promeritis capitur, nec tangitur irâ."

The Jewish Chronicles are not free from this strange obliquity of vision: it is sad to read (I Chronicles, xiii, 10), that Uzza, who put forth his hand to hold the Ark, when the oxen stumbled, raised the anger of the Lord, "and He smote him . . . and he died"; and in other passages, the Anger and Jealousy of the Deity are alluded to. So imperfect was the conception of the Hebrew Chronicler of the Deity.

What an imperfect Idea they could have had of Sin? In I Samuel, xiv, 34, I read:

"Sin not against the Lord in *eating with the blood*": they killed their neighbouring tribes by the scores, seized their land, plundered their cattle, burnt their houses, enslaved their females: this was apparently no Sin. They killed women and children; when Achan stole a Babylonian garment, not only was he killed, but the Hebrews killed his wife and children also. Then the awful phrase occurs frequently, that the Deity sold His people into the hands of their enemies: it seems impossible to conceive such things of the Deity, even in a moment of suffering; but to record such phrases centuries afterwards for the teaching of the people, seems to pass beyond all comprehension. We read in Kings how Jehu slaughtered, in the most deliberate and treacherous way, the Royal children of Ahab, the Royal children of the Kings of Judah only coming on a visit, the Priests of Baal: nothing but praise was heaped upon him for such dastardly conduct.

When the pious Jews of the time of Jeremiah were denouncing Idolatry in their own Nation and the Heathen, they were unwittingly falling into as great a theological error as those, whom they denounced: they believed, that Disease and Death were the chastisements of the offended Deity on those who would not recognise Him. So Horace writes, III, ii, 31, Odes:

" Raro antecedentem scelestum
Deseruit pede Pœna claudo."

In the Psalms we find devout men forgetting charity so far as to pray God to punish their enemies: they chose to suppose, that they knew the secrets of God, and that all, who did not believe with them, were in the wrong, and justly visited by punishment: their theory was unjust and cruel.

4. Signs from Heaven.

Nothing appears so often in pre-Christian Religions, or in mistaken views of the precepts of Christianity, than the connection of the Religious conception with phenomena of Nature, such as Thunder and Lightning, Rain and Storm, Eclipses, Earthquakes, Eruptions, Wells of Naphtha, and with the incidents of Human Life, such as Accidents, Sickness, Death by what is called Visitation of God: such phenomena and incidents are attributed to the Deity to mark His favour to the so-called good, and His aversion to the so-called evil.

In Him we live and move and have our being; He is about our path and about our bed, but Sickness and Death are blessings in disguise, for "He giveth His beloved sleep," and "Whom the Lord loveth He chasteneth." The pages of the Greek and Latin secular and Religious writers furnish endless instances of the feeling, that thunder and lightning contain a message from the Deity, that sudden death, such as that of Ananias and Sapphira, and Arius, were punishments. Only this year, during a strike at Hull, the manager of a firm was struck by paralysis and death, and the strikers attributed it to a visitation of God. In Bangál the appearance of a Comet heralded a disaster: the poor agriculturists anticipated a dearth and famine; the corn-dealer could not consider a famine a misfortune, and thought that the Comet indicated something else.

In India grants used to be made by the British Government

to the Brahmans, and Mahometan officials, to pray for Rain: this was stopped. In Great Britain the custom seems still to prevail, though contrary to all reason. A light crop of grain in South Russia is a great blessing to the people of India. A short crop of cotton in the Southern States, owing to want of Rain, makes the fortune of other countries.

The Jews were not free from this delusion, as we read in Samuel of the Lord sending thunder to discomfort the Philistines, and sending thunder and rain at time of harvest with a view of confirming the power of Samuel.

An eclipse of the Sun or Moon in India is still an event of solemn importance: the Greek Historian tells us how combatants engaged in battle left off fighting on account of an eclipse. Earthquakes and eruptions were deemed messages from the Deity. Hailstones are described as falling on an enemy during a fight, and killing more than fell by the sword. The arrest of the Sun and Moon in their progress to help on a greater slaughter can scarcely be seriously treated, for as the Sun never moves, there was no occasion to arrest its progress: this is one of the stories, the survival of which is to be regretted, and, as a fact, is only a quotation from a book, of which nothing is known, and which can scarcely claim to be inspired.

Lucretius, who wrote before Anno Domini, remarks that the gods often destroyed their own temples with lightnings. Professor Sayce writes, Hibbert-Lectures, p. 300: "The pro-"phetic voice of Heaven was heard in thunder by Accadians, " as well as by Semites: the sounds of Nature were to them " a Divine message: the roar of the ocean was an oracle; " subterranean noises were messages from Hades."

Only within the last few years I read in a Missionary Report how in South India a Missionary pointed out to a Hindu the inferiority of the Deity, whom he worshipped, who could not protect his own temple from being destroyed by lightning? Have the steeples of Christian Churches never been struck by lightning? To doubt that thunder was the voice of God seemed impious. Æneas is described by Virgil as seeing in Tartarus a certain King, named Salmoneus, who was undergoing punishment for the following reason:

"Demens! qui nimbos, et non imitabile fulmen
Ære, et cornipedum cursu, simulârat equorum."
(*Æneid*, VI, 590.)

The utter ignorance in ancient time of the physical world, and their inability to explain what they saw by natural causes, and the pre-occupation of their minds with the paramount importance of their own private, tribal, or National, affairs, led poor weak men to imagine, that the Stars, the Planets, the Comets, Rainbows, Eclipses, fire falling from Heaven, had no other object but to benefit or injure them, or their neighbours, or their enemies. A sign from Heaven was a thing demanded, as a voucher of authority, or a proof of innocence. It is difficult to bring the mind to the standpoint, whence such things were possible: they were part of the stock-in-trade of the Prophet, and the Augur. With such wonderful allies how utterly kings, and great men, failed in what they had to do! In II Chronicles, vii, 1 it is narrated how fire came down and consumed the burnt-offering: the Chronicler lived about six hundred years after this event, which took place in a totally illiterate and exceedingly credulous age.

We read in the Kings, that the Sun went back on the Dial of Ahaz to assure Hezekiah of the truth of Isaiah's message. The Pharisees demanded of Christ a sign from Heaven as a voucher for His authority, for even at that late period the world had not outgrown the old notions. In Latin Poets we read .

" Sol tibi signa dabit : Solem quis dicere falsum
" Audeat ? ille etiam cæcos intrare tumultus
" Sæpe monet, fraudemque et operta tumescere bella."

The eclipse of stars was supposed to portend a change of the flourishing condition of Carthage. (Justin, XXII, 6.)
In Ovid's Metamorphoses, XV, 782,

" Signa tamen luctus dant haud incerta futuri:
" Solis quoque tristis imago
" Lurida sollicitis præbebat lumina terris."

5. CONCEPTION OF FATE, NEMESIS, 'E$\rho\iota\nu\nu\grave{\nu}s$.

In elder days there was a strong feeling of this kind, and to a certain extent a salutary feeling. The Mahometan bears ills patiently, because he says that it is his "kismat." In Christian Poetry mourners are consoled by allusion to the common lot: "Sic voluere Parcæ" settled the matter. Still more important in restraining the hand of violence and injustice was Nemesis, or "A$\tau\eta$, the displeasure of the Deity at something that was wrong, and the power of the 'E$\rho\iota\nu\nu\grave{\nu}s$, or Fury, to whom was committed the punishment of criminals by exciting the tortures of conscience. We have a grand instance of this in the tale of Orestes. Nothing could justify matricide: an erring mother must fall by some other hand than that of her son: but the existence of such feelings, or convictions, argue a state of mental culture above that of the savage or barbarian. King Mtesa, of U-Ganda, ordered one of his wives to be led out and killed for some petty offence, and his conscience was not troubled. So on the Niger a man killed his Mother, because her conduct was vexatious to him, and felt no compunction, and had no 'Ερινύς after him; in fact, he could not see that he had done wrong any more than a brute beast. It might be well if individuals, and especially those in Power, had the thought of Nemesis, and 'Ερινύς, more before their eyes, as the lookers-on see so many instances of sorrow following sin with unerring certainty.

CAP. IV. EARLY HUMAN PRACTICES AND NOTIONS.

1. Disposal of Dead.
2. Eschatology.
3. Mutilation or Disfigurement of Body.
4. Strange and Abominable Customs.

1. DISPOSAL OF DEAD.

In no other quarter is there such a variety of customs, as in the disposal of the dead, but always under a Religious sanction: the Egyptian embalmed, and enveloped the departed in a mummy; the Etruscan laid him away in a rock tomb, with all his mortal comforts around him; the Jews buried; the Greek, and Roman, and Indian, burnt; the followers of Zoroaster exposed the body to the birds to be devoured. More barbarous Races packed them up, and stowed them in the roof of their houses, or on frame-works of wood prepared to receive them. If civilized Nations have hitherto preferred burying, they have for the future to confront the difficulty of finding space for the ever-increasing cemeteries. However different the practice, the reason for the practice is always attributed to Religion, and is somehow or another connected with the Resurrection of the body, though it is obvious, that in a very short time after sepulture in the ground the body is consumed, nor does the precaution of the rich in embalming, and placing in leaden coffins, arrest the progress of decay.

The urgent necessity of funeral rites of some kind is evidenced by passages in the Sixth Book of the Æneid, which describe the sad state of the Souls of those, whose bodies have not been properly disposed of after death. In China to this day the Spirits of the dead, who have not been honoured properly in death, become a trouble and curse to their survivors. In the lower classes in Europe there is a strong feeling on the subject. Tobit in the Apocrypha seemed to make a merit before God to have buried the bodies of his countrymen, when he found them.

We remark in the Greek Authors, that the idea of a body being left unburied, and not properly mourned, was deemed sad and terrible :

" ἀλλ' ἄρα τόν γέ κύνεστε, καὶ οἰωνοὶ, κατέξαψαν
" κείμενον ἐν πεδίῳ ἑκὰς ἄστεος, οὐδέ κε τίς μιν
" κλαύσεν Ἀχαιιάδων· μάλα γὰρ μέγα μήσατο ἔργον."
(HOMER: *Od.*, III, 258.)

We find traces of this in the Tragedians: Orestes in Iphigenia in Aulis deplores that there will be no sister to perform the usual rites to his body: Iphigenia, being warned in a dream, that Orestes was dead, proceeded to perform the usual rites, though absent.

The echo of the same sentiment comes to us in the Latin Poets :
" Non hic mihi mater,
" Quæ legat in teneros ossa perusta sinus;
" Non soror, Assyrios cineri quæ dedat honores,
" Et fleat effusis ante sepulchra comis."
(TIBULLUS.)

Perhaps, after all, Cremation, and collecting the remnants in a vase labelled with the name of the deceased, is the most sanitary method, and most conducive to respect for the departed. When I stood lately beside the Mummy of Rameses II at Cairo, the Pharaoh of the Hebrew oppression, it occurred to me, that it would have been better for his poor remains, had they been burnt at the time of his death : so in modern time Earth to Earth in a simple wooden coffin is better than the leaden receptacle. The New Guinea - custom is certainly the nastiest, where the body of the Grandmother laid up in the roof of the single room is permitted to decay, and drip down over the persons of her descendants. A traveller, while writing in his journal in a hut, found the paper of his note-book soiled by this ancestral rain.

Custom, no doubt not distinct from Religion, in some cases urges the stronger to put an end to the lives of the weaker: I have already disposed of Human Sacrifice. Cannibalism is credited with three causes : (1) want of animal food. Where there are plenty of goats there is no occasion to eat men ; in India the wolves creep into the inclosure and carry off infants, but, where there are plenty of goats, they prefer kid-flesh : (2) the second cause is the desire to add to the greatness of the triumph, and to the horror of the enemy in his dying moments : (3) if the slain is distinguished for bravery, or strength, it is hoped by eating him to get a portion of his physical gifts: an English Governor of a West African Colony was eaten with that view.

In the eleventh volume of Gibbon's "Decline and Fall" I read, how the Germans many centuries ago had no scruple in bringing the life of their parents to a close, if they lived too long. In India a Religious motive is added: until made punishable by British law, pious children would take their aged relatives down the ghats of Banáras, fill their mouths with mud, and push them off into the Ganges, with a sure and certain hope of eternal bliss for them. In Sumátra, which is not a Realm of Law, annually all the old and infirm, when there is abundance of lemons, are gathered together, and placed on the branches of the trees, under the shadow of which there are large vessels full of water: the branches are shaken by the younger members of the family, while they sing: "When the fruit is ripe, then it will fall," and the old bodies fall into the vessels, are cooked, and eaten, just as years ago they had eaten their own parents.

Sometimes in Europe the way of disposing of the dead seems strange. In Naples there are 365 deep wells: one is opened each day, and the dead are thrown into it, and it is fastened up for one year. In some Monasteries, at Palermo and Rome, the dead Monks are still visible in their Monkish dress, sad and loathsome objects. In Austria the remains of the Imperial dead are divided: the body goes into a lead-coffin, the heart into a separate lead-heart-box, and the brain is disposed of elsewhere. In England I have been down into family vaults, and found myself in the midst of dead ancestors, or connections: some coffins were standing upright; one lady, who died in foreign parts, came home in a leaden coffin fitting like a riding habit. The sexton, like a ghost, was quite at home amidst his charges, and handed to me the coffin of a baby, who had died in the reign of Charles II, which had a little shelf of its own; above the vault was the Family Pew, from which one by one the living representatives of the old Race were taken down to join the general rendezvous below.

All this should cease, and the remains of the dead should be consigned to Holy Earth, or Holy Fire, and disappear.

2. ESCHATOLOGY.

The Egyptian "Book of the Dead" reveals to us the conceptions of that Nation of life beyond the grave. Homer and Virgil conduct the reader into the Elysian Fields. The Brahmanical and Búddhist substitute the Doctrine of Transmigration of Souls in an endless chain, until non-existence is gained. The Red Indian expects, that his dog will accompany him to another world; the African Chief goes to the grave, accompanied by slaughtered wives and slaves, who will make him comfortable in his new abode; so also was it with Attila and his Huns. The Hebrews alone up to the time of the return from Exile had no consolation for the woes of this world beyond the grave: the hope held out was, that their days might be long in the land given; and even up to Anno Domini, and beyond, when Paul addressed the Sanhedrin, the question of a Future State was allowed to remain an open one. If Moses were learned in all the learning of the Egyptians, it is wonderful to think, that he was not acquainted with Egyptian Eschatology; had he been so, he would hardly have been silent on the subject, for the tribes of Ephraim and Manasseh were descended through the wife of Joseph from an Egyptian Priest, and must have had Egyptian relatives, and heard of the Mummies, the Book of the Dead, and the popular sentiment, evidenced by the Pyramids and the Catacombs.

I quote the condensed expression of an esteemed Author: We cannot hope to understand the dogma of the Resurrection of Christ without bearing in mind the theories of the Jews, and early Christians, concerning the structure of the world, and the cosmic localities of departed souls. Since the time of Copernicus modern Christians no longer attempt to locate Heaven and Hell; they are conceived of merely as mysterious places remote from the earth. The theological Universe no longer corresponds to that, which physical Science presents for our contemplation. To the Jews the Universe was like a sort of three-storied house: the flat earth rested on the water, and under its surface was Sheol, where the souls of all went, righteous as well as wicked; a land peopled with flitting shadows, suffering no torment, but experiencing no pleasure. Sheol is the first story; the earth is the second; above was a firmament, and above that Heaven, where Jehovah reigned. Two only of the Human Race had been admitted to the third story. Sheol was the destined abode of all after death; all rewards and punishments known to the early Hebrew Writers before the Captivity were earthly. According to the new Doctrine, the Messiah was to free the righteous from Sheol and cause them to ascend in *new* bodies, while the wicked were to be punished: this doctrine was Pharisaic: the Sadducees rejected it to the last. Paul grasped the deep significance, and it became the kernel of the new Idea; something more than a mere intellectual assent was required; there must be an emotional striving after righteousness, a developing conscience of God in the soul, a subjugation of the flesh to the

Spirit. It was to this new Idea, spiritually set forth, that the new Religion owed in great part its rapid success, for it met the requirements both of Jew and Gentile. When Saul made use of a woman with a familiar spirit to bring up Samuel (I Samuel, xxviii, 15), the deceased is reported to have said: "Why hast thou disquieted me to bring me up? . . . . . to-morrow *shall thou and thy sons be with me*": he meant that, whether good or bad, all men went to Sheol. More than a thousand years afterwards Paul wrote as follows: "If there " be no resurrection of the dead, then is Christ not risen . . . . " for if the dead rise not, then is not Christ raised . . . . then " they also which have fallen asleep in Christ are perished; " if in this life only we have hope in Christ, we are of all " men most miserable" (I Corinthians, xv, 13–19).

The comparison of the sentiments of these two holy men, Samuel and Paul, who spoke according to Ideas of their Epoch, indicate the vast change, which had taken place in the eschatological conceptions.

It appears to some (Dale: North American Review, April, 1893), that, in spite of all the alleged physical difficulties, there must be a future state, because an adequate purpose is required for the Universe. Of what good is all the beautiful order, if it worked out nothing but death? Besides, Hope is an essential to mankind, and this can only co-exist when Life, not Death, is the destiny of Man. It is incredible, that the lives of good men should utterly perish, and that so much suffering should be endured by those who deserve it not, if there be no hereafter compensation: we have, however, no certain knowledge; no one ever came back from the dead to tell us, nor, if they had told us, should we understand, for our knowledge is limited to our earthly requirements and experiences. It is impossible to realize what union with God hereafter may mean, unless we have some faint Idea of what is union with Him in this world. It is impossible to say whether personal memory of things of the world, of beloved ones, will survive; those, who have known God best here, and felt His reality here, will find Him there also. It is impossible to conceive what becomes of poor savages, and the ignorant, of children who die in infancy, of idols and lunatics who are scarcely, or not at all, conscious of a personal identity, for after all the evidence must be spiritual, not physical.

In common conversation, or even in Religious teaching, there is great vagueness: some people entrust dying people with messages to their loved ones; some believe, that the dead are still cognizant of what takes place on earth; some enthusiasts elevate poor dead ones to the rank of a demi-god, and invest them with Spiritual power. The Hebrew Idea of

Sheol, and the Græco-Latin Idea of Hades, were most shadowy; the use of the word Hell, for instance, in the Creed, is most unwarrantably applied. Poetry has taken great liberties: take for instance Longfellow's beautiful poem on the death of his daughter; Dante's three great poems are monuments of the strange mediæval conceptions, more than half Pagan, of the future State. Such books as "Letters from Heaven," and "Letters from Hell," and many other attempts to lift up the curtain, indicate how great is the uncertainty of the Human mind. And yet the subject is spoken of by votaries of all Religions with certainty: a Brahmin speaks of his dead friend as baikunth-bash, "dweller in Heaven"; so does a Mahometan as bihisht-manzal; the Church of Rome imagines, that by Masses and prayers it can modify, and improve, the position of a departed Soul; the sensational Evangelical talks and writes of his dear one, as already in Heaven, ignoring the caution of Paul, I Thess. iv, 13–15. Such poems as "Saints in Paradise" are familiar to us all.

Once in India in my office some papers were read to me in one of the Vernaculars of Northern India. I remarked on the use of two or three expressions, to imply Death, and the following day one of the officials brought me a list of between thirty and forty terms in Persian, Urdu, and Hindi, for expressing the fact: some exceedingly expressive, some needlessly unkind to the dead. Being a great reader of Evangelical periodicals and books, it occurred to me to collect the terms sentimental, emotional, sensational, used to record the death of Missionaries, or others, in whom friends were interested:

1. Entered into glory.
2. Called home.
3. Went to see the King.
4. Went no more out.
5. Mr. Spurgeon entered Paradise this morning at 4 p.m. (telegram).
6. My Mother is in Heaven.
7. The Lord took him home.
8. He passed to see the King.
9. He fell asleep in Jesus.
10. He was called up higher.
11. He was called to higher service.
12. Her Spirit fled.
13. She passed through the gate into the city.
14. He promised to follow his wife to Heaven.
15. She rests from her labours till the day dawns.
16. She passed away, absent from the body, present with the Lord.

17. She went from the far East to Paradise.
18. Gathered home from the Missionary harvest.
19. Has gone to be with Christ.
20. He passed away.
21. Her Spirit departed like a child falling asleep.
22. The departure of a servant of Christ.
23. Is with the Lord.
24. His sun has set.
25. Entered into rest.
26. Started on his journey.
27. Passed across the borderland.
28. She saw the Sun set on the other side.
29. My dead husband has one child with him to keep him company.
30. All those have long been in Paradise.
31. God called him home to a better country.
32. She passed from death unto life.
33. Called to leave the great harvest-field.

Whatever may be said to the contrary, the doctrine of Rewards and Punishments in a future state, though absolutely ignored by the Hebrews, appears from evidence beyond doubt, to have been believed by the Egyptian, Hindu, Zoroastrian, Greek, and Roman: the echo of the same strain is caught up elsewhere: the oral legends of the North American Indians, and of the Polynesian and Melanesian Islanders, tell the same story. It is, indeed, part of the Spiritual outfit of the Human Race. It is difficult, indeed, to arrive at the standpoint, whence the opposite doctrine was susceptible of argument, for it has been well said that "it seems to be the spontaneous outcome of the Human mind, when brought face to face with the mystery of Death" (Max Müller: Gifford-Lectures, 1892—*Theosophy*, p. 231).

Travellers and Residents among barbarous tribes have systematically inquired: (1) What was their view of the world of Spirits? (2) How do they speak of the Soul after separation from the body? (3) Where does the Soul go to after death? (4) Do Spirits appear on earth, where, how, and by what name called? (5) Do they influence the lives of the living for good, or for bad? The Idea of the bliss of Heaven varied with the climate, customs, and habits, of each Nation: the Northerner looked forward to unlimited drinking of ale; the Mahometan to an abundance of female companions, but no liquors. Kong-Fu-Tsee gives no explicit utterance on the state of man after death: he held that, though disembodied, he somehow or other continued to live on (Legge's Religion of China, p. 112).

The transmigration of the Soul to another body is asserted by a great many, both in Asia and Europe. (Rhys Davids: Hibbert-Lectures, pp. 75, 90; Tyler's Primitive Culture, vol. ii. pp. 4–11.) The Idea of the Hindu may be gathered from the following poetic rendering of a passage of the Vishnu Purána:

MAITRÉYA (the pupil).

" Parásura, you've told me
 " All that I wished to hear,
" How out of chaos sprung this
 " God-made hemisphere.

" How zone on zone, and sphere on sphere,
 " In ever-varying forms
" The wondrous egg of Brahma
 " With living creatures swarms.

" All great and small, all small and great,
 " On their own acts depend:
" All their terrestrial vanities
 " In punishment must end.

" Released from Yama they are born
 " As men, as beasts, again,
" And thus in countless circles still
 " Revolving they remain.

" Tell me, oh! tell me, what I ask,
 " What you alone can tell:
" By what acts only mortal men
 " Can free themselves from Hell?"

PARÁSURA (the teacher).

" Listen, Maitréya, best of men :
 " The question you have brought
" Was once by royal Nákula
 " Of aged Bhisma sought.

" And thus the hoary sage replied:
 " Listen, my Prince, this tale
" A Brahman guest once told me
 " From far Kalinga's vale.

" He from an ancient Múni too
  " The wondrous secret gained,
  " In whose clear mind of former births
  " The memory remained.

" Never before had human ear
  " The tale mysterious heard:
" Such as it was I tell it you,
  " Repeating word for word.

" As from the coil of mortal birth
  " Released the Múni lay,
" He heard the awful King of Death
  " Thus to his menials say:

" ' Touch not I charge thee, anyone,
  " ' Whom Vishnu has let loose;
" ' On Madhu-súdan's followers
  " ' Cast not the fatal noose.

" ' Brahma appointed me to rule
  " ' Poor erring mortals' fate,
" ' Of evil and uncertain good
  " ' The balance regulate.

" ' But he, who chooses Vishnu
  " ' As spiritual guide,
" ' Slave of a mightier lord than me,
  " ' Can spurn me in my pride.

" ' As gold is of one substance still,
  " ' Assume what form it can,
" ' So Vishnu is the self-same power,
  " ' As Beast, as God, or Man.

" ' And as the drops of watery spray,
  " ' Raised by the wind on high,
" ' Sink slowly down again to earth,
  " ' When calm pervades the sky,

" ' So particles of source divine
  " ' Created forms contain:
" ' When that disturbance is composed,
  " ' They reunite again.'

" ' But tell us, Master,' they replied,
" ' How shall thy slaves descry
" ' Those, who with heart and soul upon
" ' The mighty Lord rely?'

" ' O! they are those, who truly love
" ' Their neighbours, them you'll know,
" ' Who never from their duty swerve,
" ' And would not hurt their foe.

" ' Whose hearts are undefiled
" ' By soil of Kali's age,
" ' Who let not others' hoarded wealth
" ' Their envious thoughts engage.

" ' No more can Vishnu there abide,
" ' Where evil passions sway,
" ' Than glowing heat of fire reside
" ' In the moon's cooling ray.

" ' But those, who covet others' wealth,
" ' Whose hearts are hard in sin,
" ' And those, whose low degraded souls
" ' Pride rampant reigns within;

" ' Whoever with the wicked sit,
" ' And daily frauds prepare,
" ' Who duties to their friends forget:
" ' Vishnu has nothing there.'

" Such were the orders, that the King
" Of Hell his servants gave:
" For Vishnu his true followers
" From death itself can save."

(ROBERT N. CUST:
Banda, Aug. 1853.   *Poems of Many Years and Places*, p. 80.)

But some admit a future state, but make no mention of future Rewards and Punishments. On the Egyptian monuments we read, that Osiris is to be the Judge of the Quick and the Dead at the time of the Day of Account: the dead are brought before the Judge, himself clad in mummy-clothes, as having himself risen from the dead; those, who are acquitted, are united to the Lord, and become one with Him. We are not much nearer the solution of the riddle of Human life than was the Egyptian: he laid his dear ones in their rocky tomb sixty centuries ago with the same sorrow, and received no reply, no whisper of what happened to them; he looked out on the course of the Sun, and the flow of the great River, and the return of the Seasons, and we gather from the Inscriptions, that he prayed for more light, as we do at this day.

The Egyptian Idea was of this kind:

Man was composed of four different entities, each having its separate life and function:

(1) The body, which was embalmed, so that for ages it would not suffer decomposition.
(2) The "ka," or "double," was saved from extinction by prayer and offerings.
(3) The "bi," or "ba," or Soul, saved in the same way.
(4) The "khoo," the "lumm," a spark from the fire down in the Soul.

The "ka" never left the place, where the Mummy reposed; the "bi" and the "khoo" went forth to follow the gods, perpetually returning like travellers to their home; the mortal dwelling was only a wayside inn; the tomb was the eternal home, and was built solidly to meet this requirement; in it was the room, where the Mummy was; there was also the private room of the Soul, which could not be visited; and the reception room of the "ka," to which friends brought offerings; the two rooms were connected by a passage.

Hades, in Babylonian legends, is a gloomy realm, a land of forgetfulness, and darkness, where the good and evil deeds are remembered no more; its occupants are mere shadows of men, who once existed, very much as described in the Poems of Homer and Virgil, except that there were Rewards and Punishments in the Græco-Roman conceptions, which were undreamt of by the Babylonians. All moral responsibility ended with death: good or bad, heroes or serfs, were all condemned to a dreary lot; the Spirits of the dead flit about in darkness with dust and mud for their food and drink. (Sayce: Religion of Babylonia, p. 364.)

Æschylus has no hope of assured happiness beyond the grave; he was a contemporary of the Jews of the Exile: they had none either: it would have been a reply to Job's questions, if they had known it: but to them the fulness of life was on earth: there might be unbroken rest,

εὕδομες εὖ μάλα μακρὸν ἀτέρμονα νήγρετον ὕπνον,

but no possible joy. Homer describes Achilles saying to Odysseus in the Elysian fields:

"Scoff not at death, he answered, noble Chief;
"Rather would I in the Sun's warmth divine
"Serve, a poor churl, who drags his days in grief,
"Than the whole lordship of the dead were mine."

(WORSLEY's Homer: *Od.*, XI, 488.)

Centuries later, Virgil takes up the strain:

"Quam vellent æthere in alto
"Nunc et pauperiem et diros perferre labores."

(*Æneid*, VI, 436.)

And later on Shakespeare echoes the thought:

"Ay, but to die, and go we know not where:
"To lie in cold obstruction, and to rot;
"This sensible warm motion to become
"A kneaded clod;
.   .   .   .   .   .
"To be imprison'd in the viewless winds,
"And blown with restless violence round about
"The pendent world."

(SHAKESPEARE: *Measure for Measure*, III, sc. 1.)

We gather from Prescott's volumes, that the Mexicans had an Idea of Rewards and Punishments after death. (p. 56).

On the pictures on the walls of Hindu temples we have distinct information of the current Ideas of after-death Rewards and Punishments. In the life of Baba Nanak, who lived in the sixteenth century of the Christian era, and founded the great Sikh Sect of the Brahmanical Religion, we read how pious men were being carried to Heaven in palanquins, while wicked men were stripped naked, and driven with blows into Hell. He adds this striking circumstance: A looker-on saw a sinner being taken in this way to Hell; half an-hour later he recognised the same man being brought back in a palanquin towards Heaven. How did it happen? As they went along, they passed over a spot, where Nanak had rested, and the mighty change took place. In Plato's Republic, Gorgias, and Phædo, we have the fact distinctly stated, that men go after death to the Isles of the Blessed, or Tartarus, according to the lives led by them. The three Judges sit at the point, where the road divides: the Soul becomes tainted by the evil conduct of the body: some punishments are remedial, consisting of a few stripes; some are exemplary, so as to warn others; there are some, who cannot hope for forgiveness in this world or the next. Some are saved by the intercession of a Saviour, such as Vishnu, the merits of a Saint, like Nanak, as already described. However narrow was Plato's knowledge of the physical world, and contemptible compared to our knowledge was his acquaintance with Geography, History, and Ethnography, yet he had in him the inspiration of a Divine Life, and bowed humbly in the presence, the immanence, of a perfectly wise, and perfectly holy God, and never let go the unflinching conception of Human responsibility: there was more Christianity in him than in many nominal Christians, accurate and precise in dogma, but devoid of the perception of Divine things.

"There are no traces of scenes of future happiness, or
" misery, or of Judgment, on early Greek funeral sculptures; all
" that we see is the farewell of the traveller, who is bound for
" some unknown realm: the hand is laid on the shoulder of
" the beloved one in the moment of parting; the future finds
" no place in the Inscription; the world to come is out of sight
" as too visionary, when men come to deal with business such
" as death." (Westcott's Religion in the West, p. 136.)

In the Nineteenth Century, 1891, October, Mr. Gladstone propounds two questions, worthy of earnest consideration:

(1) Was the knowledge of a future state evolved by man subjectively from his own thoughts, or was it dimly imported?

(2) Did the knowledge progressively increase along with the general growth of intelligence, or did it on the contrary decline?

He lays aside for the time the first question, and considers the second:

(A) Enoch walked with God, for God took him: does not this show, that life in an unseen world was a conception accepted by the writer? But when was it written? After the Exile or before?

(B) Elijah was corporally translated somewhere.

(C) The witch called up Samuel: where did he come from?

It is clear that the Hebrews did not believe in the extinction of the Soul, or even the body, at death.

There can be no question, that in the Middle Ages the conception of a Day of Judgment, and Rewards and Punishments, was a strong weapon in the hands of unscrupulous priests, and that the necessity of making large donations to the Church was pressed upon persons of property in the hour of their departure. Even in modern times I read that to some it seems hard to believe that rich men, who leave nothing to the Church, and the poor, and the suffering, are genuine believers in a future state of Rewards and Punishments.

Let us ponder over the Emperor Adrian's dying words to his Soul:

" Animula vagula blandula,
" Hospes comesque corporis,
" Quos nunc abibis in locos ?
" Pallidula, rigida, nudula,
" Nec ut ante dabis jocos ?"

Let us now reflect upon the view taken of Life, as a term of years preceding Death. As our acquaintance with the private history of mankind in ancient days increases, many of our previous notions take wing and flee away, and it is well, that they should go. Contemporaries, and even predecessors, of Abraham lived holy lives, or at least there was a standard for them to live up to of holy life. Let us read, and read with humility, the inscription recorded on the tomb of Ameru, the rock tomb of Beni Hassan on the Nile: its date is placed at 2500 B.C.: we dare not affirm, that he lived up to the standard of goodness described, any more than we can of those, who lie under Monuments in Westminster Abbey: no doubt their survivors flattered them: be it so: from that flattery we gather what the ideal was of contemporary goodness:

(1) He was justified, weighed in the scales of Osiris, and cleared at the great tribunal, an indication of the need of righteousness, wherewith to appear before God.

(2) He never wronged any poor man: let us contrast the words of Isaiah, "The Lord looked for judgment, but behold oppression" (v, 7).

(3) He never oppressed a widow.

There was not a poor man ever seen, and no one was hungry: in time of famine he made the people to live by making provision : he gave to each widow the property of her husband: in great rises of the Nile, bringing prosperity, he did not exact arrears of rent.

If we examine the books of the Hebrew Prophets, we find, that the Princes and Nobles of Jerusalem and Judæa did just the contrary down to the very time of the Exile.

What shall be said of the words of a modern divine ? "I " have nothing more to do with him, for he has passed to the " bar of his Sovereign-Judge. I humbly trust that the " Sovereign-Judge has reserved to Himself the right to make " allowances : I have no power to make reservations : *He that* " *believeth not, shall be damned.*" (Canon Sadler, p. 32.)

What, again, is the view taken of death ? Did they consider it a punishment, or a release from labour, or a reward ? We can find passages supporting all these views. The Idea of death being a punishment is very forcible; we find such a phrase as "God slew him," and frightful exterminating passages in all the Sacred Books. An Indian historian of even this century would think it good style to describe all the slain on the side of the party, whom he favoured, as "going to Heaven," and the slain of the other side, as a matter of course, "going to hell." I have read these phrases in the descriptions of battles fought in the beginning of this century.

The Idea of release from labour comes out in the oft-repeated phrase, "he fell asleep" (ἐκοιμήθη), "He giveth His beloved sleep."

" ὃν γὰρ θέοι φίλουσιν ἀποθνῄσκει νέυς,"

"felix oppurtunitate mortis": how many live too long for happiness!

The echo has been caught up by modern poets:

"No pain, no passionate grief,
"No anger burning hot,
"Will vex her quiet spirit more:
"She's gone unto that silent shore,
"Where grief is not."

"Take me, oh! take me, while my life is glory;
"Ere I be weary, take me to my rest;
"Ere love be feeble, or my locks be hoary,
"E'en in my beauty take me to be blest.

"Leave me not, leave me not in this world of sadness,
"When the friends of my youth are gone to their doom:
"Take me, oh! take me, while still in youth's gladness,
"Into Thy garden there for ever to bloom."

Men shrunk from Death as beyond their experience:

"Men long to look upon the coming day
"Bearing a burden of unnumbered woes,
"So deep in mortals lies the love of life;
"For life we know, but ignorant of death
"Each fears alike to leave the Sun's dear light."

Euripides: fragment of *Phœnix*, 813.

(WESTCOTT: *Religious Life in the West*, p. 124.)

The Nirvana of the Búddhist is not the annihilation of death, as the Saint may live on after having obtained it; it is rather the extinction of that sinful grasping condition of mind and heart, which is the root of all evil, and cause of all pain and sorrow. Paul seems to have realized the idea : " To me to live is Christ."

Euripides, Cresp, p. 452, strikes another note :

" It were well that men, in solemn conclave met,
" Should mourn each birth, as prelude to great woes,
" And bear the dead forth from their home with joy
" And thanksgiving, as free at last from toils."

(WESTCOTT : *Religious Life in the West*, p. 123.)

Euripides again writes in a sad strain :

" τίς δ'οἶδεν, εἰ τὸ ζῆν μέν ἐστι κατθανεῖν·
τὸ κατθανεῖν δὲ ζῆν."

It is difficult to discover the motive of the Court-practices in modern days on the death of a great person.

Paris, November 2, 1894.

"A special Cabinet Council was held this morning at the
" Elysée, at which it was decided, that the President of the
" Republic and the Ministers should attend the funeral service
" for the repose of the Soul of the Emperor of Russia."

November 4, 1894.

"Late last night *The Official Gazette* published the Imperial
" manifesto announcing the entry of Princess Alix into the
" Orthodox Church as follows : ' The bride of our choice has
" ' to-day been anointed with the *holy chrism*, and has accepted
" ' our Orthodox faith under the name of Alexandra, to the
" ' great comfort of ourselves and all Russia.

" ' After the painful trial, imposed upon us by the inscrutable
" ' will of God, we believe, together with our people, that the
" ' Soul of our well-beloved father *from its celestial abode*, has sent
" ' down a blessing upon the choice of his heart and of our
" ' own for consenting to share in a faithful and loving spirit
" ' our incessant solicitude for the welfare and prosperity of our
" ' Fatherland.

" ' All our loyal subjects will join with us in imploring God's
" ' blessing upon our destiny, and that of the people confided to
" ' our care.

" ' In announcing this much-wished-for event to all our
" ' faithful subjects, we command, that henceforth our august
" ' betrothed Princess Alix be called by the name and title

"'of Her Imperial Highness the Orthodox Grand Duchess "'Alexandra Feodorovna. Given at Livadia, November 2.'"

Moreover, Protestants, Mahometans, Pagans from China and Japan, all in full diplomatic uniform, attended these services: we seem transported back to the time of Trajan and Marcus Aurelius.

The funeral ceremonies of the deposed and discredited Khedive present another variety; at any rate, Ismail Pasha is not described as looking down from his Mahometan Paradise:
" The procession itself presented the same contrasts, the same
" curious jumble of Eastern and Western life. Its very
" composition reflected all the anomalies of modern Egypt.
" Behind detachments of mounted police and Egyptian cavalry
" came the Sirdar and staff of the Egyptian Army, unmistakably
" English in spite of their Egyptian uniforms. Immediately
" behind them walked readers of the Korán, reciting the sacred
" verses in a high nasal chant, deputations from the native
" Guilds and Corporations bearing flags and banners em-
" broidered with sacred devices, descendants of the Prophet in
" green turbans and flowing robes, mollahs and ulema in long
" kaftans, dervishes in tall felt caps, students from El-azhar;
" in fact, the militant and uncompromising Islam in all its old-
" world picturesqueness. Then, in sharp contrast to the
" mediæval scholasticism of the great Mahometan University,
" came hundreds of black-coated youths from the modern
" schools and colleges, with their European masters. Behind
" them again, in curious alternation, native and European
" notables, Judges from the Native and Mixed Tribunals, gold-
" laced pashas and beys, English Government officials in plain
" Stambouline, long-robed clergy of the different Christian
" denominations and Rabbis of the Jewish community, red-
" coated officers of the British Army of occupation, the
" Diplomatic Corps in full uniform, the Ministers and English
" Advisers for Finance, Justice, and the Interior, and the
" Imperial Ottoman Commissioner, the Khedive, followed by
" all the male members of his family. Behind the chief
" mourners and the household of the deceased Khedive a
" double row of youths sprinkled perfumes and burned incense
" in front of the coffin. Covered with an embroidered pall, on
" which were displayed the uniform and decorations of the
" deceased, the mortal remains of Ismail were borne on the
" shoulders of 20 men from the Khedivial body-guard, hard
" pressed by a weird crowd of hired female mourners, who rent
" the air with their shrieks of woe. Another body of troops,
" with arms reversed, closed the strange pageant.

" The ladies of the ex-Khedive's harem, who, to the number
" of some 800, have been holding funeral-wakes for the past

" week at the Kasr-el-Nil Palace, had expressed their intention
" of following barefooted the remains of their former lord and
" master, but orders from the Palace ultimately forbade such a
" public manifestation of their grief."

3. MUTILATION OR DISFIGUREMENT OF BODY.

Circumcision is one of the oldest, most wide-spread, and extraordinary, conditions precedent of Religious convictions: it is scarcely credible, that any educated Christian European could have accepted "ex animo" the Jewish persuasion, or Islam, so it is impossible to find out, whether such a one in the Nineteenth Century, under Religious influences, submitted to such a disgusting initiatory rite. It was practised in Egypt, but chiefly among the Priests. It prevails among the barbarous tribes of Africa, quite independent of Islam. It seems beyond hope, that this old-world, and degraded, mutilating of the body, will die out. Extracting the teeth, boring the ears, painting and tattooing the body, passing rings through the nose, painting caste-marks on the forehead, shaving off the hair, placing the limbs in a position of torture by way of penance: all such practices, based on Religion, must, and will, have their way out, and die: one of the not sufficiently recognised merits of Christianity, as a Human association is, that the sacred body is entirely set free from disfigurement in the name of Religion; and no dis-qualification on account of blemish or infirmity is admitted. The Hindu married woman still pierces her nose to hold the marriage ring; some foolish women in Europe, and even men, still pass rings through the lobe of their ears, and deem it a decoration. These are only bad survivals, and in no way connected with Religion.

Paul the Apostle boldly got rid of circumcision, not only of Gentile converts, but of the reputed children of Abraham. None of the great Races of Eastern Asia would have submitted to this degraded ceremonial. It does not appear, that Abraham brought it from Mesopotamia, but introduced it when he was in Canaan: that it should have been tolerated in the Mosaic code is remarkable, when we read, Leviticus, xix, 28, the law forbidding the cutting of the flesh for the dead, or putting any marks on the body; that the Egyptians practised it, is evidenced beyond doubt by examination of statues, which have been found. A Clergyman in my presence justified it, as being the command of God: if so, how did Paul find himself justified by his own authority to abrogate it: on one occasion John (Gospel, vii, 22, 23) alludes to it in a marked manner, and not only all proselytes to the Jewish faith were circumcised, but during the century preceding Anno Domini the Jews had forcibly circumcised members of the neighbouring tribes, which had fallen into their power.

4. STRANGE AND ABOMINABLE CUSTOMS.

The annals of every country teem with customs, such as burning widows, killing female children, burying alive lepers, of which three customs I am personally cognizant, and to which I helped to put a stop in 1846 in North India; also passing sons through the fire, as Manasseh, King of Judah, did; killing twins, a custom still frequent in West Africa; burying alive unhappy wives and slaves of deceased men, to accompany them to the next world, still practised in Africa; burying men alive under the four corners of a new palace, as was the practice of King Thebau in Burma; castrating boys to supply the service of Eunuchs, which apparently was practised by the Hebrews in the time of King Josiah; Slave-hunting, Slave-dealing, Slavery with all its horrors; gladiators' shows, bull-fights, cock-fights. No Religion, not even the Christian, seems to have been free from some or other of these disgraces and degradations of the Human Race, and many were done under the influence of Religion, and with the encouragement of the Priests; for instance, the Koptic Priests still do all the work of castration of Eunuchs in Egypt. I have before me a Spanish notice, that a rich widow in Andalusia offered some bulls of her own breeding for the bull-fight, "come un' ovra piedosa," "as a pious offering."

Other abominable customs I pass over in silence.

One would have supposed, that the killing of all female children would not have been tolerated by the wealthy, educated, and so-called pious; but it was precisely this class that did it. I reasoned in 1846 with a venerable old Priest, a descendant of Baba Nanak, the Reformer, on the enormity of female infanticide; his answer was, that the terms daughter, sister, aunt, had never been known in their sacred families; when I pleaded for the lepers, I was told that they were used to it. Even now the Government of India are striving to introduce the notion of Matrimony into certain classes of Southern India, as for the convenience of the Priesthood all the women have been deemed common property, and the child of the Sister succeeds to property, as no man can have a legitimate child of his own; and Religion is put forward as the motive of this abominable custom.

A kind of Nemesis has followed the benevolent attempts of the Anglo-Indian officials half a century ago. The Census reports twenty-two Millions of widows, and a vast number of unmarried females, a thing unknown in former years, and a great misfortune in an Indian family, and a perfect invasion of armies of lepers.

Another strange custom is that of males and females moving about in perfect nakedness. In Africa that is an ordinary feature. A Missionary reported the extreme discomposure caused to him by having to preach to a congregation of adults, male and female, standing round him entirely nude. In British India there was one tribe, the Juang, in which the women refused to wear clothing from a superstitious feeling, that the tigers would destroy them, if they did. A large supply of clothes was made by the Government, and engagements taken from the men, that the women should wear them.

CAP. V. RECORDS OF PAST GENERATIONS.

1. Written.
   A. Necessity for Higher Criticism.
   B. Connection between Language and Religion.
   C. Advantages derived from perusal of Sacred Books.
   D. Description of Sacred Books.
   E. Was there a Divine Afflatus?
   F. Blemishes in literary style of the Books.
2. Oral: Tradition.

1. WRITTEN.

In the Religions of barbarous tribes there is no record of the past beyond the uncertain recollection of a totally illiterate, and uncultured, community: this is called Tradition, or Legends. In all the great Religions there exists a considerable, important, and interesting, literature: documents written contemporaneously, or committed to writing after several generations of oral transmission, are found in a dead, and imperfectly-known, Language, and a Written Character difficult to read, quite distinct from the vernacular of the people: the narrative is in a style of exceeding exaggeration, interspersed with expressions of great coarseness, and stories quite incredible to an age when people think. The mode of transmission of such a literature has been threefold:

(1) By an effort of memory of succeeding generations of Bards.

(2) By Inscriptions on rocks, stone tablets, papyri, or clay bricks, which have survived to the present date.

(3) By copies of copies of copies, versions of versions, translations of translations, the documents themselves being imperfect and mutilated, and generally violated by a succession of copyists, editors, interpreters, or bonâ-fide falsifyers. We are uncertain whether we have lost portions, or what portions ought to be excluded from, or included in, the recognised volume, or whether they are in the right order of sequence.

The works of Plato, as a fact (B.C. 347), older than the Greek

Septuagint, have reached us in a most perfect condition: the text must have been reverently watched from the first (Davis's Republic of Plato, 1890, Preface). In many other cases the Records have come down in a fragmentary state; there was a prejudice among the custodians of such literature against translating them into a modern vernacular, with the exception of the Jewish Records, which were translated into Greek, and Aramaic, and a portion into the Samaritan; similarly the Avesta Records were translated into Pahlavi.

A century ago the Old Testament stood out as the only representative of the pre-Hellenic period. When men read it, they seemed to lay aside all links of habit, all canons of criticism, all conceptions of probability; the existence of the relations of the Deity with man was presumed to have been totally different from that of modern times. Moreover, the atmosphere, which surrounds the Old Testament, is totally different from that of the New Testament. Paul writes in a style, which might be equalled, but could not be surpassed, in later ages. Now Egypt, Assyria, Babylonia, Persia, India, China, Japan, have leapt into a new existence, and present phenomena analogous to those of the Old Testament. The Religious conceptions of the elder world represent the communion of man with a Deity bearing a particular name. Portions of the Records of India, China, and Persia, have survived in their original form; the Monumental Inscriptions of the others are accessible.

Great liberty is taken with the awful person of the Deity in all these Records: in the childhood of mankind there appears to have been no respect for accuracy, or probability. Words are placed in the mouth of the Deity in the Veda, and in the Avesta: it was the form of literary expression, which ancient men were audacious enough to adopt: they conceived an Idea, no doubt in a reverent spirit, and then placed it in the mouth of the great Ruler of the Universe. In Jeremiah, xl, 1, the usual formula is given: "The word that came to Jeremiah"; but the whole chapter is mere History: the Speaker's Commentary is obliged to suggest, that History of the Past was inspired, as well as Predictions of the Future. Every verse of the Achemenian Tablets at Behistûn begins: "Darius said." These Records give conversations, as if there were reporters standing with pencil in the hand behind the curtain, though the context shows, that no third person was present, and those, who were present, could not write: the actual words are given, but not in the Language of the speaker, but of the Chronicler. The Chronicler, who compiled the Book of Samuel centuries after the death of Samuel, describes Samuel as in constant communication with the Deity about the choice of a king of the

Hebrew Nation: he does not tell us in what form it was made, whether by words or suggested thoughts. In the Epic Poem of the Hindu we are invited to a discussion in Heaven betwixt the Deities on the subject of sending an Incarnation in the person of Rama to save the world; very much in the style adopted by Milton in "Paradise Lost," with this difference, that the utterances of Milton are accepted as Poetry, those of the ancient Chroniclers were deemed to be absolute Truth. This leads us to reflect on how far the alleged Inspiration extends to the subject of the Narrative, or to the literary form. One thing is clear, that in such ancient carefully-treasured Records we read perhaps only one, perhaps only two, syllables of the great Word, which the Deity in divers Languages, far distant climes, at different Epochs, has allowed to be uttered, and to survive, when temple and tower went to the ground. A recent writer remarks with truth, and I quote his words, though many will not agree with him, as they run counter to deep-rooted prejudices, and a general feeling, that the Creator does not care equally for all His poor creatures:

"When we read the utterances of the Sacred Books of the
" East we learn, that no Human Soul was ever quite forgotten,
" and that there are no clouds of Superstition, through which
" the ray of Eternal Truth cannot pierce: they reveal the fact,
" that God has not forsaken any of His children, if only they
" feel after Him, if haply they may find Him." (Gifford-Lectures, 1893, *Theosophy*, p. 23.)

It is clear that the Assyrian emissary Rabshakeh considered, that he also was Heaven-directed in his expressions: whether he was so in reality, is not the question: he thought that he was so, and speaks thus: "Am I now come up without the Lord against this place to destroy it? The Lord said to me, Go up against this land, and destroy it" (II Kings, xviii, 25). No doubt the Hebrews would say, that he was deceived by a false Prophet, and, when the Hebrews asserted, that their Prophet spoke the truth, he doubted it, and returned the compliment of the Hebrew Prophet being false.

The subject is so large that I must subdivide it, and treat each subdivision separately. No one, who has not examined the parchment Synagogue-Rolls, now collected in the Museum of St. Petersburg, or Indian Manuscripts on slips of the Talipat leaf, can realize the difficulty, which surrounded literary work in ancient days. They were written for the most part in one continuous line, with no separation of words, or sentences. In Sanskrit there was something worse, for by the law of Euphony the last letter of one word coalesced with the first letter of the next word: there was no punctuation, no division of verses, sections, or chapters, no facilities for marginal references, or indices: if a Commentary existed, it seemed to make the matter worse by its bulkiness, and it being written in the same manner: a second elephant was tied to the first. Consider the Written Characters: the Hebrews changed theirs to the well-known Square Character about a century before Anno Domini; the Samaritan text is in the old Character. In India the Written Characters are numerous: some for the learned, some for the shopkeeper, a third for the Sacred Books.

What influence did Sacred Books have *directly* upon the Soul of the common people, if any indirectly through the Preacher? I should reply, before the invention of Printing "*none*"; before the beginning of this century "little." We are so familiar now with beautifully clear editions in every child's hand, that we unconsciously transfer this state of things to former times: some passages of the 119th Psalm unintentionally deceive us.

Let anybody, who has seen a MS., whether in uncials, or cursive, in minuscules, or tachygraphy, consider what a small portion of the community could read at all, and of those who could read, how few could read such MS.:

(1) The Veda: absolutely none; the first knowledge of great portions has come from the European translation to the Hindu Nation.
(2) The Buddhistic Books: none but the Priests.
(3) The Confucianist and Taouist Books: the literati only.
(4) The Zoroastrian Books: none.
(5) The Korán: as regards non-Arabian Mahometans only those who read, and of these only a small percentage can understand.
(6) The Old Testament: none but those who had acquired the Hebrew Language, which ceased to be a living Language after the return from Exile at Babylon.

When translations into living Languages existed, there was still the formidable difficulty of the Written Character, and the absence of all the facilities of Capital Letters, punctuation, Paragraphs, and References. We know what difficulties are presented by the written MSS. of the New Testament in the familiar Greek, written in a literary age, 300 A.D., and the study of a MS. in an Indian Written Character, even in this century, is no easy task: in the centuries before Anno Domini the difficulties must have been infinitely greater, and the resources of Memory were more made use of, as indeed they are to this day, when men can repeat large portions of their Sacred Books by heart.

The two classes of Records are:

(1) Those that are immoveable on rock, and carved on metal, brick, or stone-tablets.

(2) Those that are on perishable materials, moveable, and liable to all the incidents of Human existence, fire, water, ravages of insects, decay, rough handling, wilful destruction by petulant kings (Jeremiah, xxxvi, 23), or by intolerant religionists, as happened to the early translations of the Bible in England.

The Rock-Inscriptions, such as those in many parts of India by King Asóka, and at Behistûn in Persia by King Darius, bring us face to face with the Monarchs themselves: in all probability they looked on, and touched the identical objects, which we can see and can touch at this day. Any attempt to falsify is detected. How priceless would be the two Tables of Stone of Moses' Law, or some dedicatory Statue put up by King Solomon in the Temple at Jerusalem: there is nothing, absolutely nothing, earlier than the Moabite Stone of the ninth century B.C. in the Alphabet then used by the Hebrews. The Egyptian and Mesopotamian Inscriptions go back to the time of Abraham and beyond. Buried away in safety, they have escaped decay, and bring messages to this generation. The Indian Inscriptions of King Asóka have been preserved sometimes by moss-covering. We feel that we are dealing with positive unadulterated facts.

How different is the position of all moveable Manuscripts on fragile materials! The bricks of Mesopotamia are indeed fresh from the writer's hands; the papyri in Mummies are coeval with the dates of the tomb, in which they are found; but as regards other Manuscripts, there is no certainty, that they have not been tampered with, intentionally or unintentionally. No Hebrew, or Sanskrit, Manuscript in existence is much older than the Norman conquest of England. Emphatically we have the treasures, which haughty Time has spared to us, as the outcome of the genius of the great men of past centuries, in earthen vessels.

A. *Necessity for Higher Criticism.*

Higher Criticism is the peculiar right of this Epoch: we are told to prove all things, and not to lend our ears to old women's fables. Archbishop Benson thus expressed himself, September 22, 1893, in his Visitation-Charge:

" The thirty-nine Articles throw no discouragement in the
" way of the most rigid Criticism of the Sacred Books; they
" set forth, that these Books must ever maintain their place,
" as tests of Truth, but, as their meaning must be arrived at by
" the reverent use of Sanctified reason, they do not put the
" Bible up, as the antagonist, but as the guiding help, of man's

"reason. How far questions of physical science, or other "matters, quite irrelevant to the principles, by which the "Human Soul lives, have any place in the revelation, which the "Bible contains, they do not consider... We are to read the "Sacred Records, as intelligent men, with a full right to judge "of their meaning by all help, which an enlightened reason, "and an enlarged observation, and experience, and the "judgment of the wise of the past and present time, may "place within our reach."

In this critical age a literary fraud is a fraud, but it was not so in the centuries preceding, and immediately following, Anno Domini. A person, who wished to publish his views, had no hesitation in assuming the "nom de plume" (for it was no more) of Enoch, Moses, Solomon, Baruch, Daniel, or even of the Sibyl; no one of his contemporaries was deceived for a moment, any more than by a letter in *The Times* signed Brutus, or Socrates; it was a pious fraud, but later ages have taken the names of Books too seriously, as we should rightly do as regards a modern author. Had Milton published his "Paradise Lost" in those days, his utterances would have been accepted by a credulous age as revelations, just as the Drama of the Book of Job is deemed to be a narrative of real conversations, in which the Ruler of the Universe is made to take a part. The difficulty was felt very acutely at the period, when Greek and Semitic Thought were impinging on each other. The abstract Philosophic Conception of Plato on the subject of the Logos was idealized and sanctified by Philo, and then passed into dogmatic Christianity in the Gospel of John. The Greeks had long before recognised the literary habit of introducing into serious History, such as the Peloponnesian War of Thucydides, entirely fabricated orations, or written despatches: it would seem monstrous in the present Epoch to do so, but it was not deemed so in that Epoch: can we place entire credit on the despatches of Roman Authorities quoted textually in the Acts of the Apostles, any more than on the speeches, attributed to Members of the House of Commons last century, but actually written by Dr. Johnson, or other Editors of News-letters.

Educated man is a reasoning being, and there are some demands on Faith, such as provoke an unqualified rejection, as inconsistent with ordinary common-sense, unless the person, who hears them, is willing to swallow anything that a Priest tells him. Sanctified common-sense rejects the notion, that Moses wrote the last chapter of Deuteronomy, describing his own death. This is but the principle, on which all Higher Criticism proceeds.

There were no Libraries worth calling by that name: the travellers, who have visited the Convents of Mount Sinai, Athos,

and the Natron Lake in Egypt, tell us of the state, in which
documents, the value of which is inestimable, are found. The
writings of Aristotle were placed away by one of his admirers in
a safe place, and bricked up, and lost sight of for 180 years:
even now, at this late date, fragments of classical authors are
coming to light. We may find additional books of the Old
Testament or New Testament, which were not known to the
early Christians. There is no historic testimony to the authorship of the Peloponnesian War by Thucydides until more than
two hundred years after he died.

Pass from the Public Library to the ἐργαστήριον of the writer,
and mark the difference of the environment. In each and all of
the Sacred Books of the Zoroastrian, the Brahman, the Buddhist,
the Confucianist, the Hebrew, we can picture to ourselves, how
some great genius, or high official, or a succession of such,
occupied for generations the same office, a room in the Temple,
or the Priest's office, or a Convent, and placed away their
autograph, or dictated, Manuscripts, in some chest, or shelf,
or drawer, behind the Image of the Idol, under the bed of the
Priests, amidst the clothes and the furniture: they were quite
forgotten when the authors died: somebody, in a later century,
of a curious disposition, came upon them, examined them, sorted
them, arranged them to the best of his ability, made a clean
copy of them with his own hands, or that of his clerks, and
let the old fragments perish: nor did he limit his interest
to copying, for he corrected what seemed to him mistakes,
supplied omissions, intercalated notes: the next generation
accepted this revision as the original, and the train of connection
of one fragment with the other was hopelessly lost till the
time of Higher Criticism came.

No chain is stronger than its weakest link, with no disrespect
to the holy men, who more than two thousand years ago
committed to parchment, or papyrus, or the talipat leaf, or the
skins of beasts, their thoughts in the Written Characters of their
Epoch. The Inscriptions on stones and rocks remain as they
were on their first day: whatever they are worth, they are
genuine articles. We know, however, that they also can be
tampered with; for the Inscriptions of Queen Hatásu had been
deliberately tampered with by her brother, who succeeded her,
but the alteration made is palpable. Manuscripts carry in
themselves the seeds of decay, and can be replaced by others,
and the fragments of one mixed up with fragments of another;
this is not possible with documents on stone, or burnt brick.

At any rate, the altered point of view of the Hebrew Scriptures,
which formerly had the sole monopoly of Sacred Books, must
be considered: they are the same Scriptures, as a house is the
same house, whether standing alone on a plain, or surrounded

by houses. There is now a wider orbit than that of the old Roman Empire: Syria is no longer the Orient "par eminence," the type of everything in Asia. The shores of the Mediterranean, and the Region of Mesopotamia, no longer comprise "the whole world." The Religious conceptions, and the Sacred Books, of the ancient Nations of Asia and Egypt, are no longer things to be despised or talked lightly of; their objects of Worship can no longer correctly be called evil Spirits and devils; their Worship and Prayers can no longer be described as abominations and lies, but as the early crying out of Nations in their childhood to their great Creator, the greatest proof of the greatness of that Creator, and illustrations of the innate piety of His poor creatures, for every Nation has tried to find out the great Power, which rules the world, and has failed.

The rise of new difficulties is as essential to the Progress of Truth as the removal of old puzzles: it sometimes happens, that Truth, Everlasting, Unchangeable, is confused with the opinion of one man, one coterie, one school of thought. In Higher Criticism that word which appears so fearful, "New," is really nothing but the "Old," better understood and further developed. The aim is the recovery of the true meaning of the Bible. Every Truth is better than even the most edifying error, and a Faith, which is irreconcilable with Truth, cannot possibly be the right one. A perfectly free, but none the less devout, Criticism is the best ally of Spiritual Religion, and of a sound apologetic Theology.

The license, which was taken by early Chronologers, not from dishonest, or base, or lying, motives, but merely from their idea of correcting what appeared to them to be a mistake, is illustrated by Dr. Hincks' remarks on the Book of Manétho, which were clearly doctored so as to meet the wishes of the Chronologer, and to bring the books of the Egyptians into harmony with what the writer deemed to be the correct interpretation of the Old Testament. There was an utter disregard of literary propriety: in modern times a critic would write a pamphlet; in those days the critic altered the Manuscript, which seemed to him to be wrong, and said no more about it.

A late writer, Mr. Bellars, in his "Our Inheritance in the Old Testament," expresses himself to the following effect:

"From a sincere and reverent and unprejudiced and truly learned Criticism the believer has nothing to fear." From a review of his work in *The Record*, 1894, I quote the following:

"The mischief has been partly due to the unintelligent way, "in which many have read the Bible. They have practically "ignored the Human element. In spite of the clearest "difference of style, and manner, and genius, they have viewed "the author merely as the pen of the Holy Spirit, with no

"personal individuality. That there are plain marks of
"editorial action in the Old Testament is a matter of mere
"common-sense. How far the Human element extends is a
"matter of careful study, as is the question of what is literal
"history, and what is allegory."

The peculiar features, and the weak side of Written Records,
are, that they have to be interpreted by the ever-varying
intelligence of different generations of men, who import into
what they read, or hear read, the tenets of their own environment, and intellectual status: the Jews of Palestine were grossly
ignorant; the Christians of the first four centuries, in spite of
the Greek and Roman Philosophic influences, not much better;
then came a long tyrannous period of Ecclesiastical despotic
interpretation; with the Reformation came freedom, but there
was ignorance of the world outside Europe and its frontagers;
there was an entire absence of knowledge of Comparative
Philology, Comparative Religion, and Higher Criticism. The
situation of the followers of the other Sacred Books was,
intellectually, still more degraded. A kind of worship of the
Book itself of the grossest kind followed; even to this day
I read, that one hundred and forty Christians in Armenia were
imprisoned on the charge of desecrating the Korán. The
Mahometan would think nothing of burning or destroying,
a Sacred Book of the Hindu, or Zoroastrian; and in Europe
to this day, the Priests of Rome follow the Bible-Society agent,
and tear up all the copies which they can get hold of.

Another feature is, that the Sacred Books of all Religions
are understood only by educated persons, and only partially by
them, for they are old-fashioned in their phraseology, poetical,
symbolical, exaggerated, full of coarse similes or allegories,
and speculations too refined for the vulgar herd, who had to
be content with an inferior order of Divine Things, and fell
back on lower, but visible, objects of Worship.

Certain misconceptions have to be cleared away: any date
at pleasure can be assigned to the period of Job's existence:
critically it matters not, but it does matter very much what date is
assigned to the beautiful Hebrew Drama, which bears the name
of Job. Admitting that there was a Hebrew of great distinction, named Daniel, at Babylon during the Captivity, there is
great difficulty in assigning the Book, which bears his name, to
that Epoch. So also a careful distinction has to be made
betwixt the date of a book in the recognised form, in which
we have it, and the dates of the materials, on which the book
is based. This difficulty presses heavily on the Student of the
Sacred Books of the Zoroastrian. Will anyone be bold enough
to state, that any book in the sense, in which we use the term,
whether a roll, or leaves, existed before 700 B.C., familiarly used

by private owners, not liturgical Rolls of the Temple. To compose such a book there must be a graphic vehicle for conveying Ideas, such as an Alphabet, a substance like papyrus, or skin, or clay, on which the words could be impressed, a colouring-matter, by which in the two former cases the impression could be made, and a vehicle for conveying that liquid under proper control of a skilful hand. Before that Epoch, the tongue was the teacher, not the pen.

B. Connection between Language and Religion.

Language is the vehicle of communication between a man and his fellow-men; Religion is the same between Man and God. The conception of Religion, and the mode of expressing orders, opinions, wishes, are generally limited within National, or tribal, boundaries. As the Religious horizon enlarges, so does the capacity of expressing Ideas by words enlarge also. The first and most important oral legends, or written Records, in each Nation are connected with Religion. Man was born without either: his earliest thoughts were connected with his Religious conceptions, and they found expression at a very early period in Language. No other animal, but the genus Homo, has acquired the power to express his thoughts in words: intelligent animals, like dogs, clearly have thoughts, but though they live their lives, many of them, with men in the highest stage of culture, they never reach the power of articulate speech, nor can they be taught to do so. On the other hand, no Race of man, however ignorant or degraded, has been found devoid of the power of conveying thoughts to words, and of those words, few as they may be, a portion relate to their Religious conception. We come, therefore, to this, that the Creator gave man to work out in his own way his Language-making Faculty and Religious Instinct. No Race has ever been found unsupplied with these two gifts, however low their standard.

It is no fond fancifulness, that connects Language with Religion: neither apparently could exist without the other; at least, they have never been found existing alone: a deaf and dumb community could with difficulty join in prayer. The Traveller landing in a barbarous island, catches alive the sounds, that represent thoughts, calls them words, and records them; he then, through those words used by himself, probes the thoughts, and finds his way to their Religious conceptions.

Bishop Westcott thus expresses himself: " Religion must " be a solution of the mysteries, by which man is surrounded: " a solution, which shall bring into harmonious relation, Past, " Present, and Future, the seen and unseen, the conflicting " elements of our personal nature.

"A Religion and a Language, even in their simplest form,
"are witnesses to necessities in Man's constitution: no one
"Language exhausts Man's capacity for defining objects of
"thought, but all Languages give a lively and rich picture
"of his certain, yet gradual, advance in innumerable different
"paths towards the fulness of intellectual development. So
"is it with the many Faiths, which Men have adopted: these,
"in due measure, reveal something of his Religious powers
"and needs." (Westcott: Gospel of Life, pp. 18, 106.)

C. Advantages derived from the perusal of the Sacred Books.

"The central Idea of the Book-Religions was the necessity
"of harmony betwixt Man, the World, and God. Great
"Teachers in different climes accentuated and recorded this;
"but in lapse of time mistakes, misinterpretations, and gross
"ignorance, overlaid it on one side with speculation, on the
"other with material ceremoniousness. What was meant to
"be a Religion developed into a cold Philosophy, such as the
"Brahmanical and Greek, or degraded itself into an unmean-
"ing ritual, or diluted itself by incorporation of local practices
"and rural beliefs."

Professor Legge writes: "One is often grieved to read the
"incautious assertion of writers, who think, that apart from our
"Christian Scriptures there are no lessons for man about their
"duties, and that Heathendom has in consequence never been
"anything but a slough of immoral filth, and outrageous crime.
"Such writers betray their ignorance of the system and people,
"about which they affirm such things, and their ignorance
"of the sacred volumes, which they wish to exalt. Such
"advocacy is damaging rather than beneficial to Christianity."

Bishop Westcott writes: "As Christianity is universal, every
"genuine expression of Human Religious thought illuminates
"our Faith, and enables us to see in the Gospel some corre-
"sponding Truth: if we can understand what whole Races
"of men were feeling after, we shall have a clue to the discovery
"of mysteries, for which we, with our limited Religious instincts,
"should not otherwise have sought, and in the given assurance,
"that the Gospel meets each real need of Humanity, we shall
"find the highest conceivable proof of its final and absolute
"Truth." (Westcott: Gospel of Life, p. 121.)

In the posthumous volumes of the Histoire des peuple Israel,
vol. iii, p. 524, Renan thus expresses himself:

"The return of the Jews from Babylon was of general
"advantage to the Human Race: it solved a question of life
"or death. Had part of the Jewish exiles not returned, the fate
"of the two tribes of Judah and Benjamin would have been that

" of the other ten : they would have disappeared, and Christianity
" would never have come into existence: the Hebrew Sacred
" Books, such as they were when the Exile commenced, would
" have disappeared also: we should have known nothing of
" those strange stories, which have charmed and consoled
" so many generations. The little Caravan, which crossed the
" desert 535 B.C. from Babylon to Jerusalem, carried with it the
" Future of the World, and laid the foundations of the Religion
" of Humanity."

It is true, and Islam would never have come into existence either; but no doubt the Parsi of Bombay, the Búddhist and Confucianist of Further Asia, the Brahman of India, the professors of which Religions comprise more than half the population of the world, would no doubt tell in the same romantic way how the preservation of their Sacred Books during time of peril affected the character of the Millions of Asia: the Búddhist Pilgrims from China to India did something of the same kind.

The history of the people of the ancient world, if looked at from a proper point of view, is a grand procession of an ever-increasing knowledge of God; all the different Religious conceptions, and forms of civilization, contributed in their different ways to the great purposes of the Creator of Mankind, and their existence was part of the Divine Plan. Each conception was within the radius of its influence, a Schoolmaster, παιδάγωγος, leading on to something higher and better, which coming Ages, and Nations yet to be born, would mature. Unassisted man would have been unequal to the gestation of such spiritual Empires as those of the Brahman, the Búddhist, and the Confucianist. To suppose this to have come into existence in defiance of the Divine Will, and in contempt of His Commands, would indeed be a practical piling of Pelion on Ossa, as told in Greek fables. From the very first the Human Race knew of a Divine Law, of a fixed distinction betwixt Right and Wrong; gradually they became aware of their guilt, God's mercy, the necessity of Prayer and of Holiness, and all these things are set forth in the Sacred Books, which we are now discussing.

A one-sided partizan in the *Quarterly Review*, January, 1894, writes : " Despite the poetic fancy, which invests non-
" Christian Religious systems with an aureole of sanctity and
" beauty, they have been weighed, and found wanting in power
" to meet the deepest wants of mankind. Whatever their right-
" ful place may have been under Providence in the education of
" Humanity; whatever the virtues, which they are calculated
" to produce among people in certain stages of mental and
" material development; however beautiful the theory, or
" elevated the ethics, which some of them embody or enjoin,

"we cannot accept them, as a substitute for Christianity." Who asked anybody to accept them on these terms? Who asked this substitution to be made? This is only a rhetorical flourish. Compared to that Gospel preached in Galilee in the great Anno Domini, the fairest flowers of the Ancient world are as weeds; but look around at Christianity, as evidenced in the Nineteenth Century in Europe, and as deported from Europe into Africa, Asia, and Oceania, in the form of the most noxious products of the Earth. Is there anything Christian in the mode, in which Europeans deal with subject Races? Take U-Ganda in Central Africa, and Ma-Tabéle-land in South Africa, as the latest specimens. The Ancient Heathen before Anno Domino erred, because they know no better. The Moderns err, in spite of knowledge, warning, and example. The chief feature of Christian Life and Liberty is, that it leaves the Salvation of the Soul of each of God's creatures to his own Faith in his Saviour, that it spurns Ritual and Sacerdotalism; that it will have nothing to do with the old illusions, which existed before Anno Domini; that it is so reasonable, so sweetly simple, so suitable to man in every stage of Human culture; not limited to any Race, any Country, any Language, or any period of Human life. Will not, however, the enforcement of Higher Criticism reduce the estimation of the Scriptures, and injure Religion. Prof. Driver objects to the Bible (at least the Old Testament) being called the "Word of God," and would substitute "the Word of God mediated by Human instrumentality." My own view has always been the same. As the Λογος Himself came to us in Human guise, subject to the infirmities of hunger, thirst, fatigue, grief, tears, Human love, and even Human anger, so the Bible has come to us in the envelopment of perishing vocables, Human sounds, logical sentences, subject to the perils of copying, editing, correcting, transposing portions, omissions, additions, all which perils do not exist in our literary age. Milton's Poems come down to us practically intact in his own MS.

In *The Expositor* of October, 1894, there is a paper called "Prof. W. Robertson Smith's Doctrine of Scripture," by Prof. Lindlay, of Glasgow. Robertson Smith maintains, that his doctrine as regards the Old Testament is identical with that of Calvin and the Reformers:

"The Bible brought man into personal fellowship with a "redeeming God [p. 245], who through the ages had spoken to "His people, telling His Salvation, and giving the promise of "it, sometimes in direct words, sometimes in pictures of His "dealing with the Hebrews." But these Scriptures were *historical* (p. 247).

"Just as the principle of personal Faith is the foundation

" of all the fresh life of the Reformation, so the principle of
" *a historical treatment* of Scripture is at the bottom the principle
" of the whole Reformation-Theology." (p. 247.)
So there are two sides to Biblical Records:
(1) "They are historical documents, subject to the ordinary career of historical research."
(2) "They are the medium, whereby the Personal God reveals Himself to His people."
Calvin and the other Reformers held firmly by the doctrine of the witness of the Spirit, yet they treated the Record with boldness. Calvin speaks out boldly, that in Matthew, xxvii, 9, the attribution of the prophesy of the 30 pieces of silver to Jeremiah instead of Zedekiah was an *error* (p. 249).

We must distinguish between the Record, that is to say the sheets of paper and vellum covered with writing, and the Divine communication of God's heart and will, which the Record conveys (p. 250).

" The Revelation of God's will is a Spiritual manifestation of
" a Supernatural reality to be apprehended by Faith; but the
" witness of the Spirit does not attach to the outward Characters
" of the Record." (pp. 256, 257.)

" In outward form the Scripture is like other Human writings;
" the Supernatural reality is incased in Human realities: to
" apprehend the former, the use of Faith enlightened by the
" Holy Spirit is necessary: with regard to the historical credi-
" bility of Scripture, it *is sufficient to use the ordinary methods of
" Research*. It is not a matter of Faith, when the Books were
" written, by whom, in what style, or how often they were
" edited or re-edited; it is not a matter of Faith whether
" incidents happened in one century or another, whether Job
" is a history or a poem: all such things belong to the Human
" side of the Record. The Bible is part of Human literature
" as well as the Record of Divine Revelation. It is our duty
" to examine it as literature, and to determine all its Human
" and literary characteristics by the same methods as are applied
" to the analysis of other ancient Books." (pp. 258, 259.)

" The value of the Bible is not affected by the fact, that the
" Text, as we now have it (after the lapse of ignorant centuries),
" contains some marks of Human imperfection, some verbal
" and historical errors." (p. 260.)

" The Bible is a direct gift of God to us; it is not a mere
" inheritance from the earlier Church: God has *employed a series
" of Human agencies*, and in the use of these agencies has not
" excluded every Human imperfection." (p. 260.)

" The *Evangelicals* have used typology as freely as the mediæval
" Theologians employed the fourfold sense, extracting truths
" from the description of the Temple and its functions.

"The Broad Church distinguished clearly betwixt the Word of God contained in the Scripture, and the Scripture, the Record of that Word, and they went further and declared, that those parts of the Scripture, which did not appear to them to be Divine utterances, were *not* the word of God, thus leading to the conclusion that part of the Scripture was, and part was *not*, the Word of God." (p. 263.)

D. *Description of the Sacred Books.*

Let us consider what are these Sacred Books: they divide themselves into two classes:

    A. The contemporary Written Records.
    B. Poetical and Philosophic Works of a later date.

A. Here a second division introduces itself:

        I. Dead Religious conceptions.
        II. Living Religious conceptions.

I. Records of Dead Religious conceptions have come down to us from

           (1) The Egyptians.
           (2) The Assyrians.
           (3) The Babylonians.

II. Records of Living Religious conceptions have come down to us from

           (1) The Zoroastrian.
           (2) The Brahmanical.
           (3) The Hebrew.
           (4) The Búddhist.
           (5) The Confucianist.
           (6) The Taouist.
           (7) The Jainist.
           (8) The Mahometan, long after Anno Domini.

B. Poetic and Philosophic Works of a later date.

The Græco-Roman cults were represented by no Writings, to which the name of Sacred Books could be applied, but a clear idea of the nature of that cult can be formed from the great Dramatic, and Poetic, and Philosophic Works, which have survived of the great literatures of those countries.

It lies outside the purport of this Essay to do more than allude to the wonderful Writings, which Science in the last half century has revealed to us, copies of Inscriptions on tablets, and burnt bricks, Manuscripts on Papyrus, Parchment, and the Talipat Leaf: it seems incredible, if it were not a fact: in the case of the stone and brick survivals of the ravages of centuries, we can handle and see. Professor Sayce writes: "In these "late years Chaldea has given up its ancient stores of know-"ledge: it seems not without design, that, when temple and "tower went to the ground, the Sacred Books of the early and "forgotten Nations should have survived, carved in stone, or "in burnt-clay bricks: they are of three kinds: (1) magical "texts, (2) hymns of a spiritual character, (3) penitential "psalms; and in two Languages: the non-Arian Akkadian, and "the Semitic-Assyrian: this was the Babylonian Bible in the "time of Nebuchadnezzar" (Religion of Babylon, p. 313).

Some analogies arise betwixt the handling of these ancient books by their successors. Kong-Fu-Tsee arranged, annotated, and edited, with possible improvements from his point of view, the old Religious Books of the Chinese, known as the King, just as Ezra edited such books of the Old Testament as came back with the Exiles from Babylon (Legge's Religion of China). At a certain period in the long History of India, Manu codified the laws of the Indian Nation, very much as Ezra codified the unwritten laws of the Hebrew Nation, which we know as the Priestly Code: there was no idea of forgery, or imposition: they considered, that they were doing a good service in developing, and arranging, on scientific orderly plans the scattered effusions of their predecessors, who lived in a non-literary age.

The writers of those remote years were not without a deep spiritual undertone: in the Bhágavadgita, of the Sankya School of Hindu Philosophy, "the duty and necessity are put neatly "before us of living in the world, but not of the world, of "keeping our hearts free from overpowering interest in the "world, of fixing our love on the Supreme Being; we should "do our duty in the world, and yet morally renounce the world "by rejecting all its fascinations" (Thompson's Edition, cxxxi).

In past History there are only two Nations, who developed a real Philosophy, that is to say "a desire for knowledge," the Indian and the Greek: at a given moment in their History, they produced a class of men with leisure, knowledge of the phenomena of their environment, intellect, and a desire to think out the origin of the phenomena of the world around them, which consisted of Self, other living creatures, and the great unknown Common Cause: their search was that of observation, comparison, introspection: the questions propounded for solution were, What am I? where am I? whither am I going?

Ποῦγένομαι; τίνος εἴμι; τίνος χαρὶν ἤλθον, ἀπηλθον;

These questions, in spite of all the babbling in thousands of pulpits, have never yet been answered. The teachers of the people used then to be the wisest: it is the absence of wisdom, which now qualifies: a genius in Church-circles would get no quarter.

Búddha, Socrates, and One greater than they, left behind them not one single autograph word. What we know of them is from the pen of devoted followers, but it is difficult to free the mind from the conviction that the great Story expanded itself as time went on, that John the Evangelist had, after an interval of forty years, reached an Intellectual epoch far beyond the three elder Evangelists, just as Plato, who lived fifty years after the death of Socrates, idealized his Master by putting into his mouth the magnificent outcome of his own genius, which had advanced with an advancing age; as to Búddha, we know little for certain, though much has been written. This fact marks distinctly how the age had advanced in a literary conscience, that the followers of Mahomet, immediately after his death, A.D. 632, collected all the scattered fragments of his autograph writings, copied them all out in one authorized copy, and destroyed everything else: if there be anything false in the Korán, it is the falsehood of the epoch of Mahomet, not the accrescence of his credulous successors. It seems strange that Matthew makes no mention of the raising of Lazarus, of which he was an eye-witness. But for John, forty years later, we should never have heard of this great Miracle performed in the near neighbourhood of Jerusalem, and in the presence of Jews, who at once reported the matter to the Chief Priests.

Mr. Grote, the historian, justly remarked with regard to Greece, "that we possess only what has drifted ashore from the wreck of a stranded vessel," and the wreck has only given up fragments, or planks of Knowledge, bit by bit during the long course of centuries. It is a notable fact, that the Greeks, occupied though they were with speculation on Divine things, left no so-called Sacred Texts, to which reference could be made. Avowedly Hesiod and Homer were the first setters forth of their Theology, till the time came when Socrates acted as a dissolvent of cherished but archaic Ideas, and brought alleged Miracles to the cold ordeal of Reason: they disappeared, and were not kept in a galvanized life like the Miracles recorded in the Asiatic Sacred Books, written long before the age of Criticism.

The supercilious Greek and Roman held that their geographical environment represented the world; their conception of the Orient ceased to extend beyond the Euphrates: the March of Alexander to the Hyphasis was relegated to the same class of events as the voyage of Jason for the Golden Fleece, and the Siege of Troy. The convenient term Βάρβάροι comprised all the Millions of the population of the world, except the Region, of which the Mediterranean Sea was the centre: India and China, with half the population of the world, sate haughtily apart. Now that the whole surface of the Globe is known, we feel how narrow were the Ideas of the Roman and Greek writers as regards to spiritual as well as material things. The Hebrews, if we can judge from the lists of Nations, against whom curses were launched, had a still narrower geographical horizon, and called all the other Nations "Goi."

The beautiful Poem of the Æneid may well be called The Bible of the Romans: it is made up of Miracles, Prophecies, the interference in Human affairs of the Immortals, the anger and the kind favour of the individual members of the Immortals, Signs from Heaven, Prayer, Sacrifices, Dreams, Visions, Theophanies, and the conception of a Future State, accompanied by Rewards and Punishments: throughout the great principle inculcated is obedience to the Gods, and Virtue, Chastity, Monogamy, and Family-Duties.

I really feel afraid to express my own opinions in my own words, so I quote those of Bishop Westcott:

"The Poems of Homer were, as it were, a Bible to the
"Athenian people: everyone was more or less familiar with
"their contents, and derived from them the general view of
"the relations of God to man, of the Seen and the Unseen,
"which form the background to the common prospect of
"Life." (Religious Thoughts of the West, p. 101.)

"The myths of Plato transcend the dominion of pure Reason:
"they answer to Revelation as an endeavour to enrich the
"store of Human Knowledge, and to the Gospel as an en-
"deavour to present, under the form of facts, the manifestation
"of Divine Wisdom." (*Ibid.*, p. 48.)

What can more convince us that the Fulness of Time was at hand? Poor Human reason had, in the speculations of the Indian and Greek Seekers after God, gone as far as finite faculties would permit.

The same kind of tender feeling towards Virgil was entertained in the early centuries of Christianity: Paul landed at Appii Forum, and in his walk to Neapolis must have passed over the heights of Posilippo, now pierced by a tunnel; in this journey he would have passed within touch of the grave and monument of Virgil, who had died about half a century before his arrival. A Monkish poem in Latin describes how pleased Paul would have been to have met Virgil, and conversed with him, had he arrived a few years earlier:

" Ad Virgilii Mausoleum
" Ductus, fudit super eum
" Piæ rorem lacrymæ.
" ' Qualem,' dixit, te fecissem
" Si te vivum invenissem,
" Poetarum maxime!"

The Divine light, as it were, shone through the Human garment of words and sentences in these ancient Books. Round the Divine germ the Human writer threw the hard husk of his own individuality, his degree of culture, his idea of decency and literary fitness, the atmosphere of the environment, in which he moved; and centuries later someone moving in a totally different environment, with different tastes, experiences, and culture, took up the old Manuscript, and presumed to manipulate it, bringing it down to the level of a later age.

The Hebrew Books had this advantage over the Zend, Indian, and the Books of the extreme Orient, that Palestine was geographically situated on the frontier of the Kingdom of Socrates and Plato, and by a literary fancy of a Greek Monarch of Egypt was transferred from its own Semitic garb into one of the two greatest vehicles of Human Ideas, Greek, and Sanskrit. Six hundred years later one of the ablest and most devoted of translators, Jerome, transferred them from the original Hebrew into the great reservoir of European idioms, the Latin Language, then on the eve of extinction. For one thousand years it remained in a comatose state till Erasmus came, and with him the new Idea, the new mechanism of the Printing-Press, and the downfall of Priestcraft. Many a good soul of that period resented the idea of the Sacred Books being transferred into an unsanctified Vernacular, and kicked against Erasmus and his notions, as they do now against the Higher Criticism. During those long centuries the other Sacred Books of the Ancient World had been shrouded from the knowledge of the followers of the Religious conception, and all outsiders.

E. Was there a Divine Afflatus?

An accomplished writer has written as follows: " In all ages
" there have been enthusiasts: the Hebrew Prophets were so;
" the men in after ages, canonized as Saints, were so: there
" are certain minds capable of penetrating the uselessness of

"a purely worldly existence, and, finding it hard to live a
"double life, one material, the other spiritual, seek refuge in
"seclusion, and leave the outer world to those, whom it suits
"and satisfies."

The narrow vision of the writer could not get beyond the
Hebrew and Christian Books; we know that the same features
are evident in the other Sacred Books, and that the same
Afflatus was distinctly claimed for the Veda by the Brahmins,
and, if not claimed for the writings of Búddha and Kong-Fu-
Tsee, it was because, in a system, where no God was recognised,
the word Θεοπνευστος could not apply, but the presence of
something superhuman was recognised in the matter and style
of the Books written.

The Holy Spirit existed from the time of the Creation of the
World, striving with man (Genesis, vi, 3) long before the Hebrew
Race came into existence, and its power cannot be limited by
time, clime, or Human conditions. It sometimes has approached an individual, as the Eunuch of Queen Kandáce, or
a family, such as that of the Centurion Cornelius, or an assembly
of holy persons, such as met on the day of Pentecost, or a
Nation, when they come out and serve God. Its mode of
action is not limited also: it may come by word of mouth, by
inscribed tablet, or written document, by the example of a holy
life, round which the aureole of entire self-sacrifice sheds its
light, such as the life of Búddha, who neither worked a miracle,
nor penned a line, or by a stroke of affliction, sickness, or death.
It may come to the believer by a dream in the night, by a vision
in the day, by a chance utterance overheard in a crowd, or a line
read in some writing. Even so the Holy Spirit may humbly
be believed to have spoken to God's poor creatures made in
His own image, endowed with a capacity of uttering articulate
sounds, and congenitally endowed with the Religious instinct
from the beginning of the world, even as he speaks now to man
in an unmistakable manner, if the din of the world, the carnality
of the flesh, the careless state of mind, the life of sinfulness,
permit His poor creatures to hear. Socrates was persuaded,
that he had a high Religious Mission to fulfil, and that a Divine
Power, called by him Δαιμών, controlled him, and no doubt his
feeling was a true one. The Holy Spirit was with him.

No doubt the Hindu has always thought, and thinks still,
that the Veda was composed and written in Heaven, and com-
prises all knowledge, past, present, and future. The Mahometan
asserts, that the Korán came down from Heaven in its different
chapters, and is the "kalám illah," the Word of God. These
two Religious conceptions are believed in by Millions to the
present day. Want of vitality and long life cannot be charged
against them: but let us cast our eyes back for some five

thousand years, or more, and read what the mummy-pits have revealed to us :

"The Egyptian Religion, which in its wonderful *Book of the Dead* gives the oldest, and one of the most trustworthy, accounts of primitive belief, expresses very clearly the hopes and fears of the Egyptians with reference to the world beyond the grave. The *Book of the Dead* was considered by the Egyptians as an inspired work. It is Thoth himself, who speaks and reveals the will of the gods, and the mysterious nature of Divine things to man. Portions of the book are expressly stated to have been written by the very finger of Thoth, and to have been 'the composition of a great god.'

"The *Book of the Dead* gives us the completest account of primitive belief. We learn from this remarkable book, that the standard of morality among the ancient Egyptians was very high. 'Not one of the Christian virtues,' writes Chabas, 'is forgotten in the Egyptian code: piety, charity, 'gentleness, self-command in word and action, chastity, the 'protection of the weak, benevolence towards the needy, 'deference to superiors, respect for property in its minutest 'details,' etc. It shows that thousands of years before Christ, the Egyptians held lofty conceptions of the Deity; that they believed in one God, self-existent and omnipotent; and that their moral ideas were of the purest and best."

Certain members of the Christian Community choose to attribute all the Sacred Books of Antiquity, except those of the Jews, to Satan, with whose habits and machinations they are somehow or other so familiar; but the moral tone of these books, and occasionally a spiritual light, must disabuse all careful thinkers of such a notion : that they should have been preserved in such different ways, and revealed to this century in such a wonderful manner, seems to mark the presence of the Almighty in this and in all past ages. These revelations escaped the eyes of the Greeks and Latins in the plenitude of their intellectual Powers, and have been made known to this generation, presumably because it is prepared and qualified to make a proper use of this knowledge, which appears to justify the ways of God to men.

The genuine, the abiding, the inestimable, value of the Sacred Books, and Inscriptions, however recorded, by men of Ancient Days before the great Anno Domini, is sadly diminished by the pseudo-halo flung round them, and claims made on their behalf, by one-eyed pious men, who neither look round the world, nor can take in the fact, that God in sundry times and divers manners spake to past ages, as He speaks to us now. These priceless survivals of men, whose names are forgotten, remind us, that men were men in those days such as we are now, that they had reached a certain standard of Human knowledge, and a consciousness of the existence of God.

The traditional conception of verbal or plenary Inspiration I reverently lay aside; the men were inspired, not the Books. It may not be true, as all will admit, with regard to the Zoroastrian, Brahmanical, or Mahometan Books: this is admitted, because no one in Europe believes in those Religious conceptions; but à priori it is just as reasonable a theory, that the Ruler of the Universe should make himself known to the Millions of East Asia as to the tiny tribes of the Hebrews. Such notions do not belong to the present Epoch; we do not believe things because they come down to us as our inheritance from a credulous age. Professor Sandey, in his Bampton-Lecture, 1892, p. 424, sums up the argument with great caution: let us think it out: the Old Testament consists of 39 books, which are admitted by Hebrew and Christian authorities to belong to dates betwixt 800 B.C. and 350 B.C., or even later. The books of the Apocrypha may date as far down as 10 A.D.: they relate to different subjects, some of the highest possible interest to Human conception, some to mere traditions, misconceptions, or positive inaccuracies. Centuries ago allegory was allowed full play: that license is no longer allowed; we accept words in the meaning, which they are shown to bear, *and one meaning only, and no more:* all beyond is mere pious trifling.

Admitting that we have a fairly correct text, which is at once an assumption, and a reminder, that our treasure is in earthen vessels, the Human conception of sounds, words, and sentences, the treacherous pitfalls of dialects, and Written Characters, the quicksands of copyist, and editorial, license; we have to discriminate the passages which are totally void of Inspiration, from those with different degrees of Inspiration, remembering that no Prophecy is of private interpretation, and that it is not legitimate, or even honest, to read into passages with an obvious meaning the thoughts of subsequent generations and centuries.

We cannot read a line even of the Prophet Isaiah without feeling, that we are dealing with Human, very Human, sentences, words, and Ideas: we see a great deal of exaggeration, grossness of expression, illustrations void of good taste, gross ignorance of Geography, History, and Physical Science.

The non-Christian Sacred Books must be submitted to the same criticism: to say that they were intentional falsehoods is to fall into the same manifest error, as the one complained of above, but there will be found a residuum, which carries in itself a plain testimony, that the Message is more than

Human, not necessarily prediction, but advice, warning, promises. Prediction is not the true, or only, meaning of the word Prophecy. In the Edict of Cyrus (II Chronicles, xxxvi, 22) we read, "Thus saith Cyrus the king"; in the Behistûn tablets every verse begins, "Darius the king said": it was a common form. In some Meetings certain Sects commence their remarks with a conventional phrase: "the Spirit moves me." Stress cannot be laid on the repetition by the Prophets of the words, "The Lord said"; it is repeated too often to have any evidential value. When Paul, five centuries later, used analogous expressions, he carefully distinguishes what the Holy Spirit had taught him to say, from the thoughts and words, which were based on his own Human experience.

There is also another reason why a Divine Afflatus is always claimed by the announcers of a new Religious conception, or a new departure in an old one, for each enthusiast desires to cut all connection with the Past, and gives out that he has a new Heaven-sent Revelation to bring: so did Búddha, so twelve centuries later Mahomet, so the mediæval Saints, or Apostles of Rome, so the Mormonite, and Theosophist of this period, John Smith, and Madame Blavaski. The same necessity presses on all, who attempt to deal with matters of Faith, which is not seen.

In 1 Chronicles, xxviii, 19, we read with astonishment the following words: "All this, said David, the Lord made me understand *in writing by His hand* upon me, even all the works of this pattern."

The Septuagint renders it thus:

"ἐν γραφῇ χειρὸς κυρίου."

Archdeacon Farrar in the Expositor's Bible, I Kings, p. 150, calls this "*an amazing hyperbole*": it is just what the Hindu and Mahometan claim for their Scriptures. The Chronicler lived seven hundred years after the death of David. The destruction of Jerusalem and the long Exile had taken place intermediately.

Those, who argue for plenary Inspiration, must consider what an abyss of Human possibilities, and insufficiencies, they have to span: a chain is not stronger than the weakest link, and we have all the links of tradition, evidence in every stage, dangers to which all writings are exposed. Admitted that the Spirit of the Lord still speaks to man's Soul in present days, as in years gone by; admitted that Miracles were performed in the years, which elapsed betwixt Moses and the date of the taking of Jerusalem by Titus, in one narrow strip of land in Asia, and there and there only: we have still to depend on the Record of these wonderful events: *and this is the weakest link.*

The Hindu and Mahometan got over the difficulty, and declared, that the Veda and Korán were composed and written in Heaven, and are independent of all Human agencies. We do not assert that, but trust our faith to the dogma, that *God spoke by His Prophets*, and they made use of their material environment to communicate the word of God, dabar Yahveh, to future generations.

It is all very well for a Pope, who declares himself to be Infallible, to cry out: "Semper, Ubique, ab omnibus": these words did very well for the Middle Ages: they knew nothing of History: this qualified "Semper"; they knew nothing of Geography, which took away the meaning of "Ubique"; and they had no conception of the population of the world, so there was absolutely no meaning in "ab omnibus," unless they meant their own precious selves: all this is known now.

F. Blemishes in literary style of the Books.

In all the Sacred Books there are the great blemishes of vague terms, poetical expressions, phrases capable of ambiguous interpretation, or from which no meaning can be extracted at all, gross and filthy stories, introduced for no purpose. It appears sometimes, as if the writer did not clearly know what he wished to say, or that his amanuensis had misunderstood him, or copyists had corrupted the Text. This gave scope to ignorant, and sensational, readers of after ages to make private interpretations to suit their own views, and to import into the Text imaginary allusions, and unjustifiable deductions. Clearly none of the Sacred Books, without exception, form any sure base for History.

No impartial observer can fail to remark, that there is a strain of exaggeration running through the whole, and that there were none of the salutary checks of Criticism, and Reviews: temptations are idealized into a personal evil spirit, called Satan, and a thought suggested to the Soul is magnified into a Heavenly Message; the phraseology is often most lax, the figures of speech most unsuitable: why is Idolatry described so often in the Hebrew Books as "whoredom," to which sin it can have no possible relation or resemblance? Ample allowance must be made for exaggeration, poetical phrases, the excited state of the writer, the credulity of the people, and the sheer ignorance both of writer and reader: modern thought is more logical; modern experience is more accurate.

Take, for instance, a verse which appears twice in the Old Testament, the last verse of the last chapter of II Chronicles, and the second verse of the first chapter of Ezra:

"Thus saith Cyrus, King of Persia, the Lord God of Heaven hath given me the *Kingdoms of the Earth.*" We remark here, first, that the Hebrews admit, when it suited them, that the Ruler of the Universe made communications to Zoroastrians, and that Zoroastrians recognised such communications; secondly, that Cyrus speaks as Lord of the Kingdoms of the Earth. What would the Sovereigns of India and the Extreme Orient of the time have said to this claim of universal Sovereignty? We know that Egypt was not conquered till the time of Cambyses, successor to Cyrus, and that Greece was never conquered by Darius, the successor to Cambyses. Rome would have laughed even then at the idea of being subject to Persia: in fact, it was gross exaggeration; it must be admitted, that many utterances cannot be taken in their strict verbal meaning.

People write about the peculiarities of Oriental Nations: they do exist, but at present not to the extent to which they once existed. It is impossible to avoid seeing, that the Sacred Books of the East were written in an exaggerated, hyperbolic, and highly poetic, style which would be impossible in the present time. The importance of the Kingdom, and the wealth, greatness, and worth, of its Sovereign, the size of his armies, the number of men killed in battles, are quite beyond the control of Criticism. The whole Earth is spoken of by persons, who had the most limited knowledge of Geography; appeals are made to History by persons, who knew no History, and had no standard of comparison.

The Sovereign of Egypt, seated on the throne of Horus, claimed authority over all the Nations of the world. "All Nations are subject to me," said Queen Hatásu on her great obelisk at Karnak; "God has handed over the whole circuit of the Sun to me" (Renouf: Hibbert-Lectures, p. 162). Egypt was a great, rich, conquering Power, which lasted for centuries, and was able to raise up Monuments, which will last all time; still it used such rhodomontade, and similar expressions are used with regard to Solomon's petty Kingdom, which broke in half after his death.

No doubt Poetical rhapsody is the cause of much exaggeration of expression: the ideal is seized, and intertwined with all that is the tribal, and national, and domestic, tradition of the past, becomes amplified, and egoistic national pride caused it to grow from generation to generation: the Hebrew really believed that Solomon was a great and powerful king: we can see clearly, that he was only a petty Rajah, who would not have been thought much of in India in past or present times, as his territory was so small, and his resources so limited by the poverty of his country.

The account of the death of Búddha, as given in the Pítaka

(Journal of R.A.S., N.S., vii, viii), seems much exaggerated: long sermons are ascribed to Búddha in extreme old age just before he died: they were probably composed by the Chronicler, and included much, that was said in former years rather than at that time: the facts are no doubt true: we see an analogy in this in the three chapters of teaching introduced by John the Evangelist into the narrative of the Last Supper, which are not alluded to by the Synoptists.

When Krishna was in the chariot with A'rjuna, he bade his companion look into his throat, and there he saw the whole world, all mankind, Heaven, and all the gods. The same may be said of the Incriptions of the Assyrian and Babylonian Monarch: great allowance must be made for this feature in ancient prose, and poetical, literature of every kind, sacred or profane.

It is difficult to realize the gross ignorance of Geography, Language, Ethnology, general Science, of the Nations of that time; and in weighing the comparative value of their writings, this element must be considered: they were credulous to an enormous extent: the basin of the Mediterranean was very nearly the whole world to the Nations, which had access to it: two-thirds of the Human Race in India and the extreme Orient were utterly unknown to the people of Western Asia, and to the people of Eastern Asia there was equal ignorance of the Western Nations: that the Earth was a revolving globe, and was not the centre of the Universe, was of course beyond their wildest conception. In estimating the value of their statements on the subjects of things spiritual, it must not be forgotten, how grossly ignorant the wisest of them were of things material.

Take, for instance, the characters of David and Solomon as delineated in the Books of Samuel and Kings, written about 600 B.C., and the Book of Chronicles, written about 350 B.C., with an interval of two hundred and fifty years betwixt the two periods. The intelligence, the manners, the religious and social sentiments of the Hebrews, had changed; all hope of political independence, all prophetic visions and inspirations, had passed away, when the nameless Levite undertook to write an account of the Hebrew Nation, commencing with Adam and ending with Cyrus, the king of Persia, a period of 3500 years according to Archbishop Usher, and of 8000 years according to all reasonable inductions from actual facts of Egyptian and Mesopotamian History.

We have only to imagine the Chaplain of the Archbishop of Canterbury, or a minor Canon of St. Paul's, undertaking to write the History of the Church in Britain from the days of the foundation of the City of Rome till now. The Levite could only draw on the manners and customs of the Jews, as he saw them: he had formed high idealistic conceptions of David as the warrior king, and Solomon as the philosopher king, of Israel; he had no idea of the size of the great world, of the Millions of India and China, of the wealth there accumulated. The Kings of Israel were of about the same calibre as the Kings of Kashmír, with little or no commerce with the outer world, but maintaining a precarious existence at the mercy of the Sovereigns of the Kingdoms of Egypt and Mesopotamia: yet he describes them as the most powerful and wealthy of all the earth, "kul he aratz" (II Chronicles, ix, 23): "And all the kings of the earth sought the presence of Solomon, to hear his wisdom": he was a barbarous Sovereign of a barbarous people, the son of a king who had risen from the sheep-folds: it is doubtful, whether in his reign the art of writing alphabetically had been attained either on stone, brick, parchment, or papyrus; at any rate, the oldest survival of the Phenician Alphabet is 200 years later: at the time when the Kings of Egypt and Mesopotamia were erecting Monuments with Inscriptions in Hieroglyphics, or Cuneiform characters, King Solomon left nothing, nothing at all, most probably because he was not up to that level of culture, very much as the Afghan Chiefs of the Indian frontier at the present moment are not abreast with the culture of their neighbours Russia and British India, otherwise his Egyptian wife might have enabled him to do something, and his friend, King Hiram of Tyre, in whose dominions the Alphabetic Character was being worked out about that period, would have supplied skilled lapidary workmen.

The Levite, who wrote the Chronicles, assumes, that David wrote the Psalms, and Solomon the books attributed to him: this may be questioned. The Levite had arrived at a standard of holiness, outward holiness, to which neither David nor Solomon reached: he shrank from recapitulating the assassinations, which took place by the order of King Solomon, according to the last testament of his father King David; he makes no allusion to their gross immoralities, and the very name of Bathsheba, the wife of Uriah, is not totidem verbis mentioned: Solomon is described as having only one wife, because the Jews on their return from exile had become strictly monogamist, and the idea of a harem would have been as offensive to the Levite, as to a Clergyman of the Nineteenth Century. How unfortunate for these two Kings it has been, that the two Books of Samuel and Kings did not go the way of the Chronicles of the Kings of Judah, and the Book of the War, and the Book of Jasher, and the other Hebrew Documents of the pre-Exilic period, which perished in that great catastrophe. How different would have been their characters!

Supposing that we were now on the same intellectual and literary platform as the Levite, who wrote the Chronicles, and a Protestant Levite of an amiable and holy character and life, but devoid of any sense of historical truth, were to undertake to write the Chronicles of King Henry VIII of England: the writer would no doubt idealize the King, who broke the bonds of Rome, would omit all allusion to his brutal treatment of his wives, his judicial murder of several of his most noble subjects, his confiscation of Church-property, and distribution of it among his favourites: he would be painted as an able and patriotic and wise king, who did his country excellent service: his crimes were such as would be deemed impossible in the Victorian Era, and the pious Chronicler could not imagine his ideal hero acting in any other way than as a noble Christian: the Hebrew Chronicler has depicted David and Solomon with the same sympathetic, but strangely untrue, manner, if the Books of Samuel and Kings are to be trusted.

2. ORAL: TRADITION.

It is difficult to define the boundary, which divides History as a Science, from Legend, of the Family, of the Nation, and of the Religion. Even in this hard matter of fact age men treasure up as quasi-truths, Reports complimentary to their Families, their Country, and falling in with their Religious conceptions; but it is Faith, not evidence, on which they rely; such Legends relate generally to a remote and obscure past. The *modern* Legend is merely told without regard to exactness, but the handers down of the *old* Legends were men honest and good, worthy of our respect, but unskilled in the law of evidence, and very credulous. How often we hear people dilate on the beauty, talents, and piety, of their great grandmother, or of some remote ancestor! How from time to time springs up a National Hero, decked in feathers not his own! My remark may seem cynical, but the fact is, Truth and Untruth are hopelessly blended; there is a residuum of Truth in most narratives forming a base for large romantic developments. We see it in a marked degree, where Religious fervour, and holy men and women, are concerned. The number of believers in the Legend is no argument; so much the worse for the Truth, when all believe in it, and it bears in itself the unmistakable evidence of Falsehood. We must place it reverently aside, especially when it comes to us as a legacy from men in an early state of low culture; it might have developed into a great Legend, and been honoured by an epic poem. The raw material has reached us, and we must not despise it; we trace it back to a simple-minded period, very credulous, very ignorant of the world, delighting in the marvellous, full of reverence to their ancestors, and the great unknown Power, ready to believe anything; the more marvellous the more acceptable.

Professor Max Müller remarks on the Myths and Songs of the South Pacific: " They contain much, that will deeply " interest all those, who have learned to sympathize with the " childhood of the world, and have not forgotten, that the " child is father to the man; much, that will startle those, " who think that metaphysical conceptions are incompatible " with downright savagery; much, that will comfort those, " who hold, that God has not left Himself without a witness " even among the lowest outcasts of the Human Race."

" The sentiments [of the Vedic Hymns] are childlike, the first " sobbing and plaintive cry of the Human family to their Great " Father, who made them, and to Nature and the Elements, " the great Mother, who nourished them." This was their great environment. (R. N. Cust: Linguistic and Oriental Essays, Series I, p. 110, 1878.)

In all countries, irrespective of, and independent of, the Religious belief of the inhabitants, Legends have been handed down of the origin of the Globe, and of Mankind. Nearly every country has a Legend of the Deluge, localized to their topographical features of mountain and lake, and coloured to suit the intellectual idiosyncrasy of each population. The Legends current in India have long been well-known, but the late discoveries in Mesopotamia go behind the earliest accepted dates of the Old Testament, and the revelations of Geology pierce behind still further. We are on an inclined plane here, and cannot stop. Virgil, in a few lines in the Æneid, VI, 724, undertakes to record the current views on this subject in the Augustan age.

Myths resemble the fogs, which are exhaled in a damp neighbourhood; they are not, however, to be despised. Myths surrounded the infancy of Sargon, the first king of Babylonia, of Cyrus, king of Persia, and of Búddha; it was the usual symptom of Oriental flattery, and credulity. Sargon was born of an unknown father, like Romulus, William the Conqueror, and many others; in the Middle Ages Divine Ancestry was not claimed. Enclosed in a boat, like Danae and Perseus, and Moses, the Euphrates refused to drown young Sargon. Had they lived an obscene life, we should have heard nothing of these interesting details. So many Princes, who died young, have been glorified, like young Marcellus in the Æneid; had they lived on, they might have developed into a Nero.

The author of the "Unknown God," Mr. Loring Brace, p. 109, remarks as follows:

"The position of such deep thinkers as Socrates and Plato, "in regard to Greek Mythology, was peculiar. It was not "unlike that of some rationalistic Scholars of this day towards "the Supernaturalism of Christianity. Myths were the poetic "revelations of great Religious facts: the essential in them was "eternally true; the form imaginary and temporary: Socrates "and Plato would not rudely overthrow even the form: it was "intertwined with morality and devoutness, and should there- "fore be carefully handled: they recognised the popular "Mythology, and used it for their great moral purposes, only "half-believing it, and yet extracting from it Truths, which "were everlasting. But, wherever the Myths represented the "gods as acting contrary to the Eternal Principles of Morality, "they did not hesitate to say, that they were false."

Legends come down to us of Búddha, not in one universally recognised book, but in various narratives in different countries and Languages. He descended of his own accord, 600 B.C., into his Mother's womb: at his birth Heaven and Earth paid their homage; Angels sang songs of Victory. His Mother was the best and purest of women, and had no other son: his conception took place without the instrumentality of his father: he taught his teachers: aged Saints paid him honour. He had a great struggle to free himself from the bondage of this world. Devils came to try him, and fight him; the powers of Nature were convulsed: meteors fell; darkness prevailed, as the Sun was obscured; the Earth with its mountains, and the ocean, were convulsed; Earthquakes took place, and Rivers flowed back to their source. (Rhys Davids: Búddha, p. 37.)

There is very little scope for variety in Oriental imagery: something wonderful always takes place as regards the conception, or the actual birth, and the same natural phenomena are reported in most striking Language in the Ramáyana, when Sita was carried off from her husband Rama: I know nothing so beautiful in any Epic in any Language, as portions of this magnificent Sanskrit Poem. The beautiful Epics in Greek, Latin, and the modern Languages of Europe, are left far behind.

Of the extent to which fond credulity can be indulged, and of the crave of so-called Religious men to believe in Legends, the Apocryphal Gospels of the childhood of Christ may be cited as an instance. In modern times we know how to appreciate an historical romance, such as those of Sir Walter

Scott, or wonderful stories such as the Arabian Nights, but the composer, and copyist, of false quasi-Religious stories seem worthy of the highest reprobation. The compilers of the marvellous legendary tales, which attached themselves to some Christian Saints, are blameable, but they were only fondly, after the manner of their age, dealing with the incidents of lives of their fellow-men, but the compilers of the Apocryphal Gospels in attaching to the name of Christ tales, which were palpably false, gave a handle, and a good handle, to the unbeliever to throw a doubt on the Gospels.

Throughout Antiquity there seems to have prevailed a desire to trace back the origin of illustrious men to the Deity: to this day Rajahs in India will without scruple show their pedigrees drawn out through a countless line of ancestors to the Sun and Moon. In the great Epics of Homer and Virgil it is thought nothing wonderful to state, that Æneas was the son of Venus, Achilles of Thetis, and Bacchus and Hercules of Jupiter. Plutarch, in his work on Isis and Osiris, remarks, that at the birth of the latter there were omens, which always precede the birth of Earth's benefactors: a voice was heard announcing "that the Lord of all things had stepped into light."

" ὡς ὁ πάντων κύριος εἰς φῶς προῆλθεν."
(LORING BRACE: *Unknown God*, 1890, p. 21.)

" It is a side evidence of the spiritual inspiration of ancient
" and barbarous Races, that so many, and in all ages, have a
" tradition of a moral benefactor of the Race, who came from
" above, bore Human ills, sought to scatter happiness among
" men, and perhaps perished in the struggle with evil among
" men to appear again among the stars, or to await his faithful
" followers in the region of the Blessed. The strength, and
" purity, which gather round such memories, are the best test
" of their reality. And even, if some are only imaginary, the
" ideal shows the moral forces working on the hearts of men,
" and the Truths, which had here and there dawned upon
" them." (*Ibid.*, p. 4.)

By a singular chance, or more than a chance, the great Indian Religious System presents the conception of the Deity attempting to save mankind by repeated incarnations of himself in the form of animals in the remote past, and, as the centuries went on, in the Human form: in one of the earliest Avatára, or Incarnations, the Deity appears as a fish to save man in a Deluge: other animals succeed: Purus Rama is the first representative of the Human Race, Rama, the son of Dasáratha, the second, and Krishna, the third; Gautama Búddha is sometimes counted as the ninth and last, but there is one still to come, riding on a horse, when the world comes to an end. The whole story and character of Rama is wonderful in its sublimity and grandeur: the Son of a King, who obeyed his Father's will, and was endowed with the grace of entire Self-Sacrifice, for a given purpose, to save mankind, and conquer the great enemy of mankind. This Legend was current long before the great Anno Domini in Regions out of touch with Palestine.

In Græco-Roman Legends we read of the elevation of heroes to the position of demi-gods, for services accomplished: Hercules, Romulus, Castor and Pollux, and the flattery of courtiers added the names of Emperors, such as Julius and Augustus.

Still more striking is the Legend of Prometheus, who suffered, and suffered patiently, because he desired to benefit the Human Race; the great tragedy of Æschylus gives us an idea of what was thought of him in the palmy days of Athens; no sublimer conception is handed down to antiquity, unequalled until Socrates calmly sacrificed his life in the interests of Virtue and Morality, and escaped the indignity of being considered a demi-god, for he lived too late to attain that honour, and too early to be made a Saint of by the Vatican.

There was a great deal of Poetry in the Mythological conception of antiquity; a Poet is a creator, $\pi o\iota \acute{\eta} \tau \eta s$. Daphne unquestionably means the Dawn, which ever seems to fly from the approach of Apollo, the Sun, and dies. The laurel tree in Greek is called $\delta \acute{a} \phi \nu \eta$, and its wood is most easy to burn: this supplies ample materials for the Legend. King Arthur, Jack the Giant-Killer, and the brave Roland, have all mounted the same ladder.

CAP. VI. RELIGIOSITY AND MORALS.

1. Morality.
2. Arm of the Flesh.
3. Fanaticism.
4. Superstition.
5. Change of Belief.

1. MORALITY.

Socrates was the first in Europe, who laid down the maxim, that Morality was indispensable to Religion. In Asia, Búddha and Kong-Fu-Tsee, and some of the Brahmanical writers, had done the same. The Christian standard was still higher: "Without Holiness no one can see God." In British India, in a gross case of immorality by a Hindu, who pretended to be an Incarnation of the Deity, the Judicial Courts laid down a principle, that "nothing could be theologically right, which was morally wrong."

Nothing is more striking than the entire disrespect shown to women under the Hebrew dispensation: gross Polygamy and Concubinage were practised by David and Solomon, of an unlimited kind, compared to which the Hindu, and Mahometan, appear self-controlled. The slaughter of all the brothers (II Chron. xxi. 4) of the reigning Sovereign was a very ordinary expedient to get rid of possible rivals: a contempt of Human life, and suffering. Saul's widows were handed over to his son-in-law to be concubines, and the Prophet Nathan seems not to have disapproved of it: the marriage of brother and sister seems to have been possible (II Samuel, xiii, 13): as to any marriage ceremony, so important with the Hindu, it was not even thought of: he appropriated her, as if she had been a domestic animal, or a beast of burden. When her husband had been killed, David fetched Bathsheba to his house, and she became his wife, and the mother of the heir to the throne: he had done the same thing to Abigail, the widow of Nabal. No Sultan of a Mahometan Kingdom could have been more uncontrolled by Morality. The Gentile world appears to advantage

in the following quotation: " The superior man will watch over
" himself, when he is alone: are you free from shame in your
" own room, when you are exposed only to the light of Heaven?"
Kong-Fu-Tsee in the She-King (Sacred Anthology, p. 286).

I add the following quotation from the Dhammapada, as
illustrative of Búddhist Morality, 550 B.C.:

" 'He abused me, he beat me, he defeated me, he robbed
" me': hatred in those, who harbour such thoughts, will never
" cease.

" 'He abused me, he beat me, he defeated me, he robbed
" me': hatred in those, who do not harbour such thoughts,
" will cease.

" For hatred does not cease by hatred at any time; hatred
" ceases by love: this is an old rule.

" Do not have evil-doers for friends, do not have low people:
" have virtuous people for friends, have for friends the best
" of men.

" All men tremble at punishment, all men fear death:
" remember that you are like them, and do not kill, nor
" cause slaughter.

" Do not speak harshly to anybody; those, who are spoken
" to, will answer thee in the same way. Angry speech is
" painful; blows for blows will touch thee.

" By oneself the evil is done, by oneself one suffers; by
" oneself evil is left undone, by oneself one is purified. Purity
" and impurity belong to oneself; no one can purify another.

" Better than sovereignty over the earth, better than going
" to Heaven, better than lordship over the worlds, is the reward
" of the first step in Holiness.

" Not to commit any sin, to do good, and to purify one's
" mind, that is the teaching of the Awakened (Búddha).

" Let a man overcome anger by love, let him overcome evil
" by good; let him overcome the greedy by liberality, the liar
" by truth!

" Many men whose shoulders are covered with the orange
" gown (*i.e.*, are priests) are ill-conditioned and unrestrained;
" such evil-doers by their evil deeds go to hell.

" A man does not become a Brahmana by his plaited hair,
" by his family, or by both; in whom there is truth and
" righteousness, he is blessed, he is a Brahmana.

" What is the use of plaited hair, O fool! what of the raiment
" of goatskins? Within thee there is ravening, but the outside
" thou makest clean.

" He, who is free from anger, dutiful, virtuous, without
" weakness, and subdued, who has received his last body, him
" I call indeed a Brahmana.

" He, who is tolerant with the intolerant, mild with fault-

"finders, free from passion among the passionate, him I call indeed a Brahmana."

In the Sanskrit Bhágavadgita we find the following description of the Friend of God (Sacred Anthology, p. 59):

" He, my servant, is dear to me, who is free from emnity, the friend of all Nature, merciful, exempt from pride and selfishness, the same in pain and pleasure, exempt from wrongs, contented, constantly devout, of subdued passions, and firm resolves. He, my servant, is dear to me, who is unexpecting, just, and pure, impartial, free from distraction of mind; who is the same in friendship and hatred, in honour and dishonour; who is unsolicitous about the event of things; to whom praise and blame are as one; who is of little speed, pleased with whatever cometh to pass, and who is of a steady mind."

"The triumph of Right over Wrong in speech and action (for the same word means Truth and Justice) is the burden of nine-tenths of the Egyptian Texts, which have come down to us. In the famous Monument of the Egyptian Harps the Inscription was: 'Mind thee of the day, when thou shalt start for the land, to which one goeth to return not thence. Good for thee will have been a good life; therefore be just, and hate iniquity, for he, who loveth what is Right, shall triumph.'

"We do not believe the words of an Inscription, telling the praises of the deceased, but we must believe the Idea of Morality prescribed. None of the Christian virtues are forgotten in it: piety, charity, gentleness, self-command in word and deed, chastity, the protection of the weak, benevolence towards the humble, deference to superiors, respect for property: all this is expressed in extremely good Language on Egyptian tombs." (Renouf: Hibbert-Lecture, p. 32.)

As long as a Religious conception does more good than harm, and a standard of Morality is retained, the wise man would let the people alone; but too often a Religious conception wastes away, and dies, in an atmosphere of hideous immorality. Lucretius boldly writes as a comment on the Sacrifice of his daughter by Agamemnon:

"Tantum religio potuit suadere malorum."

And in India we have learnt lately another lesson: it may be doubted, whether the Indian youth, educated in the State-Colleges, and thoroughly purged of belief in any of the moral sanctions of their forefathers, are not less well prepared for a decent moral control of life than his uneducated contemporary.

2. ARM OF THE FLESH.

Under this head come Propagation of Religion by force of arms, Intolerance, Persecution, Spoliation, Excommunication, Civil Disabilities, Murder, Torture, Burying alive: all these atrocities performed in the name of Religion by the help of the party in power. The Books of Kings and Chronicles tell us how in that little country, occupied by the twelve tribes, the will of the King for the time being went for everything: Hezekiah succeeded Ahaz, he was followed by Manasseh, and the latter by Josiah; up and down went the Altars of Baal, and the groves; of course the Historians take the part of the so-called good Kings, and are loud in their abuse of the so-called bad ones, one of whom was only eight years old, and reigned three months, but they have all one feature in common, they killed all those, who differed from them: if Jezebel killed the Prophets, Jehu killed the Priests; there was an absolute want of tolerance: Jehu's slaughter of the Priests of Baal, and the relatives of Ahab, is the most abominable of all: the Church of Rome cries out at the least sign of Persecution, but Rome was a master of the art of Persecution, and appears quite ready to do so again, if chance offered.

" Quis tulerit Gracchos de seditione querentes?"

Some of the sufferers in the reign of Diocletian became in their old age, under Constantine, the bitterest persecutors themselves. It is an astounding fact, how Religious people forget all Ideas of Mercy, Justice, and Pity, towards those, who differ from themselves in some abstract dogma, or ceremonial practice, or even of the date of a feast-day. Men of the present Epoch have all the will to persecute, but lack the power: the dead weight of Atheism, Agnosticism, Indifferentism, renders any personal persecution impossible, but social, professional, domestic, persecution is still rampant.

In China, 460 Literati were buried alive by one of the Emperors on account of some difference of doctrine; in Egypt, a King Khuen-Atin persecuted those, who would not join him in worshipping the *disk* of the Sun, and, when he died, his followers suffered the same treatment.

" No Religious conceptions are so hard to reconcile, or to
" find a working compromise, as those, which outwardly present
" the greatest similarity to each other. The Sun was the
" object of Worship to many ancient Nations, and resolved into
" a triad :

" Atin Ra, the Solar Disk.
" Muer Ra, the Solar Ray.
" Ra, the Abstract Deity.

" They seemed to be identical, but the great so-called
" Heresy of Amenophis IV, or Khuen-Atin, turned upon this
" difference. His real name was Amen Ra, he took the name
" of Khu-en-atin, Glory to the Solar Disk." (Cooper's
Heresies of the Past, p. 41.)

Many of the differences of modern Sects are equally foolish.
" If Christians and Mahometans were in their superstitious
" fancies equally far from the Truth, they were equally wanting
" in justice and mercy. The Jesuit-ridden Court of Vienna in
" vain urged the sacred duty of persecuting the Protestants in
" Hungary on the Turkish Pasha at Buda, who treated Christians
" of all sects and sorts with the same contemptuous toleration.
" The Jews, expelled from Christian Spain, found a refuge and
" a shelter in the dominions of the Grand Turk; while the
" Corsair brigantines of Algiers and Sallee were propelled by
" sinews of Christian Slaves, the rowing-benches of the galleys
" of the Most Christian King, and of the Knights of St. John,
" were manned by fettered Turks and Moors."

But the lower grades of society are quite as susceptible of
the same bitter intolerance: they cannot be contented to leave
other people alone, if they are left alone themselves: in 1893
the Hindu mob attacked the Mahometans, because they availed
themselves of their undoubted right to kill cattle for consumption:
lives have been lost in the struggle: there is no doubt that
the new organization of "Cow-Protection Society" is but a
seditious movement under a thin veil of Religion. An attempt
has been made to capture Commissariat-cattle, collected for the
food of the British troops: the troops were called out, and
there was loss of life among the rioters. It is clear, that the
non-Christian fanatics have their Religious fads quite as much
as the Christian faddists in England, who worry about the
Opium-Trade. Of course desecration of Mosques, and
destruction of Temples, always form part of such lamentable
contests.

Civil disabilities still exist; Murder, Torture, Burying alive,
for the present, are out of fashion. Both the Hindu, and the
Búddhist, are tolerant as regards dogma, and have ever been
so. Nebuchadnezzar's golden image is a specimen of the
Religious teaching not only of that age, but of mankind till the
Reformation, and even afterwards till the Revolution; whatever
the Rulers approved, that must be enforced. We read of people
burnt because they would not believe in the Image, and then
cut to pieces because they would not believe in the God of

Israel: it is the same now: Orthodoxy means "My-doxy"; each person thinks his own form of Religion the very best form, and the only one, which ought to be allowed to exist; in fact, the common herd, gentle and simple, lays aside all Reason, Justice, and Common-Sense in matters of Religion. Christian things should be done in a Christian manner.

As I walked years ago through the streets of the great city of Banáras in North India, of which I was Magistrate, I have stopped before Temples to exchange civil words with the Hindu Priests, and watch their ritual. I listened to their prayers in an archaic dead Language, which I could understand, having learnt the Language in an English College, but of which the prostrate worshippers understood not a word. I recognised the same features, which I had witnessed in the Temples of the Greek and Roman Christianity. Whether the form was wrong or right, it was at least a service of duty to the Ruler of the Universe. It was the Religious conception of 200 Millions, and of a date earlier than Moses, tolerant, making no attempt to proselytize, peaceful, self-satisfied, and conveying a sanction to personal Morality under certain recognised laws and customs.

Then and now arose in my mind the awful question: what right had a petty Chieftain, like the King of Samaria, to slaughter the Priests of Baal, because he differed from them? Would not banishment from his kingdom, as it is presumed that they were aliens from Tyre, have been sufficient? Is it wise to read the narratives of such outrages on the Eternal Law of doing unto others as you would wish men to do unto you, in Christian Churches? Is this real Worship to a God, so full of Love and Pity, "Who hateth nothing that He has made." In times of trouble and oppression the Jew and the Christian claim Tolerance for themselves. The Missionaries in China are always raising an outcry on this subject, appealing to Treaties, and soliciting the aid of gunboats:

"Non tali auxilio."

They would be very angry if the Emperor of China acted towards them, as Ahab acted to the Priests of Baal. From the Jews came the deadly heritage of Intolerance, which lasted down to the seventeenth century A.D., of inflicting death merely on account of a conscientious difference in the appreciation of Divine Things. It took a long time for poor weak men to find out, that Religious convictions are involuntary, and that it is contrary to the first principles of true Religion to coerce them. In the time of the Prophet Jeremiah our phlegmatic indifference to the Religious convictions of our next-door neighbours would have been deemed to be dishonourable to God. Torquemáda, of Spain, who burnt 8000 Protestants, was but the lineal descendant of the assassins of Stephen, who were of the same seed, as those Priests who declared that by their law Christ ought to die.

It is clear that the spread of Christianity in the Roman Empire was brought about, not by Miracles, and Preaching, but by overbearing Sovereigns and intolerant Priests. It grew indeed by its own internal power and suitability to the age, and recommended itself by its precepts, examples, and promises: the old system had broken up; there was a vacuum in the Religious atmosphere, and Christianity filled it. Could this result not have been obtained without the frightful cruelty? The Romish persecutors at the time of the Reformation were but the legitimate successors of the original Converters. In due course, bitter complaints were made by the Christians against the Mahometans for their intolerance: in what did they differ from the Christians who converted Europe? Alcuin boldly told Charlemagne to see that "everything was done in " the right order, and that conviction of the Truth and Faith " went before Baptism, since the washing of the body without " any knowledge of the Faith in a Soul gifted with reason " would be of no use" (J. Johnston, Century of Christian Progress, p. 112).

Such were the views of the Roman Emperors in the first century of Christianity, and of the Hindu Nation always. Even an Atheist was not liable to punishment, as it was not in a man's power to believe or disbelieve at his pleasure; it was even lawful to propagate his views, but not by violence, or insult to the Religion of others. Toleration was the great primeval and Universal principle : it was lawful to every man to be of what Religion he liked. The most notable sentiment in the Annals of Tacitus for the guidance of Statesmen was the golden dictum of Tiberius:

"Deorum injuriæ Diis curæ."

What rivers of blood would not its frank acceptance have prevented? Who made poor erring man judge of the fact, whether an insult was offered to God in matters of Religion? The Missionary spares no words of abuse of a non-Christian for uttering blasphemous words with regard to his holy Religion: it is, indeed, painful to hear or read such expressions; but the Missionary does not spare the Religious conceptions of other Nations, and in their eyes is equally guilty of blasphemy, and in our eyes of ignorant intolerance.

More in his "Eutopia" gives a clear idea of the sentiments of the enlightened men of his time, such as Erasmus, Colet, and their mutual friend:

"That God's design was the happiness of man; that the "ascetic rejector of legitimate Human delights, save for the "common good, or other high cause, was thanklessness."

It must not be forgotten, that the Religious persecutor and the Religious martyr, *i.e.*, one who has courted martyrdom, are the same kind of person in a different environment. He, who is ready ostentatiously to die for his Faith, has a certainty that it is conformable to Divine law, and *to his own advantage* to make others die, if they oppose that Faith. Torquemáda could not see that there was a via media of leaving people alone: he would have courted martyrdom himself, and declined to be let alone.

Hear the words of the Bishop of London in his sermon at the Exeter Church Congress, 1894:

" If a man believed, he could not be indifferent to all that " was said against the Truth of God. But that was not Christ's " way of dealing with those, who had sinned against Him, who " were not moved in the slightest degree either by His " marvellous works or His still more marvellous teaching. In " no such way did the Lord ever allow that His Gospel should " be maintained; in no such way did He ever encourage His " true disciples to fight in defence of the Faith or of the " Church. It had been tried again and again. There had " been times, when Christians had endeavoured to maintain the " Truth by persecuting unto the death those, who dared to assail " Him, when Christians had defended the Church by the use of " such means as the Lord never used Himself, and never " authorized others to use. Was there any man who had read " Church History, who in his calmer moments was not ashamed " of what had been done in the name of Christ? Was there " any man who would not, if he could, blot out of the events " of the past all the History of those saddest of all sad days, " when Human life and comfort and happiness were counted as " nothing if there were any chance of maintaining the Divine " Institutions and Divine Doctrine? They could not think of " such things without grief of heart. No one now proposed a " return to anything like that. None proposed such intolerance " or any kind of persecution. Still they were tempted to " assume the position, which belonged to the Lord alone, and " to condemn, although they acknowledged, that they had no " right to push condemnation into punishment."

To give an idea of the feelings of a Hungarian Magnate of the Nineteenth Century on the subject of Toleration, I quote the words of Count Zichi in the Chamber of Magnates, 1894.

He stated, that it was precisely his respect to, and sympathy for, his Jewish fellow-citizens, that made him oppose the measure (to grant them freedom from intolerant laws), "because " to grant permission to Christians to go over to the Jewish " Religion was contrary to the very Idea of Christianity, while " conversion from Judaism to Christianity was already per- " mitted." This is indeed an instance of the deep degradation of the intellect and conscience of honest and educated men.

3. FANATICISM.

We have sad instances in all ages, and all climes, of Impostors, Fanatics, Enthusiasts, devotees, deliberate fabricators, perjurers. The self-imposed tortures of the Hindu Fakir is a matter of notoriety; so is the locking up in a convent of a poor young girl, whose presence is in the way of her own people; the dancing of the Durwísh in Constantinople; the swinging of the Fakir at the Charak-Puja in Bangál; the Eremites of Egypt; the pillar of Simon Stylites at Antioch; the lying miracles at Papist Shrines; the alleged Faith-healing of infatuated religionists; the believers in a Millennium. All discussion on scientific, or historical, principles is avoided, or forbidden, because it is beyond the intellectual standard of the majority. "Great is Diana of the Ephesians!" is the cry, which floats down the great River of Time in all countries and all Languages. The Protestant Missionary calls the non-Christian a fanatic, who will not listen to his arguments, or the Jew, or the Roman Catholic, but are they more fanatical than the Missionary himself? The Latin word 'fanaticus' is derived from 'fanum,' "a temple," and its primary meaning is one that is "inspired," and "enthusiastic"; as far back as the time of Cicero, it acquired the secondary meanings of "furious, mad, frantic."

4. SUPERSTITION.

In which form of Religious conception are grosser instances recorded of Superstition, Sanctimoniousness, Hypocrisy, arrogant Pharisaic pride, narrow-minded exclusion of others, claim to a monopoly of the Deity? Under each one of these heads how much could be written, gathered from the Hebrew Scriptures, the non-Christian Sacred Books, Secular Histories, Modern News-letters, or taken from life!

Religion is essentially illogical. The Psalms prove this:

they are supposed to be vehicles of Love, yet how little they have of Mercy in dealing with those, whom the Hebrew pietists please to describe as God's enemies; somebody else's "doxy." So also the purest theoretic conception of Divinity can be found flowing in the same channels with the most degraded Superstition, most worldly practice, most low morality.

5. CHANGE OF BELIEF.

There has been the same process of nominal belief, outward show, ceremonial practice, going on in the elder world, as we witness in the surface Christianity at the present Epoch. From policy, from fashion, from the influence of marriage, or education, or the result of association with other populations, changes have taken place: sometimes in the form of Religious development, or evolution; sometimes in contraction of Ideas; sometimes in sheer abandonment of the old conception, and adoption of the new. In general there has been no heart-conversion, no acceptance of a new cut-and-dried dogma; no feeling, "Behold! I am a new man." "Me eat beef, me drink brandy, me Christian": this is the cry of the Indian outcast. Circumcision fenced in the proselyte to Judaism and Islam by an indelible flesh-mark. In this they resemble cattle, which are marked with the brand of their owner. The Pagan tribes of India are gradually being absorbed into the Hindu and Mahometan system, unless Christianity anticipates the change; there is a slight modification of dress, and teaching of conventional words, and movement of the limbs, a shunning of certain foods, a keeping of certain days, a payment of certain fees, and the thing is done: whether labelled as a Hindu, Mahometan, Christain, Buddhist, Jew, he is the same ignorant Pagan, in reality, as he was before.

It seems that a powerful Religion, supported by the Ruling Power, illustrated by works of Genius, must have an influence over the Religious conceptions of other people, brought into contact; it cannot be doubted, that the conception of Angels, and perhaps of the Evil Spirit, were borrowed by the Jews during the Captivity from the tenets of Zoroaster, as exhibited by the old Persians. "It must be "admitted, that an unfamiliar Idea, when first propagated, "always and necessarily produces a popular reaction in the "social organism, which is always conscientious, and rightly "so" (*Review of Reviews*, Christmas, 1894).

The argument is: Our present Religion exists; it has worked well for a long time: let it be; we have tried it; a change may be for the worse; the reflex action of the self-preserving element in Society arms itself to resist a new Idea. We have only to imagine the feelings of a Welsh Clergyman, when his daughter announces herself as intending to be a Mormon, or an Orangeman of Ulster when his son becomes a Papist Priest. The Missionaries describe the wickedness of a Hindu, who locks up his son, so as to prevent his being baptized. What would the Missionary do, if his own wife or child were to become Theosophists?

Sometimes without actual change of terminology Sects spring into existence, like the Dialects of a Language, such as the Sikhs, Kabirpanthi, Jains, etc., among the Hindus; the Shiah and Suni, Súfi and Bábi, among the Mahometans; and the numerous Denominations of Christianity. Sometimes the new Religious conception never gets clear of the old Paganism, as is evidenced by the Church of Rome to this day: the fear is, that the same perils await Christianity in India and China; they may refuse to receive the doctrines of Christ in a Teutonic, or Græco-Roman, capsule, and form one for themselves of national and kindred elements.

The regular thing has always been for the professors of one Religion, or one Sect, heartily to abuse, and, if possible, to persecute, the holder of another: the favourite words are Orthodox and Heretic: but which is which? A man, who on conviction changes his Religion, gets no thanks for it, is frightfully abused, put to every kind of social torture, and is lucky if he escapes bodily torture and imprisonment. In the Middle Ages there was the Auto da fé: early in date the Pope issued a Bull ordering all, who had accepted Christianity, and went back, to be punished. In every form of Religion there are found to exist Sects, and they were generally persecuted.

I have myself heard an American Missionary in Northern India, in the crowded streets of a town, tell his audience that the Hindu worshipped cow-dung: the people only laughed, as we should laugh, if they were to say that we worshipped a crumb of bread. Another Missionary called upon the Hindu to change his ancient Religion for no other reason than that all the learned men in Europe and America believed in Christianity, as if that style of argument would influence any kind of believer.

Under the tombstones of so-called Heretics lie a variety of different persons, the partizans of a fallen Spiritual dynasty: they have had no mercy shown to them: Væ Victis: they presumed to do, what we all do now, think for themselves on some of the mysterious subjects presented to the Human intellect: they failed in getting a hearing, or in convincing, and were trodden down by some wilful Sovereign or Chieftain, or some imperious ecclesiastic: their books were all burnt, and therefore it is presumed, that they must have been in the wrong: the wheels of the Catholic Church went over their bones: they were anathematized in the schools by men, who had not nobility of character sufficient to credit their adversaries with benevolent intentions, and treat their so-called errors with Christian charity. Thus the Church, as left by the Apostles, has gradually deteriorated into a pretentious Priesthood with Ritual and Ceremonies: there were honest men in past centuries, as there are still, who will continue to protest, as their forefathers did, and separate themselves from the corrupted Truth.

CAP. VII. PROGRESS OF THE HUMAN RACE.

1. Multiplication and Improved Culture under all forms of Religious Belief.
2. Art, Sculpture, Painting, Architecture, Drama.

1. MULTIPLICATION AND IMPROVED CULTURE UNDER ALL FORMS OF RELIGIOUS BELIEF.

The Human Race has prospered, multiplied, and grown fat, under all conditions of Religious conception. The populations of India and China are increasing at an enormous rate, and together make up half the total of the Globe: the great non-Christian River flows on, flows on, quite unconscious of the tiny streamlet of Christian Doctrine, that leaves no trace in the colour of the waters. We read in the Books of Chronicles, that if a King or his Subjects worshipped Baal, they were at once visited by the anger of an outraged National Deity; and if a King destroyed idols, and removed high places, he received material blessing; with the Captivity at Babylon, and the conception of an Idea of Rewards and Punishments in a Future State, this style of describing the course of Human events fell out of practice: something of the kind reappears in the Annual Reports of Evangelical Missionary Societies: any temporary success of a Mission is described as "receiving God's manifest blessings." When, a few years afterwards the Missionary dies, or is killed, and the Mission uprooted, the Chronicler is silent: yet the balance of success and failure is held by the same wise, kind, and unerring, Hand: there are blessings in disguise: I have known the death of a Missionary to be a gain to the Mission, the greatest possible gain.

One thing is quite clear, that the current of Religious belief has no relation whatever to the material prosperity of a country, and it is well that this should be the case. Nor does it depend entirely on the intellectual position of the Race: none is so degraded as not to be capable of Religious influences, but the lower that they are, the lower is that influence: this makes the position of the degraded Races of mankind so peculiarly the objects of our sympathy and pity. Their existence is a wonderful phenomenon: the chariot of the great moral and political conquerors of the world in past centuries has passed them by; they have had only faint opportunities of developing the good, that most certainly is in them; they have but a dim Idea of an unknown Great Power, at whose mercy they live.

Their service is not of Love, but of Fear: the Past has brought them no lessons, the Present no enjoyment, and no certain Hope lies in their Future: here we see the necessity of a civilizing influence brought about by contact with neighbours, and the power of transmission of the experience of one age to the next by the means of literature.

And yet in the whole Race of man, whether Christian, or non-Christian, or pre-Christian, from the time of Pharaoh, who ordered all the male children to be killed, down to the present year, we find the same absence of Peace and Mercy, the same desire to shed blood, the same lust and greed evidenced in the annexation of countries, and destruction of weaker Races. The Kings of Egypt, Assyria, and Babylonia, could not have evidenced more contempt for the lives of other Nations than do the Chartered Companies of Africa, South of the Equator: we read calmly in the daily papers of so many poor Africans killed by the intruding white men, of the so-called impudence of an African Chief venturing to think of expelling intrusive enemies from his dominions; add to these the awful crimes committed by the Slave-Dealer, the Scientific Explorer, and the Liquor-Dealer: the first is beyond European control, and is only the result of European example in the last century; the second and third are the peculiar outcomes of so-called Christian civilization. The story of Africa rightly told, the thousands killed by the Europeans, the evil habits taught by Europeans, the new and filthy diseases introduced into uncivilized Races by Europeans, indicate what a powerless factor any Religion, the purest, the best, is in the control of Human affairs. How often we read in the papers of the violation and murder of women in England! In India up to a late date widows were burnt, and female children killed, as a matter of Religion. We have stopped the latter, but the former still flourishes.

Deliberate ill-treatment of women and children seems to have been the feature of all Religions in ancient days: Samuel ordered all the Amalekite women and children to be killed; in the Psalms in our Churches we hear English women and children chanting out, "Happy is he, who dashes thy little ones against the stones." The whole conduct of the Hebrew Race towards women, beginning with David and Solomon, was simply disgusting. How different was the conduct of the contemporary Greek: there was no polygamy there: the scene of Andromaché parting from Hector places the relation of the sexes beyond dispute. Among the savage Races woman is but a chattel, purchased for so many cows, to be killed at pleasure.

In a paper read at the last Meeting of the British Association, 1893, we find, that the women of the tribes in the Kongo basin are not credited with having any future state. In England women are disqualified from services, public and private, for which they are fully qualified, simply because they are women, while every foolish, half-witted, man is admitted as a matter of course. And no one class presses the heel down on women more than the Religious Classes. Some, if not all, of the greatest of Religious and Missionary Associations have scornfully rejected the rights of women to take their full share in the work of Committees. Municipal Bodies have long ago admitted women to their share of the control of Poor Law Boards, School Boards, Hospitals, and Charities. Any male old woman is fit to be on a Missionary Committee, but women are under tabu.

There seems to have been a marked change after the Captivity in the treatment of women. The compiler of the Books of Chronicles omits all allusion to the gross immoralities of David and Solomon; he belonged to an Epoch, when such things were impossible. At the time of Anno Domini women were treated with respect, and in the time of Paul with a feeling of love and honour. This was the effect, not of Judaism, but of Hellenism, which eventually was to expand into Christianity. Women were excluded from the Covenant in Judaism, but admitted by Baptism: women were subject to Polygamy in Judaism before the Captivity: Monogamy has ever been the law of Christianity: women were put to death for the offences of their male relations in Judaism; in Christianity there is no such vicarious punishment.

I should have lived with my eyes shut for a quarter of a century in the midst of an Asiatic people, scattered in hundreds of towns, and thousands of sequestered villages; I should have read in vain the writings of sacred and profane Authors of the elder centuries, if I had not come to a conviction, that the Human Race is not without a large portion of goodness, loving-kindness, docility, purity, humility, and striving after forgiveness of errors, without reference to their Religious conception. On the other hand, with reference to such conceptions, History, ancient and modern, teems with instances of staunchness, and dauntlessness, of confession before men, and martyrdom of old and young of both sexes. Paley must have been ignorant of History and the world generally, when he instanced martyrdom as a proof of the Truth of one Religious Belief: it appears that votaries are most ready to suffer and die for beliefs, which appear to us to be obviously the most false. A modern writer has told us of the universal hunger and thirst for Truth, Righteousness, and Love, exhibited by men, at intervals of centuries, showing the continuousness of the innate influence, and occurring at distances of space never traversed by mortal foot. We cannot but humbly believe that hearts, such as that of Socrates, Búddha, Zoroaster, and Kong-Fu-Tsee, were touched by the Holy Spirit, however much the Christian Pharisee may arrogate to himself the monopoly of Virtue. God has not left Himself without a witness: not without His permission, and design, has the spread of Christian Truth been delayed for so many centuries, and restricted by so many impediments. Paul testifies to this both at Lystra (Acts, xiv, 16, 17) and at Athens (Acts, xvii, 27).

I quote the words of Bishop Selwyn the elder: "I have "myself seen the lowest type of humanity, the Australian blacks; "I have seen the men of Erromanga, who have twice killed "Missionaries on their own shore, but I am sure, that these "men have the same capacity for the reception of Divine Truth, "that any of us is gifted with by God. I have been present, "when one of these despised Races was sentenced to death, "and I attended him at his execution: he left on my mind the "impression, that he died with just as much of simple Faith, as "was accepted by Jesus Christ from the penitent thief on the "Cross."

The appearance of great Philosophers, and Founders of new Religions, simultaneously in different parts of the Globe about the sixth and fifth centuries B.C. indicated that the Human Race was passing from the Animistic conception of early days, and the childhood of mankind, into full manhood. It grew in knowledge of itself, its environment, and other men, and felt after an unknown Ruler, a Dispenser of Good and Evil, one who creates, preserves, and has the power to destroy, yet is merciful, slow to anger, and full of fatherly kindness. It had been compelled to look inward and outward, and to moralize, speculate, and formulate, and all thoughtful men even to this day are troubled with the same thought, why so many hundred, apparently innocent, at any rate unprepared, thoughtless, creatures are hurried into Eternity without a moment of preparation, by a wicked War, a Storm, a Railway-Accident, a Pit-Accident, or something going wrong in a Manufactory.

Plato points out that "Knowledge is only recollection, the "soul being immortal: what men called 'Dying' was passing "from one state of existence to a new state, which men called "'Birth'; it remembers all its stages, and recalls them. In the "Royal procession of Gods and Souls of Mortals in the highest "Heavens, 'the Soul, which follows God closest, and is made "'more like unto Him, lifts the head of its charioteer into the supercelestial realm, and so he is carried round, and having gained a clear vision of Truth, remains in the society of the Gods' and apprehends absolute Truth." (Westcott: Religious Thoughts of the West, pp. 28, 29, 30.)

Leigh Hunt's beautiful lines are to the point: Abu ben Adhem, a holy man, saw an Angel writing the names of those, who love the Lord, and to the inquiry, whether his name was there, received a negative reply:

" Abu spoke more low
" And cheerily still, and said: " I pray thee then
" Write me as one that loves his fellow-men :"
" The Angel wrote, and vanished. The next night
" It came again with a great wakening light,
" And showed the names, which love of God had blessed,
" And lo! Ben Adhem's name led all the rest."

Can we not all agree in these additional lines, which I suggest?

" For we best love our God and Father, when
" We most entirely love our fellow-men."

Altruism was the great principle introduced into the world, 600 B.C., by Gautama Búddha: before it had been Egoism; "save yourself, and let the world take its chance." The secret of the power of the Búddhist was in the fact, that he was perfectly unselfish, that the greatest joy was to do good to others, that the thought of self was evil: at the time of the great Anno Domini this principle was enforced by a higher sanction, and a Divine aid promised to those who practised it.

2. ART, SCULPTURE, PAINTING, ARCHITECTURE, DRAMA.

All Religions, and more especially the Christian, have suffered much from their contact with Art, Art Pagan in its conception, half-Pagan to this day: what else but Pagan is the halo of glory round the heads of holy figures? it is but the brass plate fastened on the heads of Pagan Statues to prevent the features being defiled by the deposits of birds. The early Christians opposed the Paganizing of their Faith by contact with Art: witness Eusebius' letter to the Empress Constantia (Westcott, " Religious Thought in the West," p. 294): " We may not seem, like Idolaters, to carry our God about in an

Image." How many of the errors of the Romish Church are but the outcomes of the gross realism of Sculpture and Painting! If Christ in His agony at Gennesareth cried out, "let this cup pass from Me," was it right in a Statuary to represent an Angel forcing the Sacramental cup on Him? If the Evangelist records, that Satan entered after the sop into Judas, was it right in a Painting to delineate a rat leaping into Judas' mouth?

Ruskin ("Stones of Venice") remarks, that he never yet met a Christian, whose heart was thoroughly set upon the world to come, and, so far as Human judgment could pronounce, perfect and right before God, who cared about Art at all: at the best it is Human, false, and meretricious. The Greek Church allows no Statues, but sins more deeply as regards Pictures.

The Mahometan will not allow the figure of man to be pourtrayed. The Paintings and Statuary of the Hindu and Buddhist seem to the European eye so gross, as to be incapable of doing harm, but to the Asiatic eye they are as baneful as the finest work of European Sculptor or Painter. In the Greek and Roman Churches the effect is monstrous and lamentable. Pictures are exhibited to illustrate false Doctrines, the stories of false Miracles, such as the Miracle of Bolséna, in which blood flowed from the wafer to prove the Doctrine of Transubstantiation, or to record false facts, and false dreams. Pictures are exhibited, in which ancient and Oriental people are represented in European dress, and surrounded with European furniture, such as the birth of Christ in a four-post bed; the Last Supper is drawn as a feast of modern times, and the wine is exhibited in a Sacramental cup. Other Pictures, called Religious, are merely exhibitions of female beauty, imperfectly draped, in indelicate positions. Such stories as Potiphar's wife, Susanna and the Elders, David and Bathsheba, should have been shunned by Painters with any spark of Religion. The same thought to a less degree applies to Statues of Religious subjects: they deceive the vulgar: that is their object.

In an educated community pictures can do little harm, but among an ignorant peasantry, such as the Italian, they are productive of infinite mischief: in the Basilica of St. Agnes, at Rome, a picture is exhibited of Pope Pius IX being saved from a fall by the Apostle Peter putting his arms round him, at the same time, that Agnes is praying to the Virgin to intercede for his safety: the ignorant populace believe, that this took place. In the Vatican is a large picture of the dogma of the Immaculate Conception-Bull being proclaimed in St. Peter's by the Pope: the scene down below is what actually took place: up above is the Trinity, the Apostles, and the Prophets, looking on with satisfaction, and the Virgin coming forward and bowing her thanks to the audience below: what can be thought of such a conception! Awful pictures are seen everywhere of the pains in Hell, and poor people in Purgatory, to induce people to pay money for Masses. Mahomet saw how the influence of Pictures and Statues had led the Greek and Roman Churches into Polytheism in a veiled form, while the uncultured Semites clung to Monotheism, and he had the courage to resist it, and forbade the material representation of the Human body. Before the invention of Printing, and the spread of literature, it may have been expedient to represent Scripture scenes in statuesque full-size forms; but it is so no longer necessary or expedient.

Now that Toleration exists it may be found, that the Art of the Sculptor and Painter may be used for the purpose of deriding Scripture-stories: I saw in Holland a picture of the birth of Christ in a manger, in which it had been so arranged, that the horns of an ox should fit exactly over the head of Joseph, his reputed father, and the guide pointed out with glee this arrangement to show that Joseph wore horns. The ill-judging Missionary in India circulates offensive descriptions of Mahomet and Krishna: a free Press will soon learn to retaliate, and use the same weapons. The erection of magnificent, and highly decorated, places of Worship, with valuable ornaments of metal, is to be deplored: it is a remnant of Judaism and Paganism, and of the Religious conceptions of the elder world, when Religion was National, not individual, external ritual, not inward Spirituality. Theatrical performances of Scripture stories are to be deplored. In the streets of Banáras the great Hindu story of the Avatára of Rama is annually enacted amidst rejoicing thousands, and sometimes the great Mahometan festival of Husan and Hosein falls on the same day, and Christian Rulers have to keep the peace: all such things belong to a Past, and should under no circumstances be made use of in the great Religious conception, which now dominates the world, as it is unworthy of the civilization of the Nineteenth Century.

CONCLUDING REMARKS.

I have come to my final remarks: it is of no use, like the ostrich, thrusting our eyes in the sand, and seeing nothing. The population of the whole world is now for the first time in the annals of mankind brought into personal contact. The word Christian has now become merely a Census-term: it is not uncharitable to say, that thousands and thousands, who bear the name, have no personal knowledge of Him, whose name they bear. The effect of State-Education in British India, and of Commerce, and social intercourse and general Progress and Enlightenment in the whole world, is having the same effect on the non-Christian population. There is gradually forming a great arena, in which men nominally of all Creeds meet together, have no objection to make to each other: there may be a little backwardness in Matrimony and Commensality, but there it ends. There is the possibility before us of the great majority of the Human Race being absolutely without any Religious tie. An accomplished student of the Subject (Tiele, p. 244) remarks, that "the decay of the Roman State-"Worship, and the hunger of the Roman people for foreign "gods, Artemis of Ephesus, the Great Mother of the gods, "Mithra, Serápis, were the expression at that time of a real "and deep-seated need in the Human mind, which could not "find satisfaction in a moribund State-Religion. Men longed "for a god, whom they could worship with heart and soul, "and with this god they longed to be reconciled." This is not a characteristic of this Epoch. While the sections, the denominations, the parties, in the Christian Church are fighting with each other, the great mass of the community is slipping out of all Religious Worship whatever, and there is much reason to believe, that this means all Religious Belief also. In the face of so much blank *unbelief* in the Christian Revelation, and so much *nominal belief*, accompanied by entire absence of practical obedience, yet co-existent in both instances with morally consistent lives, free from outward stains of carnal failing, it is clear, that we are entering into a new phase of the Religious Idea. There may be an inward light shining brightly in the heart of true believers, and a feeling of the Infinite Love of the Creator to His poor creatures in sending them His Son; there may be an experimental testimony to the truth of these convictions in the lives of the believers, a fortitude under adversity, and a self-restraint in prosperity, an unfeigned kindness to man and animals, a power of gentle speech under all circumstances; hours of silent meditation may have deepened the Religious conviction of Repentance, Faith, Justification, and Holiness, quite independent of the dogma of Creeds, the shibboleth of Churches, the rubric of Worship, for verily and indeed God searches the heart, and knows His own children. But to the non-Christian emerging from Heathenism, there may be inducements, which may lead him to broad unbelief, or formal Worship, without an atom of saving Truth in his conception of Religion. Still he will be outwardly moral, and free from the cruelty and intolerance of his ancestors.

Not without reason the party, which calls itself "Conservative," is called the "stupid party" by its opponents, for its ways are stupid, both in things spiritual as well as material: "damnat quod non intelligit": it cannot see, that the thoughts of men grow wider, as the world advances, that the eyes grow keener in proportion to the increasing strength of the intellectual microscope. I quote the words of Dr. Butler, Master of Trinity College, Cambridge, at a late Annual meeting of the Christian Evidence Society:

"The marked reluctance among their ablest students to "take holy orders was caused, not by fear of hard work, or "poverty, or loss of worldly pleasures, but mainly by the fear "of losing their freedom, by the thought that they would "cease to be inquirers, and *be turned into advocates of one side* "*in a controversy*. Some of the chief causes, which set young "people against revealed Religion and the clerical position, "were to be found in certain old quarrels. He could never "forget the dismay and indignation among serious young "men when, in the name of orthodoxy, Maurice was expelled "from his professorship, Jowett's salary at Oxford was long "withheld, Dr. Temple's appointment to the see of Exeter "was protested against by leading Bishops to the very hour of "his consecration, and Darwin's great and epoch-making Work, "the 'Origin of Species,' was denounced, as a presumptuous "attack on Christian truth. Unbelievers were made by well-"meant errors of this kind. Just now we had before us the great "question of the authority of the Old Testament. Unfortunately, "few in England were competent to deal with it, as we had so "few Hebrew scholars. But this conflict as to the age and "authorship of the various books and as to the Human objects "of their authors might be left to learned experts without any "anxiety for the Christian faith. We should not take sides, as "if some Religious interest were imperilled. The only *Religious* "*interest was the victory of Truth.* The mistake of making the "Godhead of Christ a bar to the discussion of matters of history "and criticism should not be repeated. The argument was used, "that Christ quoted a psalm as David's, that Christ shared the "omniscience and infallibility of God, and that, therefore, David "wrote the psalm. This argument was most earnestly to be "deprecated, staking as it did the true doctrine of our Lord's "person on a matter of no spiritual import, which ought to be "left to the Human reason. For successful Christian evidence "work they needed an eager and unbiassed love for Truth at "any cost, intellectual power backed by adequate learning, "warm sympathy with every form of spiritual conflict, and "courtesy and fairness towards opponents. Hardly anything "repelled and disgusted the young more than books on the "so-called orthodox side which dealt discourteously with "opposition."

We live in a world of thought infinitely widened. Even since the Reformation, Astronomy, Geology, Anatomy, Comparative History, Geography, Statistics, have come into existence: we cannot assume the Religious attitude of an ignorant Hebrew, whose Ideas were restricted to his petty Province, or accept the dicta of Paul, wise for his time, and who yet expected the Millennium in the first century A.D., which has not arrived at the close of the Nineteenth. The old Fathers, and Mediæval writers, had not the physical facts of the great Globe, the great Human Race in all its colours, white, black, brown, red, and yellow, the still greater Kosmos, the handiwork of the Creator, before them. They wrote up to the level of the talents committed to them. We have the Truth, or at least a larger portion of it, but alas! it is overlaid by fond mediæval padding, and incrustated by centuries' deposit of misconceptions. Unless the great mass of mankind are to be allowed to slip out of all Religion, we must reconsider our intellectual position. One thing is clear: the uniformity of law, as valid in the revolutions of the most distant Planet, as on the Earth's surface in the smallest operation of Nature, is as valid now, as in the time of Abraham, and was as valid then as it is now. Miracles are possible, because to God all things are possible, but there is evidence in the Field of Nature, that His laws are not ordinarily suspended. We cannot assume, that our Heavenly Father dealt in a different way with His poor creatures before Anno Domini, than He does since that great event. We have, therefore, to weigh in a Christian balance the prodigies recorded in the Legends of the elder world: at any rate, they do not happen now.

We may open our eyes to what is coming when we read in

Dr. Martineau's "Religion of Intellect," published by him at the age of 85, the following:

"A conclusion is forced upon me, on which I cannot dwell
" without pain and dismay, that Christianity, as defined and
" understood by *all* the churches which formulate it, has been
" mainly evolved from what is transient and perishable in its
" sources, from what is unhistorical in its traditions, mythological
" in its preconceptions, and misapprehended in the oracles of
" its prophets. From the fable of Eden to the imagination
" of the last trumpet, the whole story of divine order of the
" world is dislocated and deformed. The blight of birth-sin,
" with its involuntary perdition; the scheme of expiatory
" redemption, with its vicarious salvation; the incarnation,
" with its low postulates of the relation between God and man,
" and its unworkable doctrine of two natures in one person;
" the official transmission of grace through material elements
" in the keeping of a consecrated corporation; the second
" coming of Christ to summon the dead, and part the sheep
" from the goats at the general Judgment: *all* are the growth
" of a mythical literature, or Messianic dreams, or Pharisaic
" theology, or sacramental literature, or popular apotheosis.
" And so nearly do these vain imaginations preoccupy the
" creeds, that not a moral or spiritual element finds entrance
" there except 'the forgiveness of sins.' To consecrate and
" diffuse, under the name of 'Christianity,' a theory of the
" world's economy thus made of illusions from obsolete stages
" of civilization, immense resources, material and moral, are
" expended, with effect no less deplorable in the promise of
" Religion than would be in that of science, hierarchies, and
" missions for propagating the Ptolemaic astronomy, and incul-
" cating the rules of necromancy and exorcising. The spreading
" alienation of the intellectual classes of European society from
" Christendom, and the detention of the rest in their spiritual
" culture at a level not much above that of the Salvation-Army,
" are social phenomena, which ought to bring home a very
" solemn appeal to the conscience of stationary churches. For
" their long arrear of debt to the intelligence of mankind, they
" adroitly seek to make amends by *elaborate beauty of Ritual Art*.
" The apology soothes for a time, but it will not last for ever."
("Seat of Authority in Religion," p. 650. Longman, 1890.)

Five years later, on the 90th anniversary of his birth, he replied to a deputation from Manchester College, Oxford, of which he had been a Professor:

"He could not too much insist on the necessity for keeping
" the teachers of Religion *in touch with the highest thought of*
" *their time*, and for giving them an insight into the *rival*
" *systems* which too often take hold of the public mind through

"an inability on the part of the people generally to compare
"one method with another. He had always insisted upon a course
"of logic as necessary before entering upon the discussion
"of Religious philosophy; he recognised more and more how
"inevitably the basis of Christian teaching would have to be
"sought less and less in the letter of Scripture. The Bible and New
"Testament would have to be regarded as literature, and the
"mind must be trained so as to fasten securely upon the abiding
"elements among its varied constituents; while the Religious
"sense must be cultivated, if we would hope to rescue the
"imperishable from what was sure to go, and to find the way
"clear to the one central Divine personality of Jesus."

We talk of Buddhism being defiled by the contact of lower Pagan elements; but has not Christianity suffered from similar defilements? Can we justify some of the accretions, when we consider them calmly? It is admitted, that the great work to be performed by the Christian Religion is the restraint and correction of the corrupt nature of man, and yet in the arguments used in theological and Religious discussions how grave appears the corruption of the Human intellect, so merciless to opponents, full of excuses for facts on their own side, which cannot be denied. The study of the Comparative Religion of the world in a calm, thoughtful, and judicial, spirit cannot fail to open out new vistas of Religious and serious thought, and a tenderer love to our fellow-creatures, eventuating in a greater desire to share with them the advantages of our privileged knowledge. "Formality in Religion, the cold, unintellectual, or even "unintelligent, assent to the Church-Creed, the formality of "Public Worship, while there is no private Worship at all, is "rearing a crop of Atheism, for it throws the veil of its own "respectability over unchristian, godless, lives, eaten up by "ambition, greed, or love-of-ease." These are the words lately uttered by a Bishop: of course a professor of Christianity of the type sketched by the Bishop, when brought into contact with a professor of a non-Christian Religion, is, or pretends to be, greatly shocked: "so disreputable, so formal, so meaningless," would be the description given by him of Hindu Worship; yet the Hindu would say very much the same of Christian Worship in the light, in which he would regard it. Both forget what the distinctive feature of a real Religion is: nothing less than the Soul's response to the Deity, who has taken notice of the Soul; a loving intercourse of the closest, and sweetest character, or as Paul puts it: "the body is the temple of the Holy Spirit." Σὰρξ and Πνεῦμα are united in one entity.

The application of scientific principles, and the reflection of the order of events in Comparative History, cannot fail to influence a mind capable of the power of Reason and Analogy, whether applied to the study of an Egyptian excavation, or the examination of an ancient written document. The Religions of the World before the great Anno Domini, instead of deserving censure and contempt, stand out amidst the loftiest conceptions of the Human Intellect, foreshadowing, symbolizing, preparing the way for, the coming in the Fulness of Time of One greater than all.

At the very time that we are spelling out the Inscriptions of Assyria, Babylonia, the Hittite, the Egyptian, the Indian, the Yenissei nations of Central Asia, the Chinese, and the Mexican, and rendering them into the Languages of Europe, which did not come into existence till centuries after the tablets of these Inscriptions had fallen out of Human sight, and recollection, and had been absolutely forgotten; at this very time we are poring over, for the purpose of fixing the true text, settling the true order, and finding out the right meaning, the MSS. of the Jewish Scriptures in Hebrew, Aramaic, Samaritan, Greek, Latin, Syriac, Ethiopic, Mæso-Gothic, Armenian, Georgian, and Anglo-Saxon, books, parts of which are contemporary with those Inscriptions, which have fallen out of sight, but which by God's special favour to some of His poor creatures have never fallen out of the thoughts and lips, and pens, of generation after generation, but which have grown with the growth of each Language, twined themselves round the hearts of each Nation, have supplied a law in life, and a hope in death, to countless Millions, and are now being rendered into the Languages of hundreds of tribes, whose existence and names were unknown to the elder world, even to the writers of the New Testament, being only darkly hinted at in the Book of the Revelation as "nations, and kindreds, and tongues," which were to come into existence hereafter.

We must recollect, that the early thoughts, Religious conceptions, and Ancestral Customs before King Cyrus broke with the Past, were National: the individual went for nothing: if a Hebrew had dared to use his private judgment, he would have been run through with the javelin of an assassin, such as Phineas, or sent to the rear to be killed, like the young Amalekite murdered by David. As to the outside world, such as India, China, Africa, or Europe, the Hebrew knew nothing. In the Religion of those times it was the duty of the local deity to look after the welfare of his worshippers, just as the local Romish Saint is expected to look after the village, which pays him, or her, by prayers, offerings, and genuflexions. The Worship of Yahveh as a tribal God made the Hebrews a peculiar, and peculiarly offensive, little Nation, surrounded by tribes, who hated them, and governed by a combination of weak and yet tyrannical kings, under the casual influence of irresponsible

Prophets, which made administration impossible. It is difficult to imagine how commerce could have thriven, when one small tribe assumed such a ridiculous attitude towards its neighbours, expecting the most perfect Toleration, and giving none. The Hebrew assumed, and rightly assumed, that their law was given to them by their God, but all the Races of the ancient world assumed the same in their own interest, whether the Assyrians (II Kings, xviii, 25), or the Egyptians (II Chronicles, xxxv, 21), or the Hindus. These lines are penned with a double object: (1) To conciliate some interest in the Religious conceptions of the elder World, and to check the ignorant abuse of all, who have not had the small grace conceded to them of wearing the cloak of outward Christianity, which is fondly supposed by the Evangelical middle classes to co-exist only with the social customs and apparel of their own class, and their own level of wisdom or unwisdom. (2) To point out how reasonable the way of Salvation traced by Christ is, if we can only clear it of the Pagan environment, which has hardened round the living germs: the real secret is, that we in these happy generation of men have found what the men of old, in spite of their goodness, wisdom, and devotion, blindly felt for, and in vain.

In argument (oh! that Missionaries would think of this!) we should seek the common ground, on which both sides can stand, the Adamantine Truth, so far as it is revealed to us: those, who have recourse to abusive language, show that their resources of argument are exhausted; the most ignorant clergy are always the most arrogant. I quote an anonymous writer: "It is the fancy of an ignorant man, that Creation was made "for him: there are few things, of which he is so utterly "ignorant, and of which he thinks so little, as that mystery "of Himself, incarnated in the temporary prison-house of his "flesh and blood." No prison-house is so fast-bound as the bondage of ignorance, false preconceptions, and obstinate refusal to give play to Sanctified Reason.

Even among men, professing the same Religion, belonging to the same Church, there are found the strongest differences in the very essentials of Religious Belief and Worship; there are men of cultivated and uncultivated minds, of strong, and weak intellectual power: so of Races some are stupid and lethargic; some wonderfully quick in apprehension, and mercurial: the effect of climate has to be considered also, the social environment, access to, or seclusion from, foreign contact, degree of leisure, or total absorption in lawful worldly business. Every mirror does not reflect the object with the same degree of clearness, but all do reflect: so the sweet reasonableness of the doctrine promulgated in Galilee is intelligible by, and is good for, all, whatever may be their degree of culture, or want of culture, on whatever platform they may be standing of wisdom or unwisdom. This cannot be said of the other two Universal Propagandist Conceptions: in Buddhism there is no God, and it cannot therefore coexist with modern culture, which postulates the existence of a God. Islam fails, as unable to free itself from the bondage of Paganism in still inculcating the worship of a stone, the Kaaba, at Mekka, in still enforcing the degrading rite of mutilating the body of the male sex, made in God's own image, and in refusal to elevate the female sex to the full dignity of a companion to man by the hateful practice of Polygamy, and cannot therefore coexist with modern social and civilized conditions.

The Jewish Idea of God was purified by contact in the Schools of Alexandria with Greek Philosophy, especially Platonic. Anthropomorphic Ideas (which disfigure the Old Testament) were discarded, and the Logos introduced as intermediary between God, the author of all good, and matter which is transitory and evil. (Conybeare's Review of Friedlander's "Entstehung Geschichte"—Jewish Quarterly Review, April, 1895, p. 554.)

The World has not yet learnt to understand the man, who places Christ above all the shibboleths of Churches, who cares a great deal for, in fact has no thought for anything but, Religion, yet places no value on particular Church-organization. There is so much hypocrisy, time-serving, fashion, carelessness of all things, and pretence to be righteous, and therefore to be ready with damnatory opinions of our neighbours. It is well to include among the real followers of Christ all the good and wise of all ages, whether they ran their mental course before the great Anno Domini, and only saw Him far off, or whether they tried humbly to follow Him. It would be well for us all to read and ponder over the following extract from Bishop Beveridge's "Private Thoughts on Religion," Part I, Art. 2:

"The general inclinations, which are naturally implanted
" in my soul, to some Religion it is impossible for me to shift off;
" but there being such a multiplicity of Religions in the world,
" I desire now seriously to consider with myself to which of them
" all to restrain these my general inclinations. And the reason
" of this my enquiry is not, that I am in the least dissatisfied with
" that Religion I have already embraced; but *because 'tis natural
"for all men to have an overbearing opinion and esteem for that
" particular Religion they are born and bred up in*. That, therefore,
" I may not seem biassed by the prejudice of education, I am
" resolved to prove and examine them all; that I may see and
" hold fast to that which is best. . . . .

"Indeed, there was never any Religion so barbarous and

" diabolical, but it was preferred before all other Religions
" whatsoever by them that did profess it; otherwise they would
" not have professed it. . . . .
 "And why, say they, may not you be mistaken as well as we?
" Especially when there is, at least, six to one against your
" Christian Religion; all of whom think they serve God aright;
" and expect happiness thereby as well as you. . . . . And
" hence it is that in my looking out for the truest Religion, being
" conscious to myself how great an ascendant Christianity holds
" over me beyond the rest, as being that Religion, whereinto
" I was born and baptized, that which the supreme authority
" has enjoined and my parents educated me in; that which
" everyone I meet with all highly approve of, and which I
" myself have, by a long-continued profession, made almost
" natural to me: I am resolved to be more jealous and suspicious
" of this Religion, than of the rest, and be sure not to enter-
" tain it any longer without being convinced, by solid and
" substantial arguments, of the truth and certainty of it. That,
" therefore, I may make diligent and impartial enquiry into
" all Religions, and so be sure to find out the best, I shall for
" a time look upon myself as one not at all interested in any
" particular Religion whatsoever, much less in the Christian
" Religion; but only as one who desires, in general, to serve
" and obey Him that made me, in a right manner, and thereby
" to be made partaker of that happiness my nature is capable of."
 A great French Author, who has lately died, has left us
these remarks in a posthumous work: let us all reflect upon
them, and ask ourselves whether as regards the exterior form
of every Religious conception it is not sadly true. (Renan,
" Israel," v, p. 106.)
 " Religion is a necessary imposture: no means of throwing
" dust into the eyes can be neglected in dealing with such a
" race of fools, as the Human Race, who seem created for the
" purpose of imbibing error, and who, even when they admit
" the Truth, never do so for the real good reasons." The great
majority think nothing about the reasons of their Belief: they
accept it.
 The Holy Spirit speaks in the Written Word, and to the
conscience and intelligence of all, but He speaks as much now
to hearts, which have accepted Him, as He did by the mouths
of Prophets, holy men of old: there is an unbroken continuity
of Revelation, and Illumination, unrestricted by time or space:
the Religious experiences of the sanctified thinkers of the
present age are entitled to as much respect as those of the
ignorant Hebrew a few centuries before Anno Domini, or the
early Christian Fathers of the few centuries after Anno Domini,
whose view of the World and mankind was limited to their

own environment. It is quite clear, that there is a distinction between the Word of God, which unquestionably exists in Holy Scripture, and the assertion, that the Scriptures in their totality are absolutely the Word of God. There is a great deal in Professor Driver's remarks, that the proper expression is, "the Word of God mediatized by Human instrumentality"; the book itself is not inspired, but the men, who wrote it, were inspired.

That only one-third of the population of the Globe is even nominally Christian, is a lamentable fact to record at the close of the Nineteenth Century after Anno Domini. Boasting is excluded. The period of the Jewish Dispensation, from Moses to Anno Domini, barely covered twelve centuries. In that Record there was nothing but Ritual, Miracles, Theophanies, Prophecies, Cruelty, Persecution, Disobedience of the Divine Law, and Ignorance of a Future State of Rewards and Punishments. The Sadducees, including the Priests, denied the Resurrection till the last, as is clear from the account of Paul's trial at Jerusalem (Acts, xxiii, 8).

One of the greatest features of the present Epoch, the close of the Nineteenth Century, is the Historical Spirit, and the domain of History has been enlarged by extending historical principles, and critical analysis, to the History of Religion. Up to this time, Christians on such subjects had a distinct bias one way, and violent opponents of Christianity went to the other extreme. They are now taken up in a cold, secular, impartial spirit; evidence is weighed, legends exposed, falsehoods called by their right name. The Church of Rome very soon recognised in such writers their real and greatest enemies, for the History of Religion, truly told, struck a blow at the exaggerated assertions of Revelation and the Supernatural, thus alienating the grossly superstitious, but attracting the really devout seekers after God. A new taste was thus created, and the new Science of Religion sprang into existence. Some illusions have been dispersed; *great and mighty Truths stand out in their full proportions.* The Philosophy of History has been correctly described, as being only an attempted interpretation of the acts, and thoughts, and works, of men in past ages by the modes of thought and accepted standard and principles of our own. Men in the times of the wars of Assyria and Egypt, of King Asóka in India, of the Emperors of China in the time of Kong-Fu-Tsee, were men of like passions, powers, and weaknesses as ourselves, and the Ruler of the World was the same yesterday, to-day, and for ever. It may be, that at the close of the Twentieth Century, other interpretations may be made according to fresh, and hitherto undeveloped, standards of our acts and writings at the present moment. During the period of a long life, the standard of most individuals, their prejudices, and predilections, have undergone change, and that change tends to increase: "The thoughts of men grow wider with the progress of the Sun." Facts are the only things which remain, facts proved by sufficient evidence, to outlive all generations. Where Tradition or Faith comes in, we seem to be walking on a quagmire.

Mr. Green, the Historian, remarked that, when he left Arthur Stanley's lecture-room at Oxford, he used to reflect on how many Faiths and Persons the lecturer had discoursed, and how he had taught his readers *to love the Truth that was in them all*. To Socrates, and Plato, the Unknown God was revealed: the Human mind cannot reach to more profound Truths than those, which they had attained: they saw, or seemed to see, through the mystery of the Universe, but we know now, that they were but the advance-guard of something infinitely greater.

The Idea has been hazarded, but by some, who have not studied History, past and present Ethnology, Language, Religious conceptions, ancestral customs, remains of Antiquity in the whole of the Round World, that Christ came in the Fulness of Time, when the Religious Education of the most progressive Races of Mankind was sufficiently advanced to appreciate the Doctrine which He brought.

But was it so?

What is called in general parlance the World is larger than the basin of the Mediterranean, and the countries on its shores within the limits of the Danube, the Black and Caspian Seas, the Euphrates, the Sahara, and the Atlantic. For many centuries the name even of Christ did not penetrate beyond the area thus defined, viz, the Roman Empire, and the Regions of the Kelts, Teutons, and Slavs. India and China were far advanced in civilization even then, but Gospel-Tidings never reached them. According to the Divine Plan it was the Fulness of Time, but this term did not imply the throwing open of the whole Globe. And now in the Nineteenth Century, when the whole round World is thrown open, the dead weight of Paganism increases annually by the mere generation of children, the repression of slaughter by overpowering Races, the precaution taken against Famines, and the Remedial Measures against Disease. New germs of Religious conception have found Life and Development, and greater enemies to Christianity have come into existence in the form of Mahometanism, Papalism, and Agnosticism. The last state of the World is infinitely worse than the first. If the watchman were asked, "what of the night?" the reply would be, "very dismal indeed": if Evangelization were a mere commercial undertaking, it had better be abandoned. Nothing, however, is impossible to God, but the foolish boasting of the Missionary platform, and the deceptive sensational literature, are excluded. The descendant of the ancient Egyptian, if there is one, will point to the Pyramids, and the long succession of magnificent Monuments, which have lasted five, six, or seven thousand years; he will point out that to him the world is indebted for the germ of the Alphabet, for the earliest Idea of a Future State of Rewards and Punishments, an Idea which the vaunting Hebrews till the time of the Exile knew not of.

The descendant of the Greek Race, if there is one of the true stock, will point to the Works of their Dramatists, their Philosophers, their Historians, the foundation of all Science, the fountain of all Poetry, the mine of all Eloquence, the groundwork of the Intellect of Future ages: what form would Christianity have assumed, if the mould of Plato had not been ready to receive the pure Semitic ore? What does Augustine of Hippo say on this subject?

Is there any product of English Art, or Intellect, which is likely to live as long, or outlive, the great Egyptian and Greek Legacies to mankind?

It may be said defiantly, that the Greek and Egyptian have passed away; but consider the Religious conceptions and the material structure of the Hindu and Confucianist, still influencing millions, evidencing no sign of decay. The Hindu system, absorbing annually thousands of Nature-worshippers, is still in situ: ancient Inscriptions, speaking from walls, from rocks, from caves, point to the imperishable monuments of Grammatical Method, the development of the Alphabet, the invention of numerals. Consider also the Poets, the Dramatists, the Philosophers, and lastly their spiritual descendants, the Buddhists, the greatest in the present Epoch in numbers.

The earnest and honest Christian preacher seems sometimes not so much to strive to deliver a man from the just judgment of God for his sins, as to deliver him over to the still more just judgment for refusing to accept the pardon held out to him: the last state of the non-Christian man is made worse than the first: in the first state it was ignorance, the result of long social isolation; in the second state it is stubborn refusal to accept a free offer: it would have been better thus for the man, if he had not received the Gospel-invitation like his ancestors for hundreds of generations; he has been called into the Light only to be scorched by that Light, and to receive more certain damnation: it is an awful problem; we can only fall back on the unlimited Wisdom and Pity of the Creator towards His poor creatures.

In *The Expositor* of July, 1893, pp. 49, 50, there appeared a paper by the Rev. H. Rashdall, on "Abelard's Doctrine of the Atonement," which I have condensed, preserving the original idea. The Church of our day is called upon to reduce Christian teaching to an intelligent, systematic, and coherent body of philosophical doctrine. The Human mind has awakened from a long slumber, and insists, that the traditional dogmas of Christianity should give an account of themselves. It is a noble and stimulating Idea to create a Science of the highest generalization, that should present the deposit of traditional and historic Faith in its due relation to other branches of Knowledge, accepting and forming into itself the Highest and Greatest Truth, that is known from whatever source, of God, the World, and Man.

Darwinism and Historical Criticism present a new starting-point: the reconstruction of Christian Doctrine is the great intellectual task of modern Christianity, and it must be done, if Christianity is to retain its hold on the Intellect, as well as on the sentiment and social activities of the time. The Religious conception, which has lost its hold on the Intellect, will not long retain its hold on the social activities. No two ages can ever be exactly alike: the wants of one age are sometimes found to have been anticipated, but the old Truth is differently expressed from the modern.

The same writer, at the Church Congress, 1894, expressed himself in this way:

"It cannot be too distinctly understood, that the
" originality of Christianity is not to be disproved, by show-
" ing that some of the most characteristic utterances of the
" Gospel maxims can be more or less closely paralleled
" by isolated sayings in Pagan moralists or non-Christian
" Sacred Books. The unique claim, which Christianity makes,
" alike in Theology and in Ethics, is to absorb into itself,
" to harmonize and combine, all that is true and per-
" manently valuable in previous systems, or, to speak in
" Religious language, in *previous and partial* revelations of
" God. And, first, a word as to the sense, in which alone
" Christianity claims to be in any sense a complete or ethical
" revelation. If our Lord and His immediate followers had
" pretended to set forth an Ethical Code, which in detail should
" anticipate the course of intellectual and social development,
" and contain definite rules of conduct capable of immediate
" application alike to the Slave-holding Society of the ancient
" world, to the feudal society of the eleventh century, and to
" the conditions of modern England, the Teacher who made
" such an attempt would be justly chargeable with having mis-
" conceived the very nature of the new message to Mankind."

The difficulty in dealing with such discussions as these is, that the one side believes everything, and the other nothing, whereas the Truth is in the midst. An old archdeacon, a few years before his death, confessed to me, that he could no longer justify the morals of King David and King Solomon, as he had done, when he took Holy Orders, for then the Scriptures, and all matters connected with Religion, were removed out of the orbit of Human events, and the Hebrew Story and Books were deemed to be unique in the History of the World.

Professor Huxley attached the following meaning to Agnosticism, which he defines not as a *creed* but a *method*: The essence of the method is as old as Socrates, and reinforced by Descartes, and the fundamental maxim of Modern Science. The principle may be expressed *Positively*: in matters of Intellect follow your reason, as far as it will take you, without regard to any other consideration. *Negatively*: in matters of the Intellect do not pretend that conclusions are certain, which are not demonstrated, or demonstrable. (Athenæum, May 4, 1895, par. 672.)

Can we imagine any Native Sovereign of an Indian Kingdom conducting his affairs in the manner described in the Books of Kings and Chronicles? one Sovereign putting up altars to one set of Deities, and *compelling* the people to worship; in a few years his son pulls them all down, and puts to death the Priests, while irresponsible herdsmen, or ascetics, appear and disappear at intervals threatening the kings, and inciting his subjects to rebellion: can we wonder that utter ruin of such a political system was the consequence?

The teaching of Christ, in whom was centred all Wisdom, Human as well as Divine, was not political: He did not object to pay tribute as a subject to an Earthly Emperor; he preached no narrow Theocracy of one petty tribe amidst the Millions of Mankind, as if the whole world was not, and always had been, governed by God. A secular Monarchy is a wiser and safer Minister of God's decrees than a debased Priesthood, whether at Jerusalem or Rome, Constantinople or Lassa: Christ came into the world, not for restoration of the Hebrew Kingdom, but for the happiness of all God's poor children: His Kingdom was not of this world; and rested on Man's love of God, and Love of his neighbour; there were to be no longer circumcised Jews, or uncircumcised Gentiles. Mankind, through His teaching in its entirety, and most remote futurity, were to be set free from the bondage of Sin, secret and open, of merciless and capricious fanatic Rulers, of old-world exploded notions of ceremonial cleanness and uncleanness, which had vexed the elder Nations, and vexes the Hindu Millions still, of Puritanic Sabbaths, washing of pots and pans, consecrated hypocrisy, domineering Priesthoods, whom He called a generation of Vipers. He abolished the fear of Death: "Fear not those who kill the body," and placed the doctrine of a Future State of Rewards and Punishments on a basis, that can never be shaken.

If the object of Religion is to bring Peace into the world, to protect the rights of the weak, to maintain purity of morals between the sexes, to bring down the proud, and exalt the humble and the weak, it must be admitted that:

I. It has as entirely failed in its object, as the Jewish Theocracy of the Kingdom of Israel and Judah.

II. The precepts of all Religions have been above the heads, and beyond the comprehension, of the great majority of mankind, even if they had wished to understand them.

III. Each Religious Conception, succeeding its predecessor in order of time, has unconsciously, but yet tenaciously, absorbed so much of the rank vegetation of its predecessor, that its power of doing good has been choked, or absolutely destroyed.

IV. At all periods of History and at the present moment, there have existed those to whom all Religious Conceptions, or dogmatic creeds, are equally false, and yet who make use of them to influence and control their foolish contemporaries, for in their opinion the sole object of Religious Conceptions and dogmas has been to deceive the unlearned, and keep them in subjection.

But what of the Future? Nothing is known, as a fact. By what measure will the dead, as they rise from the grave, be judged in the great hall of adjudication? Will it be a question of empty rites and habiliments? Will not those, who have wasted their lives in controversy about matters as trivial as the tithe of anise and cummin, moan, that they have never known Christ? Dost thou believe in Christ, and Him crucified? That will perhaps be the question. Hast thou loved God and thy neighbours? That will certainly be the qualification. The secret is unrevealed; the mystery is as dark as in the time of the construction of the Egyptian Pyramids.

" Where wert thou, Brother, those four days?
  " There lives no record of reply,
  " Which telling what it is to die
" Had surely added praise to praise.

" Behold a man raised up by Christ!
  " The rest remaineth unrevealed:
  " He told it not; or something sealed
" The lips of the Evangelist."

(TENNYSON: *In Memoriam*, xxxi.)

Just as I was laying down my pen, and adding a few references and quotations, a friend to whom I described my work, mentioned a book by the late Viscount Amberley, "An Analysis of Religious Belief, 1876," covering the same ground, which I had never seen, nor heard of: I at once sent for it, and read it as far as my subject goes: in his last 300 pages he describes the great sages before Anno Domini: I gather from the address to the Reader by a third person unknown, that the Author died before the book appeared, and "that he had parted with portions of that Faith, which in boyhood, and early youth, had been the mainspring of his life. I myself, see no reason, why such an inquiry, purely historical, as he made, and such as I have made twenty years later, with wider knowledge of the East, and of the ancient Religions of the World than he could have had, should lead to the least doubt as to the absolute Truth of Christianity: if I thought so, I should drop the pen at once.

The Author has made a very good analysis as far as it goes. His division of the Subject into "Communications Upward," and "Communications Downward," is ingenious and useful (page 15).

I. UPWARD.

A. Consecrated Actions . . (1) Prayer.
(2) Sacrifice.
(3) Ritual.
(4) Festivals.
(5) Initiatory-rites.
(6) Puberty-rites.
(7) Matrimonial-rites.
(8) Funeral-rites.

B. Consecrated Places . . . (1) Temples.
(2) Shrines.

C. Consecrated Objects . . (1) Garments.
(2) Tablets.
(3) Temple-furniture.
(4) Fetich.
(5) Land.

D. Consecrated Persons . . (1) Ascetics.
(2) Monks and Nuns.
(3) Devotees.
(4) Fakirs.

E. Consecrated Mediator . Priest.

II. DOWNWARD.

A. Holy Events . . . . . (1) Dreams.
                               (2) Omens.
                               (3) Divination.
                               (4) Ordeals.
                               (5) Miracles.

B. Holy Places . . . . . (1) Groves and Trees.
                               (2) Graves.

C. Holy Objects . . . . (1) Fetich.
                               (2) Amulets.
                               (3) Relics.

D. Holy Orders . . . . . (1) Priests.
                               (2) Faith Healers.
                               (3) Inspired Persons.

E. Holy Persons   (1) Rainmakers.
                               (2) Prophets.
                               (3) Writers of Sacred Books.

Let me add a quotation :

"We love what we are used to. We revere the ancient. We all have roots in the venerable Past. This is well. Yet the grandest arena of God's working is the future. A Christian's treasure should be there. Ours is a Religion of hope, of expectation, an onlooking to golden ages yet to come. Blessed were those Jews in our Lord's time who stood waiting for His coming ready to receive Him with open hearts. Blessed too are the *foreseeing* men and women of all ages, who are always watching for the morning; praying for great things, working for great things, expecting great things; bending forward and listening for the prophetic voices; quick to see the great light in the heavens, when it first gilds the tops of the eastern hills."

But what about the Future of the Kingdom of Heaven upon Earth ? will it bear the strain of the Twentieth Century ? The Words of Christ, and the Life of Christ, are indeed good for all time, because in them is the supreme essence of good, but the form, in which those words were delivered, the environment in which that Life was manifested, was adapted to the comprehension of Syrian Peasants, and was levelled against the low, narrow-minded degradation of Hebrew Priests, and cannot be deemed binding upon all generations of men in after ages, endued, as they are, with enlarged spiritual gifts, more exalted

Divine leadings, and greater Human possibilities. His Spirit worked with His Apostles John and Paul, and enabled the former to recall, after an interval of forty years, words of the Master previously unrecorded, and one mighty miracle, which had apparently never come to the knowledge of the earlier Evangelists; with the latter that Spirit worked in the development of theories entirely new, of which there is no foreshadowing, or even germ, in the three first Gospels, though they were written at a date later than Paul's Epistles, in which those theories, setting aside the Mosaic dispensation, are stated. At the last verse of the New Testament an absolute line must be drawn. It must be presumed that the work of Inspiration is closed for ever, through the agency of Prophets and Apostles.

It suited the powers, Civil and Ecclesiastical, of Rome and Constantinople, to erect a new edifice on Hellenic, Judæic, and Pagan foundations, and to publish Edicts, backed by anathemas and intolerant savagery. The world is not the worse for those terrible anathemas, and understands how far removed from the fundamental precepts of Christianity those men must have been, who attempted to enforce Spiritual doctrines by the help of carnal penalties and disabilities. Their game at the end of the Nineteenth Century is played out; there is an Arab Proverb, that Curses, like foul birds, come home at night to roost in the nest, which they left in the morning. The Christian is not in bondage to an ignorant and superstitious Past: he is, indeed, the heir of all the ages, but he has the grace conceded to him by the Spirit of Christ, which is immanent in each of God's poor creatures, who have accepted Him, to use his inheritance, his privileges, and opportunities wisely.

I doubt not, that the nascent Churches of Asia, Africa, and Oceania, will assert their right to sweep away the accretions of ignorant, arrogant, mediæval, European Christianity, and go back to the words and example of their Master, who lived and died amidst Asiatics in Asia. New forms of Christianity may appear from an Asiatic matrix, and free themselves from the effete ligaments of mediæval Europe.

Adapted from the Persian.

Abraham was seated just outside his tent,
Expecting friends, on social cheer intent:
Before his eyes an ancient man appears,
Weighed down with burden of long miles, and years:
Abraham in Oriental fashion rose,
Begged him to be his guest, and take repose.
In courteous conversation passed the meal,
And each for each respect began to feel:
But, when the servants cleared away the board,
Abraham stood up alone, and thanked the Lord;
And those, who sat at meat, with reverent air
Echoed his thanks, then closed their eyes in prayer;
Except the stranger, who with look benign
Looked round upon them all, and made no sign.
Abraham rebuked him: "Art thou silent, when
We thank our God for His good gifts to men?"
The stranger quietly replied, that he
Except the "Fire" knew no Divinity.
Exceeding anger Abraham's bosom tore:
He rose to drive the stranger from his door;
When a celestial light made him aware,
That a high Messenger of God stood there,
Who calmly spoke: "Abraham, thy God appears
" To grant this man a life of ninety years.
" Him has He fed with oil, and wine, and corn,
" And given him children's children to be born.
" If God, who knows each heart, restrains His ire,
" Because His creatures stoop to worship Fire,
" Are you to drive this man from your abode,
" And be less merciful to him than God?
   " Listen, while I expound the ceaseless Grace
" Of God's high dealings with the Human Race:
" 'Tis not the symbol, creed, or form of prayer,
" Which man's relation to his God declare:
" He reads the heart: full many a Saint has trod
" This earth, nor once pronounced the name of God.
" A God impersonal can thee inspire;
" He in his ignorance sees God in Fire;
" Others with simple and untutored minds

" See God in clouds, and hear Him in the winds;
" Some to the Heavenly Host their homage pay;
" Some grovelling lower bow to gods of clay.
" To each of His poor children God gives rest:
" Many the soul, which Love of God has blest.
" The heart of Man for his Creator burns,
" Just as the Sunflower to the Sunbeam turns.
" To some God sends His Revelation's light,
" And yet leaves millions in darkest night.
" He claims no homage, where He is not known;
" He will not reap, where He has never sown.
" Darest thou dispute His Wisdom, or His might?
" Shall not the Judge of all the Earth do right?
" Ask thou the heathen, whose beclouded sense
" Scarce knows 'twixt Death and Life the difference,
" Who makes the beauteous fruit on trees to grow;
" Piles up the hills; lets conquering rivers flow;
" Sends rain in season; fills the fields with corn;
" Lets cattle multiply, and babes be born?
" Will he not bow the head, and point to Heaven,
" Feel for the Hand, by which all is given?
" Millions on millions pass away unhealed,
" Because God never has Himself revealed.
" The knowledge of His Truth Man has not known,
" Because no Prophet has that knowledge shown;
" And if, till Time be full, His will He veils,
" Where is the sin, if Man in duty fails?
" If thy rash anger more restrained had been,
" This aged man his error might have seen:
" For Faith may fail, and Hope itself remove;
" Poor Human hearts are won by conquering Love.
    " Abraham, look down the vale of woe and tears,
" Through which thy children must pass many years;
" Thou wilt descry worked-out a wondrous Plan,
" Thy Lord, thy God, disguised in form of Man.
" Rejoice, that thou far off hast seen His day:
" Be still and silent: turn thee in and pray;
" Pray that, their errors and their blindness past,
" All God's poor children may find God at last."

London, December 31st, 1893.

BIBLIOGRAPHY.

Ecce Homo. *Seeley.*
Ancient Religion of Egypt. Hibbert-Lecture, *Renouf.*
Mythology of Arian Nations. *Cox.*
Sacred Anthology. *McClure Conway.*
Bible-Echo in Classics. *Ramage.*
Bhagavad-Gita and Christianity. *Tawney* (Calcutta Review, Jan. 1876).
Christianity and Paganism. *St. G. Mivart* (Nineteenth Century, 1895).
Religions of the World and their Relation to Christianity. *Maurice.*
Mexico and Peru. *Reville.*
Religion of Semitic Races. *Robertson Smith.*
Religion of a literary man. *Le Gallicne.*
Gibbon's Decline and Fall.
Homer: Iliad and Odyssey.
Virgil: Æneid, *Eclogue* No. iv.
Lucretius.
Juvenal.
Seneca.
Horace.
Claudian.
Jewish Quarterly Review.
Monuments and Higher Criticism. *Sayce.*
Religion of Babylonia: Hibbert-Lectures, *Sayce.*
Message of Man. Swan, Sonnenschein & Co., 1895.
God and Man in the Chinese Classics: a short story of Confucian Theology. *J. C. Hoare,* Ningpo, 1895.
Essay on Greek Tragedy. *Froude.*
Dionysian Mysteries. Review by *Cox.* Saturday Review, June, 1876.
Gifford-Lectures: Theosophy. *Max Müller,* 1892.
Survivals in Christianity. *Woods,* U.S., 1893.

Distinctive Messages of Ancient Religion. *Mathieson*, 1893.
Words on Existing Religions. *Canning*, 1892.
The Coffee-house of Surat. Review of Reviews, March 15, 1893. *Tolstoi*.
Fire-gleams of Christianity. *C. Newton Scott.*
Homeric Theology. *Gladstone*, 1890.
Gesta Christi. *Loring Brace*, 1883.
Unknown God. Do. 1890.
Beginning of Religion. *Bacon.*
Childhood of Religion. *Clodd.*
Fundamentals. *Griffith.*
Bases of Religious Belief. Hibbert-Lecture, *Upton.*
Natural Theology. Gifford-Lecture, *Stokes.*
Modern Scepticism compared with Christian Faith. *Kaufman.*
Christ in Modern Theology. *Fairbairn.*
Religion and Science. Bampton-Lectures, *Temple.*
    Ditto   Ditto.   *Hatch.*
The Psalms.   Ditto.   *Cheyne.*
Inspiration.   Ditto.   *Sanday*, 1893.
Genesis and Growth of Religion. *Kellogg*, U.S.
Evolution of Religion. *Caird.*
Report of Palestine Exploration.
Faith and Criticism.
Biblical Critics.
Verbum Dei. *Horton.*
Christ, and modern Unbelief.
Did Moses write the Pentateuch? *Spencer.*
Hebrew Idolatry and Superstition. *Higgins*, 1893.
Hours of Thought. *Martineau.*
The Chronicles in relation to the Pentateuch. *Hervey*, Bishop of Bath and Wells, 1893.
Gospel of Life. *Westcott*, 1893.
Lehrbuch der Religion Geschicht. *De Saussaye.*
Religion of the Future. *Momerie*, Dec., 1892.
Religious Thought in the West. *Westcott.*
Classical Essays: (1) Greek Oracles, (2) Virgil. *Meyer.*
Confucius and Christ. *Legge.*
Revue des Religions. French Periodical.
De Naturâ Deorum. *Cicero.*
Life of Cicero. *Middleton.*
Rivers of Life. *Finlay.* 2 vols., quarto.
Hibbert-Lecture, Buddhism. *Rhys Davids.*
Buddhism, S.P.C.K.   Do.
The Unseen World, and other Essays. *Fiske*, Boston, U.S.
  (1) Jesus of History, 1870.
  (2) Christ of Dogma, 1870.
Histoire de dogme de la divinité de Jésus Christ. *Reville*, 1869.

(185)

Jesus of History. Anonymous. Williams and Norgate, 1869.
Vie de Jésus. *Renan.*
St. Paul. Do.
Histoire de la peuple Israel. *Renan.*
Dawn of Civilization. *Maspero,* 1894.
Erasmus. *Froude,* 1894.
Thoughts on Religion. *Romanes.*
Studies in Biblical Archæology. *Jacob,* 1895.
Early spread of Religious Ideas in the Far East. *Edkins,* China, 1893.
Beginning of Religion. *Bacon.*
Pantheistic Philosophy. *Adol. Franck.*
Expositor. Monthly periodical.
Expository Times. Do.
Critical Review. Do.
Chief Ancient Philosophies. S.P.C.K., 1895.
 (1) Platonism. *Strong.*
 (2) Neo-Platonism. *Bigg.*
Sacred Books of the East. *Max Müller.*
Ancient Religions. S.P.C.K.
Indian Mythology: Vishnu Purána. *FitzEdward Hall.*
 ,, Classical Dictionary of. *Dowson.*
Búddhist Birth-stories or Játaka. *Fausböll* and *Rhys Davids.*
Indian Folk-lore. *Sir H. Elliott* and *Beames.*
Indian Mythology. *John Muir.*
History of Religion. *Menzies,* 1895.
Progressive Revelation. *Caillard,* 1895.
Problems of Christianity and Scepticism. *Harison,* 1894.
The Religions of the World. *Grant,* 1894.
Expositor's Bible.
Zur Entstehungsgeschichte der Christenthum. *Friedlander,* 1894.
Florilegium Philonis. Jewish Quarterly Review. *Montefiore,* 1895.
Philo Judæus. *Drummond,* 1882. 2 vols.
Via, Veritas, Vita. Hibbert-Lecture, *Drummond.*
History of Egypt. *Petrie,* 1895.

A. INDEX OF SUBJECTS AND NAMES.

(See also Classification of the Subject, page xxiii.)

A

	PAGE
Abu Simbul	35
Accadian idea of thunder	89
Æneid, the Roman Bible	129
Afflatus claimed by all Reformers	134
African, cruel treatment of	157
African, Religious acts	39
Agnosticism	13, 176
Ahaz, dial of	90
Aix-la-Chapelle Cathedral	47
Alphabet	138
Altruism	160
Amen Ra	8, 58
Ancestor Worship	28, 43
Angels	26, 28, 29
Anger of Deity	87
Animism	28, 159
Anthropology	xiii
Anthropomorphism	170
Anthrópos, derivation	3
Apollonius of Tyána	77
Aria-Somáj	13
Aristophanes	49
Ashur	8
Assyrian	2
Astrology	41, 68
Astronomy	xiii
Augurs	80
Augustus, Emperor, Worship of	43
Austrian Emperors' Burial	94
Avatára	33, 142, 162
Azteks	18

B

Bábi Sect	xviii
Babylonian idea of Future State	102

	PAGE
Balaam	67
Banáras, prisoners at	68
—— temples	149
Barbarians, conceptions of	5, 98
Beads, counting of	66
Beatification of Monks	76
Bel and the Dragon	49
Bhágavadgita	58
Bona Dea	81
Book of the Dead	132
Book Religions	20
Book Worship	120
Brahmanist	xviii
Brahmo-Somáj	13
Brittany, treatment of a Saint	79
Búddha, 5, 6, 70, 75, 131, 137, 141, 142, 144, 159, 160	
Búddhist	xviii, 170
Bull-fight, a pious offering	110

C

Calvin on Bible	124
Cannibalism	93
Caste-marks	13
Cattle-killing (India)	148
Centurion at Crucifixion	23
Charms	67
Chemosh	18
Children suffering for parents	86
China, Emperor prays for all	59
—— no Priesthood	67
—— persecution	147
Christian, a census-term	163
Christian Polytheism	24
Christian Religion, features of	3
Christian Sects	2

(188)

	PAGE
Chronicles, characteristic of	137
Churches, Pagan decorations	63
—— confiscation by other Religions	63
Cicero	1, 81
Circumcision	13, 109
Cleanness or uncleanness	68
Clement of Alexandria	8
Clergyman, prayers of aged	61
Collection of children's heads	50
Comet in India	88
Comparison unjust of Religions	xxi
Confucianist	xviii
Constantine, vision of	77
Continuance of non-Christian Religions	12
Contracts ratified by Sacrifice	51
Coptic Priests doing castration	110
Corybantes, dancing of	66
Court practices, modern	107
Covenant made by God	19
Criminal Laws, effect of	2
Criticism, Higher	xiv
Cuneiform	138
Cyrus	134, 168

D

Daniel	120
Daniel, Book of	80
Daphne, the laurel	143
Darius	134
Date of earliest book in familiar use	120
David	xv
—— character of	137, 168
Destruction of temples by lightning	89
Devils, possessed by	28
Divine Beings, minor	28, 32

E

Ecce Homo	xix
Egyptian Book of Dead	132
Egyptian idea of Future State	102
Erasmus	xix
Euripides	81, 106, 107
Exaggeration	135, 138
Expositor	124
Expository Times	82

F

Familiar Spirits	29
Farrar on Orthodoxy	4

	PAGE
Farrar, hyperbole	134
Fate	16

G

Geography	xvi, 128
Geology	xiii
God, names of	17
Goodness of Human Race	158
Gospel, Apocryphal	141
Græco-Roman cult, no Sacred books	126
Greek, sentiments of	174

H

Halo, pseudo-, of ancient books	132
Hau-Hau of New Zealand	13
Heavenly Host, Worship of	41
Henry VIII, life of	139
Heraclitus	8, 29
Heretics	150
Hero Worship	143
Hieroglyphics	138
Higher Criticism	119
Hindu Sages	xix
Hindu idea of Future State	103
History	xvi
Homer	2, 26, 58, 83, 129
Horace	xv, 2, 16, 54, 79, 80
Human Sacrifice	48, 50
Huxley	176
Hymns of the Veda	58

I

Ideas disparaging to the Wisdom of God	xviii
Idolatry called whoredom	135
Idols of the den, theatre, etc.	xvi
—— exhibition of	5
Incantations	67
Indian, remarks of a thoughtful	40
—— only father of family prays	59
Inquiry of the Lord	80
Inspiration	114
Isaiah	17, 79, 133
Isis, Worship of	13

J

Januarius, liquefaction of blood	78
Japan, spitting prayers on Búddha	59
Jerome	7
Jews	xviii, 6, 12
—— Day of Atonement	70

(189)

Job 120
John the Apostle . . xvi, 128, 137
Jonah 17
Jordánus, Monk 81
Joseph, dream 26
Jupiter 29
Justin Martyr 7, 8, 41

K

Kaaba-Stone 13, 33
—— pilgrimage to 44, 46
Kabála 68
Karma, what was it? 16
Khalifa Abdullah 76
Khama 67
Kingdoms of the earth exaggerated 136
Knowledge more or less crude . xiv
Kong-Fu-Tsee, xix, 5, 127, 131, 144, 159
Korán 120, 128, 131, 135
Krishna 19, 137, 142

L

Languages 13, 121
Later conceptions of the Deity . 33
Lazarus, raising of 138
Leaders, heavenly in battle . . 75
Legends, oral 139
Lent, dispensations 69
Lepers, burying alive 110
Libations 52
Library, dangers of ancient . . 118
Lingam 33
Literary frauds 117
Liturgical xx
Logic xvi
Λόγος xvi
Lucretius 51
Luther xix

M

Madonna Statue 33
Magical Arts 67
Mahdi 76
Manétho 119
Manichæism 13
Manu's Code 127
Maráthi Hindu observing Mahometan customs 66
Marcus Aurelius 8
Marriage ceremonies 144
Mars' Hill 1

Martyrdom no test of true Religion 158
Matrimony introduced into South India 110
Memory of Repeaters 112
Meru, Mount 24
Messages of different Nations . 6
Mexican idea of Future State . 103
Milton, Paradise Lost 117
Miracles 75
—— are possible 165
Missionaries . 12, 13, 149, 150, 154
Missionary Manual, India . . 30
Mithraism 13
Monogamy 138, 158
Montefiore 42
Moses 5, 19
Mother, Worship of the Great . 13
Myths 129, 140

N

Naini Devi 25
Nakedness of barbarous tribes . 111
Naphtha Springs, Jowála Mukhi 41
Naples, wells for the dead . . 94
Nathan, the Prophet 144
Nebuchadnezzar's Image . . . 148
Neith or Athéné 18
New Guinea, disposal of dead . 93
New Religious Conceptions . . 13
Nirvana 106
Non-Christian world . . . 4, 11
Nuk pa nuk 18

O

Object of Worship, Agni Purána 36
Offerings to demi-gods . . . 49
Old people killed by their children 94
Olympus, Mount 24
Opium-Trade 57, 86
Oracles 80, 83
Ordeals 85
Orestes and Furies 90
Orientation of Churches . . . 25
Orthodoxy 149, 154
Osiris 101, 142
Ovid 26
Outfit of Human Race 39

P

Paganism, Messages of . . . 6
—— in Christian Churches . 38, 65
Palermo, dead monks 94

Paul the Apostle	1, 109
Penance	64, 70
Perfection of God	22
Pericles	8
Persecution	xviii, 147
Peter the Apostle	150
Phidias	8
Philo	xvi, 9, 117
Philosophy, two nations only	127
Phineas	168
Pictures	161
Pilgrimage	44
Plato, xvi, xix, 1, 5, 7, 81, 112, 128, 173	
Plutarch	30
Poetical Rhapsody	136
Polygamy and Concubinage	144, 158
Population of the world	11, 12
Post-Office Bugle	68
Priestcraft	xx, 6
Primitive Revelation	30
Progress of Religious Conception	48
Prophecy in India	81
Prophets commissioned by God	17
—— interference with civil power	184
Purgatory	162
Pythagoras	xix
Pythagoreans, new	80

Q

R

Races, degraded position of	157
Rags on trees	41
Rain, praying for	89
Rama	19, 141, 142, 162
Rameses II, Mummy of	93
Ramzán fast	69, 70
Reading, limited power of	115
Relics	46
Religion, the highest outcome	5
—— the universal feature	11
Religious belief disappearing	163
—— instinct	30, 31
Rewards and Punishments	98
Rock Inscriptions	112, 115
Rome, Church of	13, 15
Romish converts	46
Romish Shrines	26
Rumour	83

S

Sacerdotalism	65, 67
Sacred Books	126
Sacrifice, sheep in Syria	48
—— savour of	48
—— female chastity	49
—— different kinds and motives	49
—— low and high view of	50
—— Hindu view of the power of	51
—— institution outgrown	52
Sacrilege, what is it?	54
Sadducees	172
Saints take place of demi-gods	43
Sanskrit	130
Sargon	140
Satan	26
Science	xiii
—— new worlds of	xviii
Scientific treatment of Religion	72
Séneca	2
Serápis	81
Shaftesbury, Earl of	60
Sign of coming events	90
Simple conceptions of early Man	42
Sins of Christian cities	21
Sneezing	83
Socrates, xix, 5, 7, 26, 49, 131, 144, 169, 173	
Solomon	xv, 136, 137
Spider's web	77
Spirits	38, 47, 92
Spurgeon	46
State Colleges, effect on youth	146
Statues	161
Stones with marks of feet	75
Superstition in modern times	84
Survey of mankind	xvi
Synagogue Rolls	114

T

Talipat Palm-leaf	118
Tattooing	13
Teraphim	43
Theosophism	13
Therianthropic	42
Tibetan Buddhist	54
—— Prayer-wheel	60
Times, places, seasons	71
Tobit	28, 76
Tolerance	3
Torquemáda	150
Tragedians	1, 17, 58
Transmigration	98
Tree and Serpent Worship	41
Troitska, Russia	63
Truth	xiv, xvii, 5, 13, 169

U

	PAGE
U-Ganda	124
—— prayers of two sides	61
Ulysses, prayer of	59
Unfair treatment of non-Christian Religions	9
Universality of Religious Truth	2, 18
Unseen and unknown Power	1
Uzza	87

V

Veda	131, 135
Vespasian	81
Virgil	2, 58, 76, 129
Voices, heavenly	29

W

Week, names of days	41
Widow-burning	110
Wisdom	xvi, 31
Worship	1
—— mockery of Nineteenth Century	37

X

Y

Yahveh, only God of Israel	32

Z

Zaragossa	47
Zeus	32
Zoroaster	xix, 26, 159

B. INDEX OF QUOTATIONS.

A

	PAGE
Abu ben Adhem (Leigh Hunt)	160
Adrian to his Soul	105
—— Statue of Memnon	29
Æschylus	102
Alcuin	150
Amberley, Viscount	178
Aratus	4
Aristotle	81
Assur-bani-pal	82
Athéné, offering to	36
Augustine of Hippo	7, 11
Aztek prayer	59
Anonymous 9, 11, 76, 77, 95, 167, 169, 179	
—— Paul at Virgil's tomb	130
—— Ποῦ γένομαι;	128

B

Beard, Hibbert-Lecture	9
Bellars	119
Benson, Archbishop	10, 116
Beveridge, Bishop	170
Bhágavadgíta	127, 146
Brooke, Bishop	15
Butler, Dr., of Trinity College, Cambridge	164

C

Carlyle	33
Cicero	xviii
Claudian	xv
Cleanthes	4
Clifton Collins (Life of Plato)	7
Conybeare	170
Cust, R. N.	ix, 99, 140, 181

D

Dale, Future State	96
Death	95, 105

	PAGE
Dhammapáda	145
Dreams, Greek	127
Driver, Word of God	124
—— pity for animals	17
Diaspora, the Jew of	65
Disease and Death as punishments	88
Divination	68
Dogmatism	xvi
Doll, illustration of idol	32
Dost Mahómed at his prayers	58

E

Easter Island, gigantic statues	35
Eclipse of the Sun	88
Egypt, monuments	7
—— Eschatology	95
—— Sovereign of	136
Egyptians, sentiment of	174
Electricity	xiii
Elijah	19
Empédocles	29
Ephod	67
Epictetus	9
Established Church	xx
Etruscan divination	83
Eusebius	7

F

Failure of Religion	177
Family vaults	94
Fanatic, what is it?	152
Fatherhood of God	17
Fasting Communion	69
Female Infanticide	110
Fergusson, James	41
Festival, Mahometan	162
Fetichism	19, 43
Finality of Religious conception	xviii
Fire-worship	40
Forbidden articles of food	168
Fulness of Time, which was it?	173

Funeral-rites, necessity of	92
Further off from God	18

G

Galileo	1
Gayatri of Brahma	41
Ginsburg on Chemosh	18
Gladstone on Future State	104
—— on Ecce Homo	xix
Green	173
Grote	128

H

Harps, Egyptian Inscription	146
Hatásu, Queen, Inscription	136
Hatch	63, 70
Hebrew at prayer	55
Herodotus	16
Higher Criticism	116
Holy life, Egyptian idea of	105
Homer	16, 27, 93, 103
Horace	23, 31, 86, 88
Hungarian Toleration	148, 151

I

Inscriptions, Egyptian	18
—— Greek, no allusion to a Future State	104
Isaiah	29

J

Jeremiah	84
Johnston, century of Christian Progress	150
Josephus	81
Julian, last Oracle of Delphi	83
Juvenal	xxi, 56

K

Keble	51
Khedive Ismail, funeral of	108
Khu-en-Atin	147
Knowledge only recollection: Plato	159
Kong-Fu-Tsee	145

L

Latin Poets on God	16
Lavigerie, Inscription	37
Lefroy of Dehli Mission	10
Legge of China	16, 122
Libation	49, 53
Lincoln, President of U.S.	27
Livy	26, 78
London, Bishop Temple	151
Loring Brace	141, 142
Lucretius	87, 89, 146

M

Mahometan apophthegm, "Son of God"	23
Malachi	12
Manchester Martyrs	66
Martineau	166
Maspero	85
Max Müller	5, 8
—— (Gifford-Lecture)	114
—— (South Pacific Legends)	140
Mekka, Pilgrim traffic	45
Mivart, St. George	38
Montefiore, Hibbert-Lecture	86
More, Eutopia	151
Mutianus Rufus	9

N

Nanak Baba	25, 58, 103
Newton, spiritual inquiry	80
Nineveh	35, 70, 103

O

Om Mani Pani Hom	55
Orpheus, description of a Prophet	82
Ovid	90

P

Pacific myths	140
Paul the Apostle, 4, 5, 15, 25, 134, 159	
Peter the Apostle	5
Pilate, Latin anagram	xvii
Plato	26, 29, 103, 159
Plutarch	142
Plymouth Brethren	85
Poetry, modern on Death	106
Porphyry	81
Prayer, act of merchandise	53
—— of Hindu	53, 55
—— of Roman soldier	53
—— flattery, threats	54
—— contradictory at same time	54, 55
—— denial by the Creator	55
—— abuse of	56, 57
—— malignant	59, 88

Purána, Agni.	36
—— Vishnu	99

Q

Quarterly Review	123

R

Rabshakeh	114
Raghuvansa	22
Rashdall	175
Renan	xiv, 21, 122, 171
Renouf, Egyptian idea of God	18
—— Hibbert-Lecture	196
Respecter of persons	5
Robertson Smith	xxi, 124
Ruskin	161

S

Sadler, Canon	105
Samuel, Prophet	96
Sanday, Professor	135
Sayce	41, 82, 89
Self, World, God	19
Selwyn, Bishop, the elder	159
Selwyn, Bishop, the younger	17, 167
Semper, ubique, ab omnibus	135
Séneca	79
Shakespeare	79, 103
Sheol	95, 97
Sin, Jewish idea of	95
—— Greek confession of	59
Socrates, dying words	xxi, 49
Solomon	25
Spirit, Holy striving with man	131
Stanley, Dean	9, 13
Stephen, dying words of	62
Strike at Hull	88
Suetonius	81
Sun's disk, Khu-en-Atin	147

T

Tacitus	80
Tennyson	177
Tertullian	81
Thales	29
Theognis	xvi
Tiberius	150
Tibullus	85, 93
Tiele	28, 163
Trench	10

U

Unknown God	141

V

Vaughan, Cardinal	4, 61, 62
Veritas, quid est?	xvii
Virgil	16, 26, 34, 79, 80, 82, 89, 103
Vishnu Purána	99
Vision on the Kongo	26
Visions, definition of	83

W

Westcott, Bishop, 8, 11, 16, 42, 62, 121, 160	
Whateley, Archbishop	38
Wisdom of Solomon	31
Wiseman, Cardinal	7, 39

X

Xenophon	85
Ximenes, Cardinal	76

Y

Z

Zoroastrian, prayers of	59

ERRATA.

Page 16, line 23, *read* ἐτελέιετο *for* ἐτελέιετυ.
,, 18, ,, 32, ,, pp. *for* ph.
,, 83, ,, 29, ,, οὗ μάντιδα *for* οὑμάντιδα.
    96, ,, 39, ,, idiots *for* idols.
,, 106, ,, 11, ,, ἀποθνήσκει νέος *for* ἀποθγήσκει νέυς.
    120, ,, 9, ,, taints *for* tenets.
    140, last line, ,, obscure *for* obscene.

www.ingramcontent.com/pod-product-compliance
Lightning Source LLC
Chambersburg PA
CBHW031828230426
43669CB00009B/1267